everything's an argument

for First-Year Writing at the University of Texas at Arlington

Seventh Edition

EVERYTHING'S AN argument

for First-Year Writing at the University of Texas at Arlington

Andrea A. Lunsford
STANFORD UNIVERSITY

John J. Ruszkiewicz
UNIVERSITY OF TEXAS AT AUSTIN

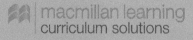
macmillan learning
curriculum solutions

bedford/st.martin's · hayden-mcneil · w.h. freeman · worth publishers

For Bedford/St. Martin's

Vice President, Editorial, Macmillan Higher Education Humanities: Edwin Hill
Editorial Director, English and Music: Karen S. Henry
*Publisher for Composition, Business and Technical Writing, and Developmental
Writing:* Leasa Burton
Executive Editor: John E. Sullivan III
Developmental Editors: Rachel Goldberg and Sherry Mooney
Editorial Assistant: Jennifer Prince
Senior Production Editor: Rosemary R. Jaffe
Senior Production Supervisor: Jennifer Wetzel
Marketing Manager: Joy Fisher Williams
Copy Editor: Steven Patterson
Indexer: Leoni Z. McVey
Photo Researcher: Sheri Blaney
Director of Rights and Permissions: Hilary Newman
Senior Art Director: Anna Palchik
Text Design: Anna Palchik and Graphic World, Inc.
Composition: Graphic World, Inc.
Printing and Binding: King Printing, Inc.

Manufactured in the United States of America.

2   1   0   9   8   7
f   e   d   c   b   a

For information, write: Macmillan Learning Curriculum Solutions, 14903 Pilot
Drive, Plymouth, MI 48170   (macmillanlearning.com)

ISBN 978-1-319-14894-2

Acknowledgments

BRIEF CONTENTS

Note: This custom edition of *Everything's an Argument*, Seventh Edition, for the University of Texas at Arlington omits Parts 3 and 4, which are not covered by your instructors. As a result, you will note a gap in pagination that is intentional.

Part 1:
Reading and Understanding Arguments 1

1. Everything Is an Argument 3
2. Arguments Based on Emotion: Pathos 28
3. Arguments Based on Character: Ethos 40
4. Arguments Based on Facts and Reason: Logos 51
5. Fallacies of Argument 71
6. Rhetorical Analysis 87

Part 2:
Writing Arguments 119

7. Structuring Arguments 121
8. Arguments of Fact 151
9. Arguments of Definition 185
10. Evaluations 210
11. Causal Arguments 240
12. Proposals 272

CONTENTS

Note: This custom edition of *Everything's an Argument*, Seventh Edition, for the University of Texas at Arlington omits Parts 3 and 4, which are not covered by your instructors. As a result, you will note a gap in pagination that is intentional.

Writing Assignments for Students at the
University of Texas at Arlington   *xv*

Part 1:
Reading and Understanding
Arguments   1

1. **Everything Is an Argument**   3

Why We Make Arguments   *6*

    Arguments to Convince and Inform   *7*

    Arguments to Persuade   *8*

    Arguments to Make Decisions   *10*

    Arguments to Understand and Explore   *11*

Occasions for Argument   *12*

    Arguments about the Past   *13*

    Arguments about the Future   *14*

    Arguments about the Present   *14*

Kinds of Argument   *17*

    Did Something Happen? Arguments of Fact   *17*

    What Is the Nature of the Thing? Arguments of Definition   *18*

    What Is the Quality or Cause of the Thing? Arguments of Evaluation   *19*

    What Actions Should Be Taken? Proposal Arguments   *20*

    STASIS QUESTIONS AT WORK   *20*

Appealing to Audiences   *21*
    Emotional Appeals: Pathos   *23*
    Ethical Appeals: Ethos   *23*
    Logical Appeals: Logos   *24*
    Bringing It Home: *Kairos* and the Rhetorical Situation   *24*
    CULTURAL CONTEXTS FOR ARGUMENT   *27*

2.   Arguments Based on Emotion: Pathos   28
Reading Critically for Pathos   *29*
Using Emotions to Build Bridges   *31*
Using Emotions to Sustain an Argument   *34*
Using Humor   *36*
Using Arguments Based on Emotion   *38*

3.   Arguments Based on Character: Ethos   40
Thinking Critically about Arguments Based on Character   *42*
Establishing Trustworthiness and Credibility   *43*
Claiming Authority   *45*
Coming Clean about Motives   *47*
    CULTURAL CONTEXTS FOR ARGUMENT   *49*

4.   Arguments Based on Facts and Reason: Logos   51
Thinking Critically about Hard Evidence   *52*
    Facts   *55*
    Statistics   *57*
    Surveys and Polls   *60*
    Testimonies and Narratives   *62*
Using Reason and Common Sense   *63*
    CULTURAL CONTEXTS FOR ARGUMENT   *66*

Providing Logical Structures for Argument   67
Degree   67
Analogies   68
Precedent   69

5. Fallacies of Argument   71

Fallacies of Emotional Argument   72
Scare Tactics   72
Either/Or Choices   72
Slippery Slope   74
Overly Sentimental Appeals   74
Bandwagon Appeals   75

Fallacies of Ethical Argument   76
Appeals to False Authority   76
Dogmatism   77
Ad Hominem Arguments   78
Stacking the Deck   79

Fallacies of Logical Argument   79
Hasty Generalization   80
Faulty Causality   80
Begging the Question   81
Equivocation   82
Non Sequitur   82
Straw Man   83
Red Herring   84
Faulty Analogy   84

6. Rhetorical Analysis   87

Composing a Rhetorical Analysis   89
Understanding the Purpose of Arguments You
Are Analyzing   90
Understanding Who Makes an Argument   91
Identifying and Appealing to Audiences   92

Examining Arguments Based on Emotion: Pathos *95*

Examining Arguments Based on Character: Ethos *97*

Examining Arguments Based on Facts and Reason: Logos *98*

Examining the Arrangement and Media of Arguments *101*

Looking at Style *102*

Examining a Rhetorical Analysis *105*
 David Brooks, *It's Not about You* *106*
  "This year's graduates are members of the most supervised
  generation in American history."

 Rachel Kolb, *Understanding Brooks's Binaries*
 [STUDENT ESSAY] *109*
  "Instead of relying on the logos of his argument, Brooks
  assumes that his position as a baby boomer and *New York
  Times* columnist will provide a sufficient enough ethos to
  validate his claims."

 GUIDE TO WRITING A RHETORICAL ANALYSIS *112*

Part 2:
Writing Arguments 119

7. Structuring Arguments 121

The Classical Oration *122*

Rogerian and Invitational Arguments *126*

Toulmin Argument *130*
 Making Claims *130*
 Offering Evidence and Good Reasons *131*
 Determining Warrants *133*
 Offering Evidence: Backing *138*
 Using Qualifiers *140*
 Understanding Conditions of Rebuttal *141*
 Outline of a Toulmin Argument *143*
 A Toulmin Analysis *144*

Deborah Tannen, *Why Is "Compromise" Now a Dirty Word?* *145*
"The death of compromise has become a threat to our nation."

What Toulmin Teaches *149*

CULTURAL CONTEXTS FOR ARGUMENT *150*

8. Arguments of Fact 151

Understanding Arguments of Fact *152*

Characterizing Factual Arguments *154*

Developing a Factual Argument *155*
Identifying an Issue *157*
Researching Your Hypothesis *159*
Refining Your Claim *160*
Deciding Which Evidence to Use *161*
Presenting Your Evidence *163*
Considering Design and Visuals *164*

GUIDE TO WRITING AN ARGUMENT OF FACT *167*

Projects *173*

Two Sample Factual Arguments *174*

Taylor Pearson, *Why You Should Fear Your Toaster More Than Nuclear Power* [STUDENT ESSAY] *174*
"We live in a radioactive world."

Neil Irwin, *What the Numbers Show about N.F.L. Player Arrests* *180*
"The numbers show a league in which drunk-driving arrests are a continuing problem and domestic violence charges are surprisingly common."

9. Arguments of Definition 185

Understanding Arguments of Definition *186*

Kinds of Definition *189*

Formal Definitions   *189*

Operational Definitions   *190*

Definitions by Example   *192*

Developing a Definitional Argument   *193*

Formulating Claims   *193*

Crafting Definitions   *195*

Matching Claims to Definitions   *196*

Considering Design and Visuals   *197*

GUIDE TO WRITING AN ARGUMENT OF DEFINITION   *199*

Projects   *205*

Two Sample Definitional Arguments   *206*

Natasha Rodriguez, *Who Are You Calling Underprivileged?*
[STUDENT ESSAY]   *206*

"The word made me question how I saw myself in the
world."

Joyce Xinran Liu, *Friending: The Changing Definition of
Friendship in the Social Media Era*   *208*

"We've created the myth of building strong relationships via
social media."

10.   Evaluations   210

Understanding Evaluations   *211*

Criteria of Evaluation   *212*

Characterizing Evaluation   *214*

Quantitative Evaluations   *215*

Qualitative Evaluations   *215*

Developing an Evaluative Argument   *217*

Formulating Criteria   *218*

Making Claims   *219*

Presenting Evidence   *221*

Considering Design and Visuals   *223*

GUIDE TO WRITING AN EVALUATION   *225*

Projects   *231*

Two Sample Evaluations *232*

Sean Kamperman, *The Wikipedia Game: Boring, Pointless, or Neither?* [STUDENT ESSAY] *232*
"Knowledge building is a connective or associative process, as the minds behind Wikipedia well know."

Hayley Tsukayama, *My Awkward Week with Google Glass* *237*
"Why? Because I'm wearing Google Glass. And I hate it."

11. Causal Arguments 240

Understanding Causal Arguments *241*
Arguments That State a Cause and Then Examine Its Effects *243*
Arguments That State an Effect and Then Trace the Effect Back to Its Causes *244*
Arguments That Move through a Series of Links: A Causes B, Which Leads to C and Perhaps to D *245*

Characterizing Causal Arguments *246*
They Are Often Part of Other Arguments. *246*
They Are Almost Always Complex. *246*
They Are Often Definition Based. *247*
They Usually Yield Probable Rather Than Absolute Conclusions. *248*

Developing Causal Arguments *248*
Exploring Possible Claims *248*
Defining the Causal Relationships *250*
Supporting Your Point *252*
Considering Design and Visuals *255*

GUIDE TO WRITING A CAUSAL ARGUMENT *257*

Projects *263*

Two Sample Causal Arguments *264*

Raven Jiang, *Dota 2: The Face of Professional Gaming* [STUDENT ESSAY] *264*
"The point is that online gaming is going to be a big deal."

John Tierney, *Can a Playground Be Too Safe?*   *268*
"Fear of litigation led New York City officials to remove seesaws, merry-go-rounds, and the ropes that young Tarzans used to swing from one platform to another."

12. Proposals   272

Understanding and Categorizing Proposals   *273*

Characterizing Proposals   *275*

Developing Proposals   *279*
Defining a Need or Problem   *279*
Making a Strong and Clear Claim   *281*
Showing That the Proposal Addresses the Need or Problem   *283*
Showing That the Proposal Is Feasible   *286*
Considering Design and Visuals   *286*
GUIDE TO WRITING A PROPOSAL   *288*

Projects   *294*

Two Sample Proposals   *295*

Manasi Deshpande, *A Call to Improve Campus Accessibility*
[STUDENT ESSAY]   *295*
"The University must make campus accessibility a higher priority and take more seriously the hardship that the campus at present imposes on people with mobility impairments."

Virginia Postrel, *Let's Charge Politicians for Wasting Our Time*   *303*
"If candidates really think it's valuable to call me, they should be willing to pay."

Glossary   *505*

Index   *518*

WRITING
assignments

for students at the University of Texas at Arlington

English 1301: Rhetoric and Composition I

Paper 1: Discourse Community Analysis

The Rhetorical Situation

Your Membership in a Discourse Community

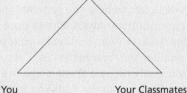

You   Your Classmates and Instructor

For this paper, you will analyze the rhetorical appeals you mastered to become a participating member of a discourse community. Your audience will be your classmates and I.

A discourse community is a group of people who share common interests, goals, values, assumptions, knowledge of a topic, and—most important for the purposes of this paper—discursive patterns (i.e., specialized vocabulary, speech genres, and ways of communicating). Examples of discourse communities include Dallas Cowboys fans, military veterans, avid gamers, members of a sorority or fraternity, Facebook users, followers of a television show or fiction writer, Reddit community members, and so on.

As a first-year college student, you have begun the process of entering the discourse community of your major field of study. Becoming an "insider" in an academic discourse community is a daunting task that takes years to complete, but the good news is that you already have experience joining numerous discourse communities. Any time you learned the lingo and began to communicate in a new school group, a new group of friends, a new workplace, a new place of worship, a new interest group, and so on, you joined a new discourse community.

The main purpose of this paper—and a primary purpose of ENGL 1301—is to demystify the process of entering an academic discourse community by demonstrating to you that this process is not so different from the process by which you've joined other discourse communities. My hope is that by having you reflect on and analyze the discursive skills you mastered as an insider in a discourse community, you will better understand the process by which you will enter the academic discourse community you pursue.

Invention

In rhetorical studies, invention refers to the systematic search for ideas that can be shaped into an effective composition. (The term *prewriting* is sometimes used to refer to the concept of invention.) This section of the assignment, then, is designed to help you generate the required content for your discourse community analysis. Please note that the following steps are not intended to serve as an outline for your paper. Rather, these steps will help you produce the "raw materials" that you will then refine into a well-organized analysis, and these steps are likely to produce more material than you can use in the draft you submit to readers.

1. Your audience for this paper (your classmates and I) will want to know the main point of your paper right off the bat, so, after deciding what discourse community you want to write about, come up with a **claim** (*Everything's an Argument*, pp. 130–31) explaining why you were successful in joining that community.

2. It's not enough just to make a claim—your audience will expect you to prove it. Thus, you need to explain why your claim is valid by supporting it with **reasons** (*Everything's an Argument*, pp. 131–33). Your reasons should state that you mastered **ethos**, **logos**, and **pathos** appeals (*Everything's an Argument*, pp.23–24) that were *specific* to this community.

3. Even after you've made a claim and supported it with reasons, your audience still won't be satisfied. Readers will expect you to provide **evidence** (*Everything's an Argument*, pp. 138–39) that you really did master ethos, logos, and pathos appeals specific to your discourse community. Please note that this step will generate the majority of content for your analysis, so this is the most important step in your invention process.

Where will you find evidence for this paper? You won't find it in the library or on the Internet because it must come from you! Reflect deeply on your own experiences. Come up with specific examples and significant anecdotes that will prove to your audience that, indeed, you learned to make successful ethos, logos, and pathos appeals to other members of the community.

For ethos appeals, provide readers with vividly drawn anecdotes and examples that demonstrate your insider status. Then, provide ample metacommentary (*They Say/I Say*, Chapter 10) that explains *why* and *how* the anecdotes you share exemplify a member of this community using ethos appeals (language-based demonstrations of your credibility, character, values, and so on) in the manner of an established insider.

Like your analysis of ethos appeals, your analysis of logos appeals should draw on specific anecdotes or examples. Then, to position these anecdotes and examples as logos appeals, provide ample metacommentary that explains to readers *why* and *how* these anecdotes and examples illustrate logos appeals (community-specific knowledge and ways of reasoning as expressed through discourse) at work.

For pathos, again you should draw on specific anecdotes and examples that you follow up with metacommentary that explains *why* and *how* these anecdotes and examples function as pathos appeals (language-based appeals to the values, emotions, and imaginations of other community members) that demonstrate your ability to sway other insiders.

Please note: this is a *discourse* community analysis, which means that the anecdotes and examples you analyze should be instances of language use. Making the football team, advancing in the military, or reading every book in a series does *not* make you a member of those discourse communities. Rather, membership in a discourse community requires that you communicate successfully with other members of the community using rhetorical appeals specific to that community.

4. The level of proficiency required for one to be considered a true insider in a discourse community is always debatable. Imagine a **naysayer** (*They Say/I Say*, Chapter 6) who questions whether your level of proficiency qualifies you to be a legitimate member of the discourse community you discuss. Offer a rebuttal that explains why you believe you have set the bar high enough, why the criteria you met are sufficient to certify you as an insider in this community.

5. The previous four invention steps will help you generate the logos appeals of your discourse community analysis, the logical proofs that will help you convince your classmates and me that you mastered the discourse conventions of the community you select. You will also make ethos appeals to your classmates and me to convince us that you are a person of good character, good sense, and goodwill. To make effective ethos appeals, make sure you:

- know what you're talking about. Provide detailed anecdotes and examples and thoughtful analysis of those anecdotes and examples to show that you've reflected deeply on your experiences and have fully accepted the burden of proof.

- show regard for your readers. Try to come across as approachable and thoughtful, not arrogant or insensitive.

- treat skeptical readers with respect—don't ignore or demean their opinions just because they expect more proof.

- are careful and meticulous in your writing, not sloppy or disorganized.

6. Finally, you will make pathos appeals to your classmates and me to sway our emotions, connect with our values, and stir our imaginations. To make effective pathos appeals, make sure you:

- draw on the lessons of Chapter 9 in *They Say/I Say* to mix standard written English with "the kinds of expressions and turns of phrase that you use every day when texting or conversing with family and friends" (121). There is no need to stick to stuffy academic prose in this paper, but you also don't want to be so informal that your classmates and I can't understand you.

- evoke emotions (sympathy, outrage, anger, delight, awe, horror, and so on) in your classmates and me that make your paper more moving.

- evoke sensations (seeing, hearing, touching, tasting, smelling) in your classmates and me that make your writing vivid and help us to experience things imaginatively.

- appeal to values (freedom, justice, tolerance, fairness, equality, and so on) that your classmates and I share.

Arrangement

In rhetorical studies, arrangement refers to the selection of content generated during the invention stage and the organization of that content into an effective composition.

To begin your paper, follow the advice offered in Chapter 1 of *They Say/I Say*: "To give your writing the most important thing of all—namely, a point—a writer needs to indicate clearly not only what his or her thesis is, but also what larger conversation that thesis is responding to" (20). The larger conversation you're responding to is our class discussion of discourse communities, rhetoric, rhetorical appeals, the rhetorical situation, rhetorical reading and writing, and so on. Indicate at the beginning of your paper—before you state your thesis—that you're writing in response to those conversations.

Once you've acknowledged the "they say" and followed it with your "I say" (i.e., your thesis), continue by adhering to the advice in Chapter 7 of *They Say/I Say*: "Regardless of how interesting a topic may be to you as a writer, readers always need to know what is at stake in a text and why they should care. . . . Rather than assume that audiences will know why their claims matter, all writers need to answer the 'so what?' and 'who cares?' questions up front" (92–93). Don't assume that your classmates and I care about what you say—*make* us care by explaining what is at stake in your paper and why it should be important to us. Feel free to use the templates in Chapter 7 of *They Say/I Say*.

After you've completed these introductory moves, the arrangement of your analysis is up to you. You should include material from each step in the invention stage, but your selection and organization of that material should follow your own judgment as to what will prove most effective with your classmates and me.

Style

In rhetorical studies, style refers to the appropriate language for the occasion, subject matter, and audience.

One purpose of ENGL 1301 is to give you practice writing in a variety of styles. For this paper, your style should be clear but informal. You should follow the advice in Chapter 9 of *They Say/I Say* and mix standard written English with "the kinds of expressions and turns of phrase that you use every day when texting or conversing with family and friends" (121). This paper will allow your classmates and me to get to know you better, so write in a style that is your own.

Readers appreciate coherent, unified paragraphs, even when reading an informal piece of writing. Your paragraphs should include a topic sentence that clearly states the main idea of the paragraph and supporting sentences that cluster around the main idea without detours.

Proofread carefully; avoid errors in grammar, spelling, punctuation, and mechanics. Visit the Purdue OWL Web site (https://owl.english .purdue.edu/owl/) for questions you have regarding style.

Other Requirements

Your paper should be no longer than *five* pages—anything beyond that length will be considered a failure to adhere to one of the assignment's basic requirements. It should be double-spaced, typed in Times New Roman font, with 12-point character size and one-inch margins all the way around.

Your first submission is due at the beginning of class on _____, and you should think of it as a final draft—something that is ready for your classmates and me to read. If your first submission does not meet every requirement of this assignment sheet, I will return it to you and count it as late. Both your first and final submissions must be turned in on time—you will be docked a full letter grade for each day either is late.

Peer reviews are due _____.

Final drafts are due _____.

Grading Criteria

The following descriptions can help you understand the difference between an excellent discourse community analysis (DCA) and an average one.

C: UTA defines a C as "average," so, since this is a 1000-level Common Core class, a C paper is what a UTA freshman who is writing at an average level typically produces when she/he gives a strong effort. To earn a C, your DCA should first indicate the larger conversation to which you're responding ("they say") before providing a thesis that claims you successfully joined a discourse community by mastering the ethos, logos, and pathos appeals specific to that community ("I say"). You should answer the "so what?" and "who cares?" questions, provide sufficient evidence to support your thesis, and respond to a naysayer who questions your membership in the discourse community. Make sure your paper meets every requirement listed on the assignment sheet, and give your paper a discernible structure. The ideas you present should demonstrate that you understand the rhetorical concepts that we have addressed in class. Moreover, show that you have responded actively and thoughtfully to peer and instructor feedback on your first submission. Grammatical and syntactical mistakes should not impede my understanding of your analysis.

B: UTA defines a B as "above average," so a B paper is what a UTA freshman who is writing at an above-average level typically earns when he/she gives a strong effort (certainly a student writing at an average level can earn a B with exceptional effort). To earn a B, first make sure your paper meets all the criteria required to earn a C. Beyond that, you should represent what "they say" more completely and provide more developed answers to the "so what?" and "who cares?" questions. Your anecdotes and examples should be particularly well selected and vividly drawn, and you should explicate their significance as rhetorical appeals through lucid, complex metacommentary. Your paper should fully represent the objection of a naysayer who questions your membership in the discourse community and respond with a strong rebuttal that defends your claim to membership. You should revise thoroughly, responding to feedback with great comprehensiveness. Finally, a B paper demonstrates strong command of word choice, voice, style, and grammatical conventions.

A: UTA defines an A as "excellent," so an A paper is what a UTA freshman who is writing at an excellent level (80th percentile or above) might produce if he/she gave maximum effort. (Again, students writing at an average or above-average level may also earn As with extraordinary effort and sustained hard work.) To earn an A, first make sure your paper meets the criteria required to earn a C and a B. Then, introduce what "they say" in a manner that conveys a deep understanding of rhetorical appeals and discourse communities. Your paper should include a thesis that is conceptually rich and should answer the "so what?" and "who cares?" questions in great depth and with keen insight. You should include numerous anecdotes and examples for each rhetorical appeal and provide sustained metacommentary that draws out the full significance of the anecdotes and examples as rhetorical appeals. Finally, your paper should engage deeply with a naysayer, make reasonable concessions, and provide a compelling rebuttal that fully defends your claim that you have met the requirements of membership in the discourse community.

u receive a **D** on your paper, carefully consider the criteria listed above for a C. I give Ds to papers when writers, while demonstrating a general understanding of the topic and concepts, have not fulfilled all the requirements listed on the assignment sheet or have failed to respond to my comments on their first submission. If you misunderstand the assignment; show little understanding of the required rhetorical concepts; or ignore the technical requirements of topic, length, or format, your paper may receive an F.

Paper 2: Rhetorical Analysis

The Rhetorical Situation

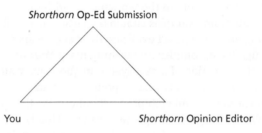

Shorthorn Op-Ed Submission

You

Shorthorn Opinion Editor

For your discourse community analysis, you conducted an analysis of the rhetorical appeals you mastered as part of a discourse community. For this paper, you will turn your attention outward, analyzing the rhetorical appeals of a writer and evaluating the effectiveness of those appeals in terms of *Shorthorn* readers. Your audience will be the *Shorthorn* opinion editor.

The purpose of rhetorical analysis is to understand how texts work to sway readers. As part of your initiation into an academic discourse community, you will need to learn the discourse conventions of your major field of study (e.g., common topics, distinctive vocabulary, field-specific values, backgrounds of participants, and so on) and understand how those conventions work to influence people in the field. The primary way you will learn these conventions is by immersing yourself in the field's textual conversations and thinking critically about the way written language functions to establish, communicate, and disseminate field-specific knowledge.

The purpose of this paper, then, is to give you practice reading the work of a writer engaged in a textual conversation you're not yet familiar with, analyzing the rhetorical moves that writer makes, and considering how those rhetorical moves will be received by readers. My hope is that this assignment will teach you a method of reading and thinking that you can then apply to all texts—academic and otherwise—you encounter.

Invention

In rhetorical studies, invention refers to the systematic search for ideas that can be shaped into an effective composition. (The term *prewriting* is sometimes used to refer to the concept of invention.) This section of the assignment, then, is designed to help you generate the required content for your rhetorical analysis. Please note that the following steps are not intended to serve as an outline for your paper. Rather, these steps will help you produce the "raw materials" that you will then refine into a well-organized analysis, and these steps are likely to produce more material than you can use in the draft you submit to readers.

1. Your editor will need to know the author's central claim. To make the most accurate identification of the central claim, consult the "Identifying Central Claims Worksheet" at the end of this assignment.

2. Your editor also needs to know what reasons the author is providing to support his/her central claim. To identify the author's supporting reasons, imagine that you could ask the writer in person:

- "Why do you believe that [central claim]?" Based on the information in the article, how do you think the writer would answer? Would the writer reply with just one reason, or would there be many? If there would be many, what would they be?

Please note that invention steps 3-6 will generate the majority of content for your rhetorical analysis because this is where you analyze and evaluate the article's effectiveness with *Shorthorn* readers. To produce such an analysis/evaluation, draw on your knowledge of the UTA community (e.g., well-educated, intellectually curious, ethnically and politically diverse, and so on). Use empathy and imagination to put yourself in the shoes of readers and make judgments about *how* they will respond to various rhetorical appeals and *why* they will respond in the way you predict.

Do not worry about whether your predictions of reader response are entirely accurate. You will not be assessed on whether your predictions are "right" but on how well you justify your predictions. In other words, you will be assessed on the reasonableness and depth of your descriptions of *how* readers will respond and *why* they will respond in the way you describe.

3. Your editor will want to know whether the author provides evidence for his/her reasons and whether that evidence will prove convincing to *Shorthorn* readers. Ask yourself the following questions:

- Will *Shorthorn* readers believe the author's reasons are true automatically? (If so, then there's no reason for the writer to provide evidence.) If not, does the writer provide evidence to support his/her reasons? If so, is this evidence sufficient to convince *Shorthorn* readers that the author's reasons are true?

4. Your editor will want to know whether the author addresses potential opponents. Ask yourself the following questions:

- Does the author anticipate objections to parts of his/her argument? If so, does the author represent opponents fairly or set up straw men? Does the author concede certain points to opponents? Does the author provide a convincing reply to opponents?

5. The previous four invention steps will help you analyze and evaluate the writer's logos appeals, but your editor will also want to know about the author's ethos appeals. Ask yourself the following questions:

- Do the author's credentials make his/her claims more credible? Does the author seem knowledgeable and well-informed on the topic? Does the author consider alternate viewpoints and treat opponents with respect? Does the author seem to have the audience's best interests at heart? Does the author draw on values he/she shares with the audience?

6. Your editor will also be interested in the author's pathos appeals. Ask yourself the following questions:

- Does the author evoke emotions in UTA readers that are likely to help his/her case? Does the author evoke sensations in UTA readers that will make the writing seem vivid? Does the author draw on values possessed by the UTA community?

7. Once you've completed the previous six invention steps, you should have a clear sense of how the article will be received by *Shorthorn* readers. Now you're ready to determine whether you will recommend the article for publication and why.

   The opinion editor is not overly concerned with whether readers will be convinced by the author's argument. Rather, the editor wants articles that readers will find interesting and thought-provoking. Ask yourself the following questions:

   - Is the article sufficiently nuanced, complex, and well-argued to engage UTA readers? Is the topic of the article relevant to the UTA community? Will UTA readers learn anything from the article? Is the article's argument controversial enough to elicit a range of responses from UTA readers?

   Based on your answers to these questions, develop a claim for or against publication and provide reasons for your decision. You will then support this thesis throughout the course of your analysis, as you break down the article and explain how it will be received by *Shorthorn* readers.

8. You yourself must also make effective ethos appeals so that you come across to your editor as a person of good character, good sense, and goodwill. To make effective ethos appeals, make sure you:

   - know what you're talking about. Make sure you read the article deeply and thoroughly, and provide sufficient evidence to support your claim for or against publication.

   - show regard for your editor. Try to come across as approachable and thoughtful, not arrogant or insensitive.

   - are careful and meticulous in your writing, not sloppy or disorganized.

9. Finally, make pathos appeals to your editor by connecting with her/his emotions, values, and imagination. To make effective pathos appeals, make sure you:

   - draw on the lessons of Chapter 9 in *They Say/I Say* by mixing standard written English with "the kinds of expressions and turns of phrase that you use every day when texting or conversing with family and friends" (121). You should adopt a slightly more formal style than in your first paper because now you're practicing a type of professional writing.

- evoke emotions (sympathy, outrage, anger, delight, awe, horror, and so on) in your editor that make your paper more moving.

- evoke sensations (seeing, hearing, touching, tasting, smelling) in your editor that make your writing vivid and help her/him experience things imaginatively.

- appeal to values (freedom, justice, tolerance, fairness, equality, and so on) that your editor and you share.

Arrangement

In rhetorical studies, arrangement refers to the selection of content generated during the invention stage and the organization of that content into an effective composition.

To begin your paper, follow the advice offered in Chapter 1 of *They Say/I Say*: "To give your writing the most important thing of all—namely, a point—a writer needs to indicate clearly not only what his or her thesis is, but also what larger conversation that thesis is responding to" (20). In this case, the conversation you're responding to is simply the one initiated by your editor's request. Indicate at the beginning of your paper—before you state your thesis—that you're writing in response to that request.

Once you've acknowledged the "they say" and followed it with your "I say" (i.e., your thesis), continue by adhering to the advice in Chapter 7 of *They Say/I Say*: "Regardless of how interesting a topic may be to you as a writer, readers always need to know what is at stake in a text and why they should care. . . . Rather than assume that audiences will know why their claims matter, all writers need to answer the 'so what?' and 'who cares?' questions up front" (92–93). Even though you're writing at your editor's request, you can still make your analysis more significant by explaining why it is important for *The Shorthorn* to publish—or not to publish—the article you're analyzing. Feel free to use the templates in Chapter 7 of *They Say/I Say*.

After you've completed these introductory moves, the arrangement of your analysis is up to you. You should include material from each step in the invention stage, but your selection and organization of that material should follow your own judgment as to what will prove most effective with your editor.

Style

In rhetorical studies, style refers to the appropriate language for the occasion, subject matter, and audience.

As mentioned earlier, you should follow the advice in Chapter 9 of *They Say/I Say* and mix standard written English with "the kinds of expressions and turns of phrase that you use every day when texting or conversing with family and friends" (121). You should adopt a slightly more formal style than in your first paper because you're writing in a professional setting. At the same time, this paper falls into the category of an inner office memo not intended for publication, so you need not adopt the highest level of formality.

Readers appreciate coherent, unified paragraphs, even when reading an informal piece of writing. Your paragraphs should include a topic sentence that clearly states the main idea of the paragraph and supporting sentences that cluster around the main idea without detours.

Proofread carefully; avoid errors in grammar, spelling, punctuation, and mechanics. Visit the Purdue OWL Web site (https://owl.english .purdue.edu/owl/) for questions you have regarding style.

Other Requirements

Your paper should be no longer than *five* pages—anything beyond that length will be considered a failure to adhere to one of the assignment's basic requirements. It should be double-spaced, typed in Times New Roman font, with 12-point character size and one-inch margins all the way around.

Your first submission is due at the beginning of class on _____, and you should think of it as a final draft—something that is ready for your classmates and me to read. If your first submission does not meet every requirement of this assignment sheet, I will return it to you and count it as late. Both your first and final submissions must be turned in on time—you will be docked a full letter grade for each day either is late.

Peer reviews are due _____.

Final drafts are due _____.

Identifying Central Claims Worksheet

One of the most difficult steps in rhetorical analysis is the first one: identifying a writer's central claim. Writers rarely announce their central claims explicitly, which means an analyst must sift through all parts of a text, apply inference skills to "read between the lines," and carefully construct a statement that accurately represents what a writer most wants his/her audience to believe.

To identify a writer's central claim, come up with the best answer (i.e., one you can make the best case for based on textual evidence) to the following question:

- Imagine that an editor forced this writer to replace the hundreds (or thousands) of words in this article with a single sentence. As compensation, the editor guaranteed the writer that readers would agree with this single sentence. What would the writer's one sentence be?

Or, to ask it another way . . .

- As with all arguments, the writer makes lots of explicit and implicit claims in this piece. But which one does the writer *most* want the audience to grant? If a genie said to the writer, "I will make your audience agree with one of your claims," which one would the writer choose?

After you answer these questions, you will have a *tentative* identification of the central claim, but you still need to test your identification to make sure it's the best option.

Test 1: All argument begins in agreement (at the very least people engaged in argument have agreed to use words rather than weapons). Consequently, a writer will make many claims that his or her opponents agree with. However, the writer's *central* claim will be one that opponents disagree with because, after all, this disagreement is what motivates the writer in the first place. After you've identified the writer's central claim, ask yourself: "Would the writer's opponents agree with this claim?" If you answer "yes," then you've probably identified a claim that serves as common ground and is *not* the central claim; if you answer "no," you may very well have identified the central claim.

Test 2: Make sure the claim you identify represents *precisely*—no more than, no less than—the minimum the writer would be satisfied with. For example, if a writer is arguing that students with concealed handgun licenses should be allowed to carry guns into UTA buildings, the central claim is *not* "everyone has a right to bring a gun to campus" (that's a much stronger claim than what the writer is advocating). Conversely, the central claim is *not* "students should be allowed to protect themselves" (that's a much weaker claim than what the writer is advocating).

Test 3: A central claim will either ask readers to change their minds (e.g., "UTA is a better university than you might think") or to act (e.g., "You should attend UTA"). First, determine whether the claim you've identified simply asks readers to understand or believe something (a conceptual claim) or whether it asks readers to act (a practical claim). If you've identified a conceptual claim, test it by asking yourself whether the writer is in fact asking for more—asking readers to act. If you've identified a practical claim, ask yourself whether the writer is in fact asking for less—asking readers to think a certain way. *Hint:* a practical claim will almost always include a verb phrase that begins with "should" or "must."

Test 4: Graff and Birkenstein point out that the best persuasive writing "is deeply engaged in some way with other people's views" (3). What this means is that a writer's central claim is often a *response* to recent events or to a previous writer's argument. For example, in the preface to *They Say/I Say*, Graff and Birkenstein don't simply claim that "it's okay to use 'I'"; rather, they claim that "in contrast to many teachers' prohibitions, it's okay to use 'I.'" For this last test, first identify the "they say" in the article you are reading. Then, consider whether the central claim you've identified is a direct response to what "they say." If it isn't, you may need to adjust your identification of the writer's central claim accordingly.

Grading Criteria

The following descriptions can help you understand the difference between an excellent rhetorical analysis and an average one.

C: UTA defines a C as "average," so, since this is a 1000-level Common Core class, a C paper is what a UTA freshman who is writing at an average level typically produces when she/he gives a strong effort. To earn a C, your rhetorical analysis should first indicate the larger conversation to which you're responding ("they say") before providing a thesis that makes a recommendation for or against publication and provides reasons for your recommendation ("I say"). You should answer the "so what?" and "who cares?" questions and provide sufficient evidence throughout the course of your analysis to support your thesis. Make sure your paper meets every requirement listed on the assignment sheet, and give your paper a discernible structure. The ideas you present should demonstrate that you understand the rhetorical concepts that we have addressed in class. Moreover, show that you have responded actively and thoughtfully to peer and instructor feedback on your first submission. Grammatical and syntactical mistakes should not impede my understanding of your analysis.

B: UTA defines a B as "above average," so a B paper is what a UTA freshman who is writing at an above-average level typically earns when he/she gives a strong effort (certainly a UTA freshman writing at an average level can earn a B with exceptional effort). To earn a B, first make sure your paper meets all the criteria required to earn a C. Beyond that, you should represent what "they say" more completely and provide more developed answers to the "so what?" and "who cares?" questions by making a compelling case that your decision on publication is significant to the UTA community. You should analyze *Shorthorn* readers' responses to the article in a particularly high level of detail. You should revise thoroughly, responding to feedback with great comprehensiveness. Finally, a B paper demonstrates strong command of word choice, voice, style, and grammatical conventions.

A: UTA defines an A as "excellent," so an A paper is what a UTA freshman who is writing at an excellent level (80th percentile or above) might produce if he/she gave maximum effort. (Again, students writing at an average or above-average level may also earn As with extraordinary effort and sustained hard work.) To earn an A, first make sure your paper meets the criteria required to earn a C and a B. Then, your paper should include a thesis that is conceptually rich and answer the "so what?" and "who cares?" questions in great depth and with keen insight. You should construct a consistent, methodical analysis of the writer's ethos, logos, and pathos appeals that describes in detail how *Shorthorn* readers will respond to each rhetorical move you analyze and explains why they will respond in the way you predict. You might even address aspects of the article that I've not noticed or in ways I've not considered. Finally, your paper should be lucid, concise, easy to follow, and should demonstrate your command of style, voice, mechanics, and usage.

If you receive a **D** on your paper, carefully consider the criteria listed above for a C. I give Ds to papers when writers, while demonstrating a general understanding of the topic and concepts, have not fulfilled all the requirements listed on the assignment sheet or have failed to respond to my comments on their first submission. If you misunderstand the assignment; show little understanding of the required rhetorical concepts; or ignore the technical requirements of topic, length, or format, your paper may receive an F.

Paper 3: Synthesis Argument

The Rhetorical Situation

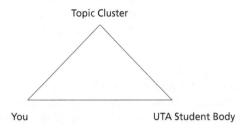

Topic Cluster

You   UTA Student Body

For your discourse community analysis, you analyzed rhetorical appeals you made as part of a discourse community, whereas for your rhetorical analysis, you analyzed rhetorical appeals an author made as part of a textual conversation unfamiliar to you. For this paper, you yourself will make written rhetorical appeals as you jump into the conversation constituted by your chosen topic cluster and contribute your own original argument. Your audience will be readers of a (fictitious) UTA student periodical that offers analysis and commentary about politics, news, and culture.

In the early stages of your entrance into an academic discourse community, you will devote most of your energies to reading about and listening to the words and ideas of others. This is how you acquire knowledge. To become a participating member of the community, however, you will transform the knowledge you have acquired as you apply it to new rhetorical goals and contexts. Such knowledge transformation requires you to synthesize the words and ideas of others with your own.

The purpose of this paper is to give you practice familiarizing yourself with a textual conversation, locating an opening for your own contribution, and making an argument that you support by combining your own ideas and reasoning with outside sources. My hope is that this assignment will familiarize you with a process of thinking and writing that anticipates the sort of knowledge transformation that will be required of you in your major field of study.

Invention

In rhetorical studies, invention refers to the systematic search for ideas that can be shaped into an effective composition. (The term *prewriting* is sometimes used to refer to the concept of invention.) This section of the assignment, then, is designed to help you generate the required content for your synthesis argument. Please note that the following steps are not intended to serve as an outline for your paper. Rather, these steps will help you produce the "raw materials" that you will then refine into a well-organized argument, and these steps are likely to produce more material than you can use in the draft you submit to readers.

1. You should begin by reading all the articles in your chosen topic cluster. A main goal of your reading should be to look for an opening in the conversation. For example, you might disagree with a claim made by one of the authors (*They Say/I Say*, pp. 58–61), you might agree with a claim but with a difference (*They Say/I Say*, pp. 61–64), you might agree and disagree with a claim simultaneously (*They Say/I Say*, pp. 64–66), or you might generate an entirely new claim that addresses an aspect of the issue that the articles fail to address. The point is that you want to *advance* the conversation, turn it in a new direction, rather than simply repeat or summarize another writer's argument.

   A second main goal of your reading is to find sufficient support for your thesis (i.e., your claim and reasons). Some of this support may come from your own experiences, observations, and reasoning, but you should also look for information from the readings that you can use to support your thesis.

2. Once you've read and analyzed all the articles, you should be ready to sketch out a thesis. Formulate a clear claim that you support with at least *three* reasons. Make sure your reasons are *good* reasons. In other words, assuming you provide sufficient evidence to prove that your reasons are true statements, those reasons should be enough to convince readers to accept your claim.

3. Once you've constructed a thesis, begin synthesizing evidence to support your reasons. As mentioned above, you should draw on your own experiences, observations, and reasoning when appropriate, but you should also incorporate words, ideas, and information from the sources that help to prove that your reasons are true statements. It's almost always a good idea to diversify evidence by drawing from multiple sources, so really mine the readings for material that helps you make your case.

4. Make sure you anticipate objections to your argument by planting at least one naysayer in your paper. To engage effectively with a naysayer, you should:

- name and describe the naysayer (*They Say/I Say*, pp. 78–86).
- represent objections fairly (*They Say/I Say*, pp. 86–87).
- make concessions when possible (*They Say/I Say*, pp. 89–90).
- answer objections (*They Say/I Say*, pp. 87–89).

5. The previous four steps will help you construct effective logos appeals. You should also make effective ethos appeals to come across to readers as a person of good character, good sense, and goodwill. To make effective ethos appeals, make sure you:

- know what you're talking about. Read all the articles in your topic cluster deeply and thoroughly, and provide sufficient evidence to support your claim and reasons.
- show regard for your readers. Try to come across as approachable and thoughtful, not arrogant or insensitive.
- are careful and meticulous in your writing, not sloppy or disorganized.

6. Finally, make pathos appeals to readers by connecting with their emotions, values, and imaginations. To make effective pathos appeals, make sure you:

- draw on the lessons of Chapter 9 in *They Say/I Say* to mix standard written English with "the kinds of expressions and turns of phrase that you use every day when texting or conversing with family and friends" (121). You should adopt a more formal style than in your first two papers because now you are writing for publication.
- evoke emotions (sympathy, outrage, anger, delight, awe, horror, and so on) in your readers that make your paper more moving.
- evoke sensations (seeing, hearing, touching, tasting, smelling) in your audience that make your writing vivid and help readers experience things imaginatively.
- appeal to values (freedom, justice, tolerance, fairness, equality, and so on) that your readers and you share.

Arrangement

In rhetorical studies, arrangement refers to the selection of content generated during the invention stage and the organization of that content into an effective composition.

To begin your paper, follow the advice offered in Chapter 1 of *They Say/I Say*: "To give your writing the most important thing of all—namely, a point—a writer needs to indicate clearly not only what his or her thesis is, but also what larger conversation that thesis is responding to" (20). In this case, the conversation you're responding to is the one constituted by the articles in your topic cluster. Indicate at the beginning of your paper—before you state your thesis—that you're writing in response to that conversation.

Once you've acknowledged the "they say" and followed it with your "I say" (i.e., your thesis), continue by adhering to the advice in Chapter 7 of *They Say/I Say*: "Regardless of how interesting a topic may be to you as a writer, readers always need to know what is at stake in a text and why they should care. . . . Rather than assume that audiences will know why their claims matter, all writers need to answer the 'so what?' and 'who cares?' questions up front" (92–93). Unlike your first two papers, this one is unsolicited, which means you must work harder to demonstrate the exigence for your argument and to attract readers. Providing compelling answers to the "so what?" and "who cares?" questions has never been more important. Feel free to use the templates in Chapter 7 of *They Say/I Say*.

After you've completed these introductory moves, the arrangement of your argument is up to you. You should include material from each step in the invention stage, but your selection and organization of that material should follow your own judgment as to what will prove most effective with readers.

Style

In rhetorical studies, style refers to the appropriate language for the occasion, subject matter, and audience.

As mentioned earlier, you should follow the advice in Chapter 9 of *They Say/I Say* and mix standard written English with "the kinds of expressions and turns of phrase that you use every day when texting or conversing with family and friends" (121). You should adopt a more formal style than in your first two papers because you're writing for publication. At the same time, you're writing for a popular periodical rather than a scholarly journal, so you need not write in stuffy, academic prose.

Readers appreciate coherent, unified paragraphs, even when reading an informal piece of writing. Your paragraphs should include a topic sentence that clearly states the main idea of the paragraph and supporting sentences that cluster around the main idea without detours.

You should introduce your sources within your text the first time you mention them, and then continue to cite them within your text whenever you refer to them, as is done in any mainstream periodical. There is no need to include a Works Cited page or to use a formal citation system (like MLA, APA, or *Chicago*) simply because this is not the convention for this genre.

Proofread carefully; avoid errors in grammar, spelling, punctuation, and mechanics. Visit the Purdue OWL Web site (https://owl.english .purdue.edu/owl/) for questions you have regarding style.

Other Requirements

Your paper should be no longer than six pages—anything beyond that length will be considered a failure to adhere to one of the assignment's basic requirements. It should be double-spaced, typed in Times New Roman font, with 12-point character size and one-inch margins all the way around.

Your first submission is due at the beginning of class on _____, and you should think of it as a final draft—something that is ready for your classmates and me to read. If your first submission does not meet every requirement of this assignment sheet, I will return it to you and count it as late. Both your first and final submissions must be turned in on time—you will be docked a full letter grade for each day either is late.

Peer reviews are due _____.

Final drafts are due _____.

Grading Criteria

The following descriptions can help you understand the difference between an excellent synthesis argument and an average one.

C: UTA defines a C as "average," so, since this is a 1000-level Common Core class, a C paper is what a UTA freshman who is writing at an average level typically produces when she/he gives a strong effort. To earn a C, your synthesis argument should first indicate the larger conversation to which you're responding ("they say") before providing a thesis that includes your claim and at least three reasons ("I say"). You should answer the "so what?" and "who cares?" questions, provide sufficient evidence to support your reasons, answer the objections of a naysayer, and incorporate outside sources effectively. Make sure your paper meets every requirement listed on the assignment sheet, and give your paper a discernible structure. The ideas you present should demonstrate that you understand the rhetorical concepts that we have addressed in class. Moreover, show that you have responded actively and thoughtfully to peer and instructor feedback on your first submission. Grammatical and syntactical mistakes should not impede my understanding of your analysis.

B: UTA defines a B as "above average," so a B paper is what a UTA freshman who is writing at an above-average level typically earns when he/she gives a strong effort (certainly a UTA freshman writing at an average level can earn a B with exceptional effort). To earn a B, first make sure your paper meets all the criteria required to earn a C. Beyond that, you should represent what "they say" more completely and provide more developed answers to the "so what?" and "who cares?" questions by making a compelling case that your argument is significant for UTA students. You should construct a complex thesis, provide ample support for all your reasons, and represent strong objections from a naysayer that you answer convincingly. You should revise thoroughly, responding to feedback with great comprehensiveness. Finally, a B paper demonstrates strong command of word choice, voice, style, and grammatical conventions.

A: UTA defines an A as "excellent," so an A paper is what a UTA freshman who is writing at an excellent level (80th percentile or above) might produce if he/she gave maximum effort. (Again, students writing at an average or above-average level may also earn As with extraordinary effort and sustained hard work.) To earn an A, first make sure your paper meets the criteria required to earn a C and a B. You should tackle the issue addressed in your topic cluster in an original and challenging way, constructing a thesis that is conceptually rich and answering the "so what?" and "who cares?" questions in great depth and with keen insight. Your paper should synthesize evidence from diverse sources in a way that provides overwhelming support for all your reasons. You should fully represent the objections of a trenchant naysayer, make careful concessions, and answer objections in a manner that might satisfy even extreme opponents. Your paper should be lucid, concise, easy to follow, and should demonstrate your command of style, voice, mechanics, and usage.

If you receive a **D** on your paper, carefully consider the criteria listed above for a C. I give Ds to papers when writers, while demonstrating a general understanding of the topic and concepts, have not fulfilled all the requirements listed on the assignment sheet or have failed to respond to my comments on their first submission. If you misunderstand the assignment; show little understanding of the required rhetorical concepts; or ignore the technical requirements of topic, length, or format, your paper may receive an F.

English 1302: Rhetoric and Composition II

Paper 1: Issue Proposal

The Rhetorical Situation

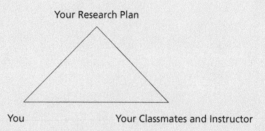

Your Research Plan

You

Your Classmates and Instructor

For this paper, you will propose a research project that will span the entire semester. Your audience will be your classmates and I.

Any academic or public policy research project begins by identifying an **issue**, which is simply an unsettled question that matters to a community. In the proposal stage, a writer takes stock of her or his current knowledge of and position on the issue and develops a research plan. A well-constructed issue proposal serves as a blueprint for the project and helps define a feasible scope for the project.

Invention

In rhetorical studies, invention refers to the systematic search for ideas that can be shaped into an effective composition. (The term *prewriting* is sometimes used to refer to the concept of invention.) This section of the assignment, then, is designed to help you generate the required content for your issue proposal. Please note that the following steps are not intended to serve as an outline for your paper. Rather, these steps will help you produce the "raw materials" that you will then refine into a well-organized proposal, and these steps are likely to produce more material than you can use in the draft you submit to readers.

1. You must first make sure the issue you've selected is arguable. Apply the "Twelve Tests of an Arguable Issue." If you cannot answer "yes" to all twelve questions, change or modify your issue until you can. Please note that all the major assignments in this course build on one another, so once you select an issue, you may not change it.

2. It's always a good idea to start a research project by taking inventory of your current knowledge of the topic. Draft answers to the following questions:

- What do you know about the topic already? Try to be as methodical and comprehensive as possible in detailing your current knowledge.

- How did you acquire your knowledge of the topic? Rack your memory to recall the specific sources of your current knowledge, and think about how your knowledge of the topic has evolved over time.

3. The most important goals of an issue proposal are to narrow the general topic to a specific issue and to construct a specific plan for research. Draft answers to the following questions:

- What are the main questions you want to answer in your final project? Be specific! Obviously, your research questions may change and evolve as you learn more about your issue, but specific research questions will give you a place to start.

- How would you answer these questions right now? Your answers may change significantly as you research the issue further, but it will be helpful to record where you stand. Your answers may be highly speculative at this point, but even speculative answers can help provide a framework for your subsequent reading and research.

- Where will you go to learn more about the issue and to find answers to your research questions? Be as specific as possible in describing the sources you'll turn to first, perhaps even mentioning specific authors, titles, Web sites, and so on.

4. You should also be thinking about potential audiences for your final project. Draft answers to the following questions:

- What audiences would be interested in your ideas on the issue?

- What types of scholars, stakeholders, decision makers, and pundits are interested in/affected by the issue?

- What sorts of people are likely to be your opponents? Your allies?

5. The previous four invention steps will help you generate the logos appeals (*Everything's an Argument*, p. 24) of your issue proposal, the logical proofs that will help you convince your classmates and me that you have selected an issue that will sustain a semester's worth of research and writing. You will also make ethos appeals (*Everything's an Argument*, pp. 23–24) to your classmates and me to convince us that you are a person of good character, good sense, and goodwill. To make effective ethos appeals, make sure you:

- are knowledgeable about the issue. Provide specific answers to the questions listed in steps 1-4 above. If you do not yet know enough about your issue to provide specific answers to those questions, you will need to conduct some preliminary research to find the information you need.

- show regard for your readers. Try to come across as approachable and thoughtful, not arrogant or insensitive.

- are careful and meticulous in your writing, not sloppy or disorganized.

6. Finally, you will make pathos appeals (*Everything's an Argument*, p. 23) to your classmates and me to sway our emotions, connect with our values, and stir our imaginations. To make effective pathos appeals, make sure you:

- draw on the lessons of Chapter 9 in *They Say/I Say* to mix standard written English with "the kinds of expressions and turns of phrase that you use every day when texting or conversing with family and friends" (121). There is no need to stick to stuffy academic prose in this paper, but you also don't want to be so informal that your classmates and I can't understand you.

- evoke emotions (sympathy, outrage, anger, delight, awe, horror, and so on) in your classmates and me that make your paper more moving.

- evoke sensations (seeing, hearing, touching, tasting, smelling) in your classmates and me that make your writing vivid and help us to experience things imaginatively.

- appeal to values (freedom, justice, tolerance, fairness, equality, and so on) that your classmates and I share.

Arrangement

In rhetorical studies, arrangement refers to the selection of content generated during the invention stage and the organization of that content into an effective composition.

To begin your paper, follow the advice offered in Chapter 1 of *They Say/I Say*: "To give your writing the most important thing of all—namely, a point—a writer needs to indicate clearly not only what his or her thesis is, but also what larger conversation that thesis is responding to" (20). In this case, the conversation you're responding to is the one surrounding the issue you've selected. Indicate at the beginning of your paper that you're writing in response to that conversation; then state a thesis that previews what you'll be discussing in your proposal.

Also mind the lesson of Chapter 7 in *They Say/I Say*: "Regardless of how interesting a topic may be to you as a writer, readers always need to know what is at stake in a text and why they should care. . . . Rather than assume that audiences will know why their claims matter, all writers need to answer the 'so what?' and 'who cares?' questions up front" (92–93). Don't assume that your classmates and I will understand why your issue matters—*make* us understand by explaining why your issue is important and why it matters to a community. Feel free to use the templates in Chapter 7 of *They Say/I Say*.

After you've completed these introductory moves, the arrangement of your analysis is up to you. You should include material from each step in the invention stage, but your selection and organization of that material should follow your own judgment as to what will prove most effective with your classmates and me.

Style

In rhetorical studies, style refers to the appropriate language for the occasion, subject matter, and audience.

One purpose of ENGL 1302 is to give you practice writing in a variety of styles. For this paper, your style should be clear but informal. As mentioned earlier, you should follow the advice in Chapter 9 of *They Say/I Say* and mix standard written English with "the kinds of expressions and turns of phrase that you use every day when texting or conversing with family and friends" (121). This paper will allow your classmates and me to get to know you better, so write in a style that is your own.

Readers appreciate coherent, unified paragraphs, even when reading an informal piece of writing. Your paragraphs should include a topic sentence that clearly states the main idea of the paragraph and supporting sentences that cluster around the main idea without detours.

Proofread carefully; avoid errors in grammar, spelling, punctuation, and mechanics. Visit the Purdue OWL Web site (https://owl.english.purdue.edu/owl/) for questions you have regarding style.

Other Requirements

Your paper should be no longer than *five* pages—anything beyond that length will be considered a failure to adhere to one of the assignment's basic requirements. It should be double-spaced, typed in Times New Roman font, with 12-point character size and one-inch margins all the way around.

Your first submission is due at the beginning of class on _____, and you should think of it as a final draft—something that is ready for your classmates and me to read. If your first submission does not meet every requirement of this assignment sheet, I will return it to you and count it as late. Both your first and final submissions must be turned in on time—you will be docked a full letter grade for each day either is late.

Peer reviews are due _____.

Final drafts are due _____.

Grading Criteria

The following descriptions can help you understand the difference between an excellent issue proposal and an average one.

C: UTA defines a C as "average," so since this is a 1000-level Common Core class, a C paper is what a UTA freshman who is writing at an average level typically produces when she/he gives a strong effort. To earn a C, your issue proposal should indicate the larger conversation to which you're responding ("they say"), provide a thesis that previews what you will discuss in your proposal ("I say"), and answer the "so what?" and "who cares?" questions. You should describe what you know about your issue and explain how you acquired that knowledge. You should list research questions, provide preliminary answers to those questions, and sketch out a research plan. Also, you should identify interested audiences, including anticipated allies and opponents. Moreover, show that you have responded actively and thoughtfully to peer and instructor feedback on your first submission. Grammatical and syntactical mistakes should not impede my understanding of your proposal.

B: UTA defines a B as "above average," so a B paper is what a UTA freshman who is writing at an above-average level typically earns when he/she gives a strong effort. (Certainly a UTA freshman writing at an average level can earn a B with exceptional effort.) To earn a B, first make sure your paper meets all the criteria required to earn a C. Beyond that, you should represent what "they say" more completely and provide more developed answers to the "so what?" and "who cares?" questions by making a compelling case that your issue is significant to a specific community. You should provide a comprehensive description of your current knowledge of the issue and explain in some detail how you acquired that knowledge. You should list well-considered research questions, provide developed (if speculative) answers to those questions, and describe a detailed research plan. Identify and describe interested audiences, including allies you might enlist and opponents you might address. You should revise thoroughly, responding to feedback with great comprehensiveness. Finally, a B paper demonstrates strong command of word choice, voice, style, and grammatical conventions.

A: UTA defines an A as "excellent," so an A paper is what a UTA freshman who is writing at an excellent level (80th percentile or above) might produce if he/she gave maximum effort. (Again, students writing at an average or above-average level may also earn As with extraordinary effort and sustained hard work.) To earn an A, first make sure your paper meets the criteria required to earn a C and a B. You should answer the "so what?" and "who cares?" questions in great depth and with keen insight into the significance of your issue. You should provide a thorough, methodical inventory of what you know about your issue and trace that knowledge to specific, named sources. You should provide numerous conceptually rich research questions that clearly justify semester-long inquiry, explain how you would answer those questions now and why you would answer them that way, and detail a research plan that includes specific sources you'll consult. Provide detailed profiles of interested audiences, potential allies, and potential opponents, and explain why these stakeholders would be interested in your work.

Your paper should be lucid, concise, easy to follow, and should demonstrate your command of style, voice, mechanics, and usage.

If you receive a **D** on your paper, carefully consider the criteria listed above for a C. I give Ds to papers when writers, while demonstrating a general understanding of the topic and concepts, have not fulfilled all the requirements listed on the assignment sheet or have failed to respond to my comments on their first submission. If you misunderstand the assignment; show little understanding of the required rhetorical concepts; or ignore the technical requirements of topic, length, or format, your paper may receive an F.

Annotated Bibliography

An annotated bibliography is a list of sources on a specific topic that includes a summary of each source. As you research your topic, construct an annotated bibliography of relevant sources. Your final annotated bibliography should include annotations for at least ten sources that represent multiple perspectives on your issue. Please note that your next paper will require you to summarize sources that advocate at least three different positions on your issue, so you can save time on that paper by including in your annotated bibliography sources that support at least three distinct positions.

The list should be complied in alphabetical order using Modern Language Association (MLA) style. Consult the Purdue OWL Web site (https://owl.english.purdue.edu/owl/) for directions on how to format entries.

Your annotation for each source should consist of two paragraphs. In the first, answer the following questions:

1. What kind of source is it—e.g., a book, journal article, magazine article, newspaper article, encyclopedia entry, database summary article, Web site, and so on?

2. What is the genre of the piece—e.g., a news report, an editorial, a report of scientific research, a summary of sources? What is the purpose of the text?

3. Who is/are the author/authors? What are the author's credentials? How does the author establish his or her authority to speak on this subject? Also consider the credibility of the publication venue.

4. Who is the intended audience? Consider where the text is published, the degree of specialized knowledge needed to understand the text, and how objective or argumentative the text is.

5. When was the text published? How does the publication date affect the relevance and usefulness of the source?

In your second paragraph, summarize the content of the piece in a way that demonstrates you have read the source and understood its content. If the source is an argument, as opposed to a purely informational text, identify its main claim and supporting reasons. In addition, explain how you plan to use the source in your researched position paper (obviously this plan may change as you conduct further research and begin drafting). Will you use the source for background information, and if so, what information specifically do you plan to use? Does the source contain evidence that you plan to borrow, and if so, what evidence? If the source is an argument, will you position it as an ally or an opponent, and why?

Sample Annotated Bibliography Entry

Estes, Todd. "The Connecticut Effect: The Great Compromise of 1787 and the History of Small State Impact on Electoral College Outcomes." *Historian*, vol, 73, no. 2, 2011, pp. 255-83. *Academic Search Complete*, http://libguides.uta.edu/acadsearchcom.

This journal article was written by Todd Estes, an Associate Professor of History at Oakland University, and was published in June 2011 in *Historian*, an academic history journal. Estes is credible because he is widely published in the discipline of history and has published numerous articles on the electoral process. Because *Historian* is an established journal in the field of history, the audience for this article comprises academic historians. That said, the article is accessible to nonspecialists who possess some prior knowledge of the electoral process and how it was formed. Because the article was published within the last year, one can assume it represents current thinking in the field of history.

The article addresses how the Connecticut Compromise, which gave smaller states disproportionate representation in the electoral college, has affected presidential election outcomes throughout the years. My plan is to use much of the information presented here as background information in my mapping the issue paper and my researched position paper. Specifically, I will borrow Estes's comparison of the ratio of electoral college voters to population in smaller states versus larger states.

Paper 2: Mapping the Issue

The Rhetorical Situation

For your issue proposal, you organized your preexisting knowledge on your issue and sketched a plan for research. You then compiled several sources and summarized their contents for your annotated bibliography. For this paper, you will map the controversy surrounding your issue by describing its history and summarizing at least three different positions on the issue—all from a completely neutral point of view. Your audience will be UTA students, faculty, and staff who read a (fictitious) UTA periodical that offers analysis and commentary about politics, news, and culture.

Before people can make an informed decision on a controversial issue, they must know the history of the controversy and the range of positions available. Major news organizations often inform their readers of public controversies by providing a neutral, unbiased description of an issue's history and the main arguments made on all sides, and academic organizations often map field-specific controversies to provide researchers with an overview of unsettled questions and unsolved problems.

Invention

In rhetorical studies, invention refers to the systematic search for ideas that can be shaped into an effective composition. (The term *prewriting* is sometimes used to refer to the concept of invention.) This section of the assignment, then, is designed to help you generate the required content for your mapping paper. Please note that the following steps are not intended to serve as an outline for your paper. Rather, these steps will help you produce the "raw materials" that you will then refine into a well-organized paper, and these steps are likely to produce more material than you can use in the draft you submit to readers.

1. Readers will need to have some background information on your issue to understand how the controversy reaches its current state. Draft answers to the following questions:

- What caused the issue?
- What prompted past and present interest in it?
- Who is interested in the issue and why?

2. Readers will also want to know the current, major positions on the issue, so reflect on the titles in your annotated bibliography, draft descriptions of *three to five* different positions, and identify which articles in your bibliography advocate the positions you've described.

3. Now that you've drafted descriptions of the background and major positions on your issue, draft a more detailed description of one position:

- What are the main claims of those who advocate this position?
- What reasons do they provide for those claims?
- What evidence do they use to support their reasons?
- What assumptions underlie their arguments?

4. Once you have described the position's argumentative structure, summarize at least one source from your annotated bibliography that advocates this position.

5. Repeat invention steps three and four with a second position. Additionally, draft a comparison of the two positions by answering the following questions:

- How do the foci of the positions intersect and diverge?
- On what points do advocates of these positions agree, and on what points do they disagree?
- What are the reasons for their disagreement?

6. Repeat invention steps three, four, and five with all the remaining positions you plan to describe.

7. The previous six steps will help you construct effective logos appeals. You should also make effective ethos appeals to come across to readers as a person of good character, good sense, and goodwill. Here are some tips:

- Describe the most significant positions across the entire field of the controversy; don't simply describe those positions that cluster around the position you favor.

- Summarize sources fairly and analyze them carefully. Accurately identify their main claims, supporting reasons and evidence, and implicit assumptions.

- Maintain neutrality. The time will come for you to take a stand on the issue, but don't do it now. Advocates of the positions you describe should feel that you have represented their views and arguments fairly, and your readers should finish your paper without any idea of where you stand on the issue.

8. Finally, make pathos appeals to readers by connecting with their emotions, values, and imaginations. To make effective pathos appeals, make sure you:

- appeal to readers' desire for information by presenting clear, well-organized, well-supported summaries that show you've read widely and closely and have developed a deep understanding of positions ranging across the entire field of the controversy.

- appeal to readers' sense of fairness by providing truly unbiased descriptions of all positions/arguments.

- Draw on the lessons of Chapter 9 in *They Say/I Say* by mixing standard written English with "the kinds of expressions and turns of phrase that you use every day when texting or conversing with family and friends" (121). Because you're writing for publication and for readers you don't know, you should adopt a more formal style and tone than in your first paper. This does not mean, however, that you need to abandon your unique ways of expressing yourself.

Arrangement

In rhetorical studies, arrangement refers to the selection of content generated during the invention stage and the organization of that content into an effective composition.

To begin your paper, follow the advice offered in Chapter 1 of *They Say/I Say*: "To give your writing the most important thing of all—namely, a point—a writer needs to indicate clearly not only what his or her thesis is, but also what larger conversation that thesis is responding to" (20). In this case, the conversation you're responding to is the one surrounding your issue. Indicate at the beginning of your paper that you're writing in response to that conversation; then state a thesis that previews what you'll be discussing in your mapping paper.

Also mind the lesson of Chapter 7 in *They Say/I Say*: "Regardless of how interesting a topic may be to you as a writer, readers always need to know what is at stake in a text and why they should care. . . . Rather than assume that audiences will know why their claims matter, all writers need to answer the 'so what?' and 'who cares?' questions up front" (92–93). Don't assume that your readers will understand why your issue matters—*make* them understand by explaining why your issue is important and why it matters to a community. Feel free to use the templates in Chapter 7 of *They Say/I Say*.

After you've completed these introductory moves, the arrangement of your analysis is up to you. You should include material from each step in the invention stage, but your selection and organization of that material should follow your own judgment as to what will prove most effective with the UTA community.

Style

In rhetorical studies, style refers to the appropriate language for the occasion, subject matter, and audience.

As mentioned earlier, you should follow the advice in Chapter 9 of *They Say/I Say* and mix standard written English with "the kinds of expressions and turns of phrase that you use every day when texting or conversing with family and friends" (121). You should adopt a more formal style than in your issue proposal because now you're writing for publication. At the same time, you're writing for a popular periodical rather than a scholarly journal, so you need not write in stuffy, academic prose.

Readers appreciate coherent, unified paragraphs, even when reading an informal piece of writing. Your paragraphs should include a topic sentence that clearly states the main idea of the paragraph and supporting sentences that cluster around the main idea without detours.

Proofread carefully; avoid errors in grammar, spelling, punctuation, and mechanics. Visit the Purdue OWL Web site (https://owl.english .purdue.edu/owl/) for questions you have regarding style.

Other Requirements

Your paper should be no longer than six pages—anything beyond that length will be considered a failure to adhere to one of the assignment's basic requirements. It should be double-spaced, typed in Times New Roman font, with 12-point character size and one-inch margins all the way around.

Your first submission is due at the beginning of class on _____, and you should think of it as a final draft—something that is ready for your classmates and me to read. If your first submission does not meet every requirement of this assignment sheet, I will return it to you and count it as late. Both your first and final submissions must be turned in on time—you will be docked a full letter grade for each day either is late.

Peer reviews are due _____.

Final drafts are due _____.

Grading Criteria

The following descriptions can help you understand the difference between an excellent mapping the issue paper and an average one.

C: UTA defines a C as "average," so since this is a 1000-level Common Core class, a C paper is what a UTA freshman who is writing at an average level typically produces when she/he gives a strong effort. To earn a C, your mapping the issue paper should indicate the larger conversation to which you're responding ("they say"), provide a thesis that previews what you will discuss in your paper ("I say"), and answer the "so what?" and "who cares?" questions. You should provide sufficient background on the issue, describe at least three different positions on the issue, summarize sources that advocate for those positions, and analyze similarities and differences among the different positions. Moreover, show that you have responded actively and thoughtfully to peer and instructor feedback on your first submission. Grammatical and syntactical mistakes should not impede my understanding of your analysis.

B: UTA defines a B as "above average," so a B paper is what a UTA freshman who is writing at an above-average level typically earns when he/she gives a strong effort. (Certainly, a UTA freshman writing at an average level can earn a B with exceptional effort.) To earn a B, first make sure your paper meets all the criteria required to earn a C. Beyond that, you should represent what "they say" more completely and provide more developed answers to the "so what?" and "who cares?" questions by making a compelling case for the significance of understanding the controversy surrounding your issue. You should construct a narrative that tells a coherent story of how the issue reached its current state. You should describe positions in a high level of detail, summarize sources fully and accurately, and provide a rich, lucid comparison of positions. You should revise thoroughly, responding to feedback with great comprehensiveness. Finally, a B paper demonstrates strong command of word choice, voice, style, and grammatical conventions.

A: UTA defines an A as "excellent," so an A paper is what a UTA freshman who is writing at an excellent level (80th percentile or above) might produce if he/she gave maximum effort. (Again, students writing at an average or above-average level may also earn As with extraordinary effort and sustained hard work.) To earn an A, first make sure your paper meets the criteria required to earn a C and a B. You should answer the "so what?" and "who cares?" questions in great depth and with keen insight into the significance of your issue. Your background section should trace the evolution of the issue in rich detail that fully contextualizes its status. You should describe positions in a fair, neutral, careful manner that clearly reveals their argumentative elements. Your summaries of sources should demonstrate how they exemplify the typical argumentative maneuvers of advocates of that position. You should pinpoint the similarities and differences among positions with great precision and in a way that captures the complexities of their relationships. Your paper should be lucid, concise, easy to follow, and should demonstrate your command of style, voice, mechanics, and usage.

If you receive a **D** on your paper, carefully consider the criteria listed above for a C. I give Ds to papers when writers, while demonstrating a general understanding of the topic and concepts, have not fulfilled all the requirements listed on the assignment sheet or have failed to respond to all my comments on their first submission. If you misunderstand the assignment; show little understanding of the required rhetorical concepts; or ignore the technical requirements of topic, length, or format, your paper may receive an F.

Paper 3: Researched Position Paper

The Rhetorical Situation

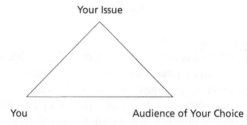

For your issue proposal, you organized your preexisting knowledge on your issue and sketched a plan for research. You then compiled several sources and summarized their contents for your annotated bibliography. In your mapping the issue paper, you traced the controversy surrounding your issue by describing its history and summarizing the major positions on it. All these assignments have been preparing you for this final paper, where you will advocate a position on your issue with a well-supported argument written for an audience that you select.

Invention

In rhetorical studies, invention refers to the systematic search for ideas that can be shaped into an effective composition. (The term *prewriting* is sometimes used to refer to the concept of invention.) This section of the assignment, then, is designed to help you generate the required content for your researched position paper. Please note that the following steps are not intended to serve as an outline for your paper. Rather, these steps will help you produce the "raw materials" that you will then refine into a well-organized analysis, and these steps are likely to produce more material than you can use in the draft you submit to readers.

1. You should first choose a publication venue for your paper. For example, will you write a letter directly to an individual, group, or organization? Or will you write an article for a newspaper, newsletter, or periodical? Perhaps a piece for a Web site, Web-based publication, or social media site? To ensure that you select a specific enough audience, make sure your venue has an address (physical or electronic) to which you could send your paper. Then, investigate the characteristics and values of the readers you will reach through this venue.

2. Once you've settled on an audience, construct a claim that *advances the conversation* about your issue and turns it in a new direction. You might disagree with a claim made by an author (*They Say/I Say*, pp. 58–61), you might agree with a claim but with a difference (*They Say/I Say*, pp. 61–64), you might agree and disagree with a claim simultaneously (*They Say/I Say*, pp. 64–66), or you might generate an entirely new claim that addresses an aspect of the issue that has not been addressed in the sources you've found.

3. Next, attach as many reasons as are necessary to fully support your claim. Your claim plus reasons, also known as "enthymemes" (*Everything's an Argument*, p. 65), will form your thesis.

4. For each separate enthymeme in your thesis, identify the implicit warrant and determine whether it represents an assumption that your audience shares with you. If so, there's no need to address the warrant explicitly in your argument. If the warrant represents an assumption some readers might resist, however, consider how you might persuade them to accept it. If you think it would be impossible to persuade your audience to accept the warrant, then you might consider changing the reason to produce a warrant that relies on an assumption that you and your readers share. Please note that each reason in your thesis will produce a different warrant, and you must assess the audience's response to each one.

5. For each of your reasons (and any warrant that needs explicit support), provide sufficient evidence to convince your audience that your reasons are true statements. Your personal experiences, observations, and reasoning count as evidence, but you should also draw extensively on outside sources for evidence to support your reasons.

6. Make sure you anticipate objections to your argument by planting at least one naysayer in your paper. This naysayer might be hypothetical or might be the actual author of an outside source. To engage effectively with a naysayer, you should:

- name and describe the naysayer (*They Say/I Say*, pp. 75–86).
- represent objections fairly (*They Say/I Say*, pp. 86–87).
- make concessions when possible (*They Say/I Say*, pp. 89–90).
- answer objections (*They Say/I Say*, pp. 87–89).

7. The previous six steps will help you construct effective **logos** appeals. You should also make effective **ethos** appeals to come across to

readers as a person of good character, good sense, and goodwill. To make effective ethos appeals, make sure you:

- know what you're talking about. Draw on all those outside sources you've been reading over the course of the semester, and provide ample evidence for your reasons.
- show regard for your readers. Try to come across as approachable and thoughtful, not arrogant or insensitive.
- are careful and meticulous in your writing, not sloppy or disorganized.

8. Finally, make **pathos** appeals to readers by connecting with their emotions, values, and imaginations. To make effective pathos appeals, make sure you:

- choose an appropriate style based on the conventions of your publication venue.
- evoke emotions (sympathy, outrage, anger, delight, awe, horror, and so on) in your readers that make your paper more moving.
- evoke sensations (seeing, hearing, touching, tasting, smelling) in your audience that make your writing vivid and help readers experience things imaginatively.
- appeal to values (freedom, justice, tolerance, fairness, equality, and so on) that your readers and you share.

Arrangement

In rhetorical studies, arrangement refers to the selection of content generated during the invention stage and the organization of that content into an effective composition.

To begin your paper, follow the advice offered in Chapter 1 of *They Say/I Say*: "To give your writing the most important thing of all—namely, a point—a writer needs to indicate clearly not only what his or her thesis is, but also what larger conversation that thesis is responding to" (20). In this case, the conversation you're responding to is the one surrounding your issue. Indicate at the beginning of your paper that you're writing in response to that conversation; then state a thesis that consists of your claim and supporting reasons.

Also mind the lesson of Chapter 7 in *They Say/I Say*: "Regardless of how interesting a topic may be to you as a writer, readers always need to know what is at stake in a text and why they should care. . . . Rather than assume that audiences will know why their claims matter, all writers need to answer the 'so what?' and 'who cares?' questions up front" (92–93). Don't assume that your readers will care about your take on the issue—*make* them care by explaining why your argument is significant. Feel free to use the templates in Chapter 7 of *They Say/I Say*.

After you've completed these introductory moves, the arrangement of your argument is up to you. You should include material from each step in the invention stage, but your selection and organization of that material should follow your own judgment as to what will prove most effective with the audience you have selected.

Style

In rhetorical studies, style refers to the appropriate language for the occasion, subject matter, and audience.

One purpose of ENGL 1302 is to give you practice writing in a variety of styles. For this paper, you should familiarize yourself with the style of pieces published in the venue you have selected. Adhere to that style as closely as possible.

Readers appreciate coherent, unified paragraphs, even when reading an informal piece of writing. Your paragraphs should include a topic sentence that clearly states the main idea of the paragraph and supporting sentences that cluster around the main idea without detours.

You should cite your sources according to the conventions of your publication venue. If you're writing a letter or an article for a mainstream periodical, then you will probably just introduce your sources and cite them within the text, much as you did for your mapping the issue paper. If you're writing for a Web-based publication, you might need to include hyperlinks. If you're writing for a scholarly journal, then you'll need to use the formal citation system (e.g., MLA, APA, or *Chicago*) that journal requires.

Proofread carefully; avoid errors in grammar, spelling, punctuation, and mechanics. Visit the Purdue OWL Web site (https://owl.english .purdue.edu/owl/) for questions you have regarding style.

Other Requirements

Your paper should be *five to ten pages*. I don't want any fluff, so construct a thesis that will require at least five pages to support. I also don't want to read a dissertation, however, so keep the scope of your thesis small enough that you can support it adequately within ten pages. Your paper should be double-spaced, typed in Times New Roman font, with 12-point character size and one-inch margins all the way around.

Your first submission is due at the beginning of class on _____, and you should think of it as a final draft—something that is ready for your classmates and me to read. If your first submission does not meet every requirement of this assignment sheet, I will return it to you and count it as late. Both your first and final submissions must be turned in on time—you will be docked a full letter grade for each day either is late.

Peer reviews are due _____.

Final drafts are due _____.

Grading Criteria

The following descriptions can help you understand the difference between an excellent researched position paper and an average one.

C: UTA defines a C as "average," so, since this is a 1000-level Common Core class, a C paper is what a UTA freshman who is writing at an average level typically produces when she/he gives a strong effort. To earn a C, your Researched Position Paper should first indicate the larger conversation to which you're responding ("they say") before providing a thesis that includes your claim and reasons ("I say"). You should answer the "so what?" and "who cares?" questions, provide sufficient evidence to support your reasons, answer the objections of a naysayer, and incorporate outside sources effectively. Make sure your paper meets every requirement listed on the assignment sheet, and give your paper a discernible structure. The ideas you present should demonstrate that you understand the rhetorical concepts that we have addressed in class. Moreover, show that you have responded actively and thoughtfully to peer and instructor feedback on your first submission. Grammatical and syntactical mistakes should not impede my understanding of your paper.

B: UTA defines a B as "above average," so a B paper is what a UTA freshman who is writing at an above-average level typically earns when he/she gives a strong effort (certainly a UTA freshman writing at an average level can earn a B with exceptional effort). To earn a B, first make sure your paper meets all the criteria required to earn a C. Beyond that, you should represent what "they say" more completely and provide more developed answers to the "so what?" and "who cares?" questions by making a compelling case that your argument is significant for your selected audience. You should construct a complex thesis, provide ample support for all your reasons, and represent strong objections from a naysayer that you answer convincingly. You should revise thoroughly, responding to feedback with great comprehensiveness. Finally, a B paper demonstrates strong command of word choice, voice, style, and grammatical conventions.

A: UTA defines an A as "excellent," so an A paper is what a UTA freshman who is writing at an excellent level (80th percentile or above) might produce if he/she gave maximum effort. (Again, students writing at an average or above-average level may also earn As with extraordinary effort and sustained hard work.) To earn an A, first make sure your paper meets the criteria required to earn a C and a B. You should tackle your issue in an original and challenging way, constructing a thesis that is conceptually rich and answering the "so what?" and "who cares?" questions in great depth and with keen insight. Your paper should synthesize evidence from diverse sources in a way that provides overwhelming support for all your reasons. You should fully represent the objections of a trenchant naysayer, make careful concessions, and answer objections in a manner that might satisfy even extreme opponents. Your paper should be lucid, concise, easy to follow, and should demonstrate your command of style, voice, mechanics, and usage.

If you receive a **D** on your paper, carefully consider the criteria listed above for a C. I give Ds to papers when writers, while demonstrating a general understanding of the topic and concepts, have not fulfilled all the requirements listed on the assignment sheet or have failed to respond to all my comments on their first submission. If you misunderstand the assignment; show little understanding of the required rhetorical concepts; or ignore the technical requirements of topic, length, or format, your paper may receive an F.

everything's an argument

for First-Year Writing at the University of Texas at Arlington

PART 1

READING AND UNDERSTANDING arguments

Everything Is an Argument

Left: Pacific Press/Getty Images; right: © Akintunde Akinleye/Corbis

On May 7, 2014, First Lady of the United States Michelle Obama turned to new media to express her concern over the kidnapping of more than 200 young Nigerian girls by the terrorist group Boko Haram. Her tweet, along with an accompanying photo highlighting the trending hashtag #BringBackOurGirls, ramped up an argument over what the international community could do to stop an organization responsible for thousands of deaths in northeastern Nigeria. In bringing her appeal to Twitter, the First Lady acknowledged the persuasive power of social media like Facebook, YouTube, Instagram, and innumerable political and social blogs. The hashtag itself, it would appear, had become a potent tool for rallying audiences around the globe to support specific ideas or causes. But to what ends?

3

Just weeks before Obama's notable appeal, a U.S. State Department spokesperson Jen Psaki drew attention with a tweet of her own aimed at countering attempts by Russian social media to co-opt the U.S. State Department's #UnitedforUkraine hashtag:

The Russian government, it seems, having just annexed the Crimea region and threatening all of Ukraine, was showing more skill than Western nations at using Twitter and other social media to win propaganda points in the diplomatic crisis. Yet Psaki's response via Twitter earned her disapproval from those who interpreted her social media riposte as further evidence of U.S. weakness. For instance, Texas senator Ted Cruz tweeted in reply to Psaki:

Even Michelle Obama took heat for her earnest appeal on behalf of kidnapped girls the same age as her own daughters. While celebrities such as Amy Poehler and Mary J. Blige posted supportive items, Obama's tweet got quick international pushback from those who argued (in 140 characters) that the anti-terrorist use of drones by the U.S. military was no less reprehensible than the tactics of Boko Haram. And domestic critics saw Obama's message as a substitute for real action, with columnist Jeffrey Goldberg chiding well-intentioned activists with a dose of reality:

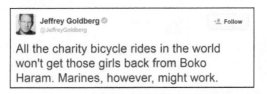

Clearly, social media play out on crowded, two-way channels, with claims and counterclaims whizzing by, fast and furious. Such tools reach audiences and they also create them, offering an innovative way to make and share arguments. Just as important, anyone, anywhere, with access to a phone, tablet, or other electronic device, can launch arguments that circle the globe in seconds. Social networking and digital tools are increasingly available to all.

We've opened this chapter with dramatic, perhaps troubling, examples of Twitter controversies to introduce our claim that arguments are all around us, in every medium, in every genre, in everything we do. There may be an argument on the T-shirt you put on in the morning, in the sports column you read on the bus, in the prayers you utter before an exam, in the off-the-cuff political remarks of a teacher lecturing, in the assurances of a health center nurse that "This won't hurt one bit."

The clothes you wear, the foods you eat, and the groups you join make nuanced, sometimes unspoken assertions about who you are and what you value. So an argument can be any text—written, spoken, aural, or visual—that expresses a point of view. In fact, some theorists claim that language is inherently persuasive. When you say, "Hi, how's it going?" in one sense you're arguing that your hello deserves a response. Even humor makes an argument when it causes readers to recognize—through bursts of laughter or just a faint smile—how things are and how they might be different.

More obvious as arguments are those that make direct claims based on or drawn from evidence. Such writing often moves readers to recognize problems and to consider solutions. Persuasion of this kind is usually easy to recognize:

> The National Minimum Drinking Age Act, passed by Congress 30 years ago this July, is a gross violation of civil liberties and must be repealed. It is absurd and unjust that young Americans can vote, marry, enter contracts, and serve in the military at 18 but cannot buy an alcoholic drink in a bar or restaurant.
> —Camille Paglia, "The Drinking Age Is Past Its Prime"

> We will become a society of a million pictures without much memory, a society that looks forward every second to an immediate replication of what it has just done, but one that does not sustain the difficult labor of transmitting culture from one generation to the next.
> —Christine Rosen, "The Image Culture"

RESPOND •

Can an argument really be any text that expresses a point of view? What kinds of arguments—if any—might be made by the following items?

a Boston Red Sox cap

a Livestrong bracelet

the "explicit lyrics" label on a best-selling rap CD

the health warnings on a package of cigarettes

a Tesla Model S electric car

a pair of Ray-Ban sunglasses

Why We Make Arguments

In the politically divided and entertainment-driven culture of the United States today, the word *argument* may well call up negative images: the hostile scowl or shaking fist of a politician or news "opinionator" who wants to drown out other voices and prevail at all costs. This winner-take-all view turns many citizens off to the whole process of using reasoned conversation to identify, explore, and solve problems. Hoping to avoid personal conflict, many people now sidestep opportunities to speak their mind on issues shaping their lives and work. We want to counter this attitude throughout this book.

Some arguments, of course, *are* aimed at winning, especially those related to politics, business, and law. Two candidates for office, for example, vie for a majority of votes; the makers of one smartphone try to outsell their competitors by offering more features at a lower price; and two lawyers try to outwit each other in pleading to a judge and jury. In your college writing, you may also be called on to make arguments that appeal to a "judge" and "jury" (perhaps your instructor and class-mates). You might, for instance, argue that students in every field should be required to engage in service learning projects. In doing so, you will need to offer better arguments or more convincing evidence than poten-tial opponents—such as those who might regard service learning as a politicized or coercive form of education. You can do so reasonably and responsibly, no name-calling required.

There are many reasons to argue and principled ways to do so. We explore some of them in this section.

Arguments to Convince and Inform

We're stepping into an argument ourselves in drawing what we hope is a useful distinction between *convincing* and—in the next section—*persuading*. (Feel free to disagree with us.) Arguments to convince lead audiences to accept a claim as true or reasonable—based on information or evidence that seems factual and reliable; arguments to persuade then seek to move people beyond conviction to *action*. Academic arguments often combine both elements.

Many news reports and analyses, white papers, and academic articles aim to convince audiences by broadening what they know about a subject. Such fact-based arguments might have no motives beyond laying out what the facts are. Here's an opening paragraph from a 2014 news story by Anahad O'Connor in the *New York Times* that itself launched a thousand arguments (and lots of huzzahs) simply by reporting the results of a recent scientific study:

> Many of us have long been told that saturated fat, the type found in meat, butter and cheese, causes heart disease. But a large and exhaustive new analysis by a team of international scientists found no evidence that eating saturated fat increased heart attacks and other cardiac events.
>
> —Anahad O'Connor, "Study Questions Fat and Heart Disease Link"

Wow. You can imagine how carefully the reporter walked through the scientific data, knowing how this new information might be understood and repurposed by his readers.

Similarly, in a college paper on viability of nuclear power as an alternative source of energy, you might compare the health and safety record of a nuclear plant to that of other forms of energy. Depending upon your findings and your interpretation of the data, the result of your fact-based presentation might be to raise or alleviate concerns readers have about nuclear energy. Of course, your decision to write the argument might be driven by your conviction that nuclear power is much safer than most people believe.

Even an image can offer an argument designed both to inform and to convince. On the following page, for example, editorial cartoonist Bob Englehart finds a way to frame an issue on the minds of many students today, the burden of crushing debt. As Englehart presents it, the problem is impossible to ignore.

© Bob Englehart/Cagle Cartoons, Inc.

Arguments to Persuade

Today, climate change may be the public issue that best illustrates the chasm that sometimes separates conviction from persuasion. The weight of scientific research may convince people that the earth is warming, but persuading them to act on that knowledge doesn't follow easily. How then does change occur? Some theorists suggest that persuasion — understood as moving people to do more than nod in agreement — is best achieved via appeals to emotions such as fear, anger, envy, pride, sympathy, or hope. We think that's an oversimplification. The fact is that persuasive arguments, whether in advertisements, political blogs, YouTube videos, or newspaper editorials, draw upon *all* the appeals of rhetoric (see p. 21) to motivate people to act — whether it be to buy a product, pull a lever for a candidate, or volunteer for a civic organization. Here, once again, is Camille Paglia driving home her argument that the 1984 federal law raising the drinking age in the United States to 21 was a catastrophic decision in need of reversal:

> What this cruel 1984 law did is deprive young people of safe spaces where they could happily drink cheap beer, socialize, chat, and flirt in a free but controlled public environment. Hence in the 1980s we immediately got the scourge of crude binge drinking at campus fraternity keg parties, cut off from the adult world. Women in

that boorish free-for-all were suddenly fighting off date rape. Club drugs — Ecstasy, methamphetamine, ketamine (a veterinary tranquilizer)—surged at raves for teenagers and on the gay male circuit scene.

Paglia chooses to dramatize her argument by sharply contrasting a safer, more supportive past with a vastly more dangerous present when drinking was forced underground and young people turned to highly risky behaviors. She doesn't hesitate to name them either: binge drinking, club drugs, raves, and, most seriously, date rape. This highly rhetorical, one might say *emotional*, argument pushes readers hard to endorse a call for serious action—the repeal of the current drinking age law.

Admit it, Duchess of Cornwall. You *knew* abandoned dogs need homes, but it was heartrending photos on the Battersea Dogs & Cats Home Web site that *persuaded* you to visit the shelter. WPA Pool/Getty Images

RESPOND•

Apply the distinction made here between convincing and persuading to the way people respond to two or three current political or social issues. Is there a useful distinction between being convinced and being persuaded? Explain your position.

Arguments to Make Decisions

Closely allied to arguments to convince and persuade are arguments to examine the options in important matters, both civil and personal—from managing out-of-control deficits to choosing careers. Arguments to make decisions occur all the time in the public arena, where they are often slow to evolve, caught up in electoral or legal squabbles, and yet driven by a genuine desire to find consensus. In recent years, for instance, Americans have argued hard to make decisions about health care, the civil rights of same-sex couples, and the status of more than 11 million immigrants in the country. Subjects so complex aren't debated in straight lines. They get haggled over in every imaginable medium by thousands of writers, politicians, and ordinary citizens working alone or via political organizations to have their ideas considered.

For college students, choosing a major can be an especially momentous personal decision, and one way to go about making that decision is to argue your way through several alternatives. By the time you've explored the pros and cons of each alternative, you should be a little closer to a reasonable and defensible decision.

Sometimes decisions, however, are not so easy to make.

www.CartoonStock.com

Arguments to Understand and Explore

Arguments to make decisions often begin as choices between opposing positions already set in stone. But is it possible to examine important issues in more open-ended ways? Many situations, again in civil or personal arenas, seem to call for arguments that genuinely explore possibilities without constraints or prejudices. If there's an "opponent" in such situations at all (often there is not), it's likely to be the status quo or a current trend which, for one reason or another, puzzles just about everyone. For example, in trying to sort through the extraordinary complexities of the 2011 budget debate, philosophy professor Gary Gutting was able to show how two distinguished economists—John Taylor and Paul Krugman—draw completely different conclusions from the exact same sets of facts. Exploring how such a thing could occur led Gutting to conclude that the two economists were arguing from the same facts, all right, but that they did not have *all* the facts possible. Those missing or unknown facts allowed them to fill in the blanks as they could, thus leading them to different conclusions. By discovering the source of a paradox, Gutting potentially opened new avenues for understanding.

Exploratory arguments can also be personal, such as Zora Neale Hurston's ironic exploration of racism and of her own identity in the essay "How It Feels to Be Colored Me." If you keep a journal or blog, you have no doubt found yourself making arguments to explore issues near and dear to you. Perhaps the essential argument in any such piece is the writer's realization that a problem exists — and that the writer or reader needs to understand it and respond constructively to it if possible.

Explorations of ideas that begin by trying to understand another's perspective have been described as **invitational arguments** by researchers Sonja Foss, Cindy Griffin, and Josina Makau. Such arguments are interested in inviting others to join in mutual explorations of ideas based on discovery and respect. Another kind of argument, called **Rogerian argument** (after psychotherapist Carl Rogers), approaches audiences in similarly nonthreatening ways, finding common ground and establishing trust among those who disagree about issues. Writers who take a Rogerian approach try to see where the other person is coming from, looking for "both/and" or "win/win" solutions whenever possible. (For more on Rogerian strategies, see Chapter 7.)

"You say it's a win-win, but what if you're
wrong-wrong and it all goes bad-bad?"

The risks of Rogerian argument © David Sipress/The New Yorker Collection/The
Cartoon Bank

RESPOND•

What are your reasons for making arguments? Keep notes for two days
about every single argument you make, using our broad definition to guide
you. Then identify your reasons: How many times did you aim to convince? To inform? To persuade? To explore? To understand?

Occasions for Argument

In a fifth-century BCE textbook of **rhetoric** (the art of persuasion), the
philosopher Aristotle provides an ingenious strategy for classifying
arguments based on their perspective on time—past, future, and present. His ideas still help us to appreciate the role arguments play in society in the twenty-first century. As you consider Aristotle's occasions for
argument, remember that all such classifications overlap (to a certain
extent) and that we live in a world much different than his.

Arguments about the Past

Debates about what has happened in the past, what Aristotle called **forensic arguments**, are the red meat of government, courts, businesses, and academia. People want to know who did what in the past, for what reasons, and with what liability. When you argue a speeding ticket in court, you are making a forensic argument, claiming perhaps that you weren't over the limit or that the officer's radar was faulty. A judge will have to decide what exactly happened in the past in the unlikely case you push the issue that far.

More consequentially, in 2014 the federal government and General Motors found themselves deeply involved in arguments about the past as investigators sought to determine just exactly how the massive auto company had allowed a serious defect in the ignition switches of its cars to go undisclosed and uncorrected for a decade. Drivers and passengers died or were injured as engines shut down and airbags failed to go off in subsequent collisions. Who at General Motors was responsible for not diagnosing the fault? Were any engineers or executives liable for covering up the problem? And how should victims of this product defect or their families be compensated? These were all forensic questions to be thoroughly investigated, argued, and answered by regulatory panels and courts.

From an academic perspective, consider the lingering forensic arguments over Christopher Columbus's "discovery" of America. Are his expeditions cause for celebration or notably unhappy chapters in human history? Or some of both? Such arguments about past actions—heated enough to spill over into the public realm—are common in disciplines such as history, philosophy, and ethics.

Mary Barra, the chief executive officer of General Motors, testifies before a congressional panel looking into problems with ignition switches in the company's cars. AP Photo/Ron Sachs/ picture-alliance/dpa/AP Images

Arguments about the Future

Debates about what will or should happen in the future—**deliberative arguments**—often influence policies or legislation for the future. *Should local or state governments allow or even encourage the use of self-driving cars on public roads? Should colleges and universities lend support to more dual-credit programs so that students can earn college credits while still in high school? Should coal-fired power plants be phased out of our energy grid?* These are the sorts of deliberative questions that legislatures, committees, or school boards routinely address when making laws or establishing policies.

But arguments about the future can also be speculative, advancing by means of projections and reasoned guesses, as shown in the following passage from an essay by media maven Marc Prensky. He is arguing that it is time for some college or university to be the first to ban physical, that is to say *paper*, books on its campus, a controversial proposal to say the least:

> Colleges and professors exist, in great measure, to help "liberate" and connect the knowledge and ideas in books. We should certainly pass on to our students the ability to do this. But in the future those liberated ideas—the ones in the books (the author's words), and the ones about the books (the reader's own notes, all readers' thoughts and commentaries)—should be available with a few keystrokes. So, as counterintuitive as it may sound, eliminating physical books from college campuses would be a positive step for our 21st-century students, and, I believe, for 21st-century scholarship as well. Academics, researchers, and particularly teachers need to move to the tools of the future. Artifacts belong in museums, not in our institutions of higher learning.
>
> —Marc Prensky, "In the 21st-Century University, Let's Ban Books"

Arguments about the Present

Arguments about the present—what Aristotle terms **epideictic** or **ceremonial arguments**—explore the current values of a society, affirming or challenging its widely shared beliefs and core assumptions. Epideictic arguments are often made at public and formal events such as inaugural addresses, sermons, eulogies, memorials, and graduation speeches.

Members of the audience listen carefully as credible speakers share their wisdom. For example, as the selection of college commencement speakers has grown increasingly contentious, Ruth J. Simmons, the first African American woman to head an Ivy League college, used the opportunity of such an address (herself standing in for a rejected speaker) to offer a timely and ringing endorsement of free speech. Her words perfectly illustrate epideictic rhetoric:

> Universities have a special obligation to protect free speech, open discourse and the value of protest. The collision of views and ideologies is in the DNA of the academic enterprise. No collision avoidance technology is needed here. The noise from this discord may cause others to criticize the legitimacy of the academic enterprise, but how can knowledge advance without the questions that overturn misconceptions, push further into previously impenetrable areas of inquiry and assure us stunning breakthroughs in human knowledge? If there is anything that colleges must encourage and protect it is the persistent questioning of the status quo. Our health as a nation, our health as women, our health as an industry requires it.
>
> —Ruth J. Simmons, Smith College, 2014

Perhaps more common than Smith's impassioned address are values arguments that examine contemporary culture, praising what's admirable and blaming what's not. In the following argument, student Latisha Chisholm looks at the state of rap music after Tupac Shakur:

> With the death of Tupac, not only did one of the most intriguing rap rivalries of all time die, but the motivation for rapping seems to have changed. Where money had always been a plus, now it is obviously more important than wanting to express the hardships of Black communities. With current rappers, the positive power that came from the desire to represent Black people is lost. One of the biggest rappers now got his big break while talking about sneakers. Others announce retirement without really having done much for the soul or for Black people's morale. I equate new rappers to NFL players that don't love the game anymore. They're only in it for the money. . . . It looks like the voice of a people has lost its heart.
>
> —Latisha Chisholm, "Has Rap Lost Its Soul?"

As in many ceremonial arguments, Chisholm here reinforces common values such as representing one's community honorably and fairly.

Are rappers since Tupac—like Jay Z—only in it for the money? Many epideictic arguments either praise or blame contemporary culture in this way. Michael N. Todaro/ FilmMagic/Getty Images

RESPOND •

In a recent magazine, newspaper, or blog, find three editorials—one that makes a forensic argument, one a deliberative argument, and one a ceremonial argument. Analyze the arguments by asking these questions: Who is arguing? What purposes are the writers trying to achieve? To whom are they directing their arguments? Then decide whether the arguments' purposes have been achieved and how you know.

Occasions for Argument

	Past	Future	Present
What is it called?	Forensic	Deliberative	Epideictic
What are its concerns?	What happened in the past?	What should be done in the future?	Who or what deserves praise or blame?
What does it look like?	Court decisions, legal briefs, legislative hearings, investigative reports, academic studies	White papers, proposals, bills, regulations, mandates	Eulogies, graduation speeches, inaugural addresses, roasts

Kinds of Argument

Yet another way of categorizing arguments is to consider their status or stasis—that is, the specific *kinds of issues they address*. This approach, called **stasis theory,** was used in ancient Greek and Roman civilizations to provide questions designed to help citizens and lawyers work their way through legal cases. The status questions were posed in sequence because each depended on answers from the preceding ones. Together, the queries helped determine the point of contention in an argument—where the parties disagreed or what exactly had to be proven. A modern version of those questions might look like the following:

- Did something happen?
- What is its nature?
- What is its quality or cause?
- What actions should be taken?

Each stasis question explores a different aspect of a problem and uses different evidence or techniques to reach conclusions. You can use these questions to explore the aspects of any topic you're considering. You'll discover that we use the stasis issues to define key types of argument in Part 2.

Did Something Happen? Arguments of Fact

There's no point in arguing a case until its basic facts are established. So an **argument of fact** usually involves a statement that can be proved or disproved with specific evidence or testimony. For example, the question of pollution of the oceans—is it really occurring?—might seem relatively easy to settle. Either scientific data prove that the oceans are being dirtied as a result of human activity, or they don't. But to settle the matter, writers and readers need to ask a number of other questions about the "facts":

- Where did the facts come from?
- Are they reliable?
- Is there a problem with the facts?
- Where did the problem begin and what caused it?

For more on arguments based on facts, see Chapters 4 and 8.

What Is the Nature of the Thing? Arguments of Definition

Some of the most hotly debated issues in American life today involve questions of definition: we argue over the nature of the human fetus, the meaning of "amnesty" for immigrants, the boundaries of sexual assault. As you might guess, issues of definition have mighty consequences, and decades of debate may nonetheless leave the matter unresolved. Here, for example, is how one type of sexual assault is defined in an important 2007 report submitted to the U.S. Department of Justice by the National Institute of Justice:

> We consider as incapacitated sexual assault any unwanted sexual contact occurring when a victim is unable to provide consent or stop what is happening because she is passed out, drugged, drunk, incapacitated, or asleep, regardless of whether the perpetrator was responsible for her substance use or whether substances were administered without her knowledge. We break down incapacitated sexual assault into four subtypes. . . .
> —"The Campus Sexual Assault (CSA) Study: Final Report"

The specifications of the definition go on for another two hundred words, each of consequence in determining how sexual assault on college campuses might be understood, measured, and addressed.

Of course many **arguments of definition** are less weighty than this, though still hotly contested: Is playing video games a sport? Can Batman be a tragic figure? Is Hillary Clinton a moderate or a progressive? (For more about arguments of definition, see Chapter 9.)

What Is the Quality or Cause of the Thing? Arguments of Evaluation

Arguments of evaluation present criteria and then measure individual people, ideas, or things against those standards. For instance, a *Washington Post* story examining long-term trend lines in SAT reading scores opened with this qualitative assessment of the results:

> Reading scores on the SAT for the high school class of 2012 reached a four-decade low, putting a punctuation mark on a gradual decline in the ability of college-bound teens to read passages and answer questions about sentence structure, vocabulary and meaning on the college entrance exam. . . . Scores among every racial group except for those of Asian descent declined from 2006 levels. A majority of test takers—57 percent—did not score high enough to indicate likely success in college, according to the College Board, the organization that administers the test.
>
> —Lyndsey Layton and Emma Brown, "SAT Reading Scores Hit a Four-Decade Low"

The final sentence is particularly telling, putting the test results in context. More than half the high school test-takers may not be ready for college-level readings.

In examining a circumstance or situation like this, we are often led to wonder what accounts for it: *Why are the test scores declining? Why are some groups underperforming?* And, in fact, the authors of the brief *Post* story do follow up on some questions of cause and effect:

> The 2012 SAT scores come after a decade of efforts to raise test scores under the No Child Left Behind law, the federal education initiative crafted by President George W. Bush. Critics say the law failed to address the barriers faced by many test takers.
>
> "Some kids are coming to school hungry, some without the health care they need, without the vocabulary that middle-class kids come to school with, even in kindergarten," said Helen F. Ladd, a professor of public policy and economics at Duke University.

Although evaluations differ from causal analyses, in practice the boundaries between stasis questions are often porous: particular arguments have a way of defining their own issues.

For much more about arguments of evaluation, see Chapter 10; for causal arguments, see Chapter 11.

What Actions Should Be Taken? Proposal Arguments

After facts in a controversy have been confirmed, definitions agreed on, evaluations made, and causes traced, it may be time for a **proposal argument** answering the question *Now, what do we do about all this?* For example, in developing an argument about out-of-control student fees at your college, you might use all the prior stasis questions to study the issue and determine exactly how much and for what reasons these costs

STASIS QUESTIONS AT WORK

Suppose you have an opportunity to speak at a student conference on the impact of climate change. You are tentatively in favor of strengthening industrial pollution standards aimed at reducing global warming trends. But to learn more about the issue, you use the stasis questions to get started.

- **Did something happen?** Does global warming exist? *Maybe not*, say many in the oil and gas industry; at best, evidence for global warming is inconclusive. *Yes*, say most scientists and governments; climate change is real and even seems to be accelerating. To come to your conclusion, you'll weigh the facts carefully and identify problems with opposing arguments.
- **What is the nature of the thing?** Skeptics define climate change as a naturally occurring event; most scientists base their definitions on change due to human causes. You look at each definition carefully: *How do the definitions foster the goals of each group? What's at stake for each group in defining it that way?*
- **What is the quality or cause of the thing?** Exploring the differing assessments of damage done by climate change leads you to ask who will gain from such analysis: *Do oil executives want to protect their investments? Do scientists want government money for grants? Where does evidence for the dangers of global warming come from? Who benefits if the dangers are accepted as real and present, and who loses?*
- **What actions should be taken?** If climate change is occurring naturally or causing little harm, then arguably *nothing* needs to be or can be done. But if it is caused mainly by human activity and dangers, action is definitely called for (although not everyone may agree on what such action should be). As you investigate the proposals being made and the reasons behind them, you come closer to developing your own argument.

The No Child Left Behind Act was signed in 2002 with great hopes and bipartisan support.
AFP/Getty Images

are escalating. Only then will you be prepared to offer knowledgeable suggestions for action. In examining a nationwide move to eliminate remedial education in four-year colleges, John Cloud offers a notably moderate proposal to address the problem:

> Students age twenty-two and over account for 43 percent of those in remedial classrooms, according to the National Center for Developmental Education. . . . [But] 55 percent of those needing remediation must take just one course. Is it too much to ask them to pay extra for that class or take it at a community college?
> —John Cloud, "Who's Ready for College?"

For more about proposal arguments, see Chapter 12.

Appealing to Audiences

Exploring all the occasions and kinds of arguments available will lead you to think about the audience(s) you are addressing and the specific ways you can appeal to them. Audiences for arguments today are amazingly diverse, from the flesh-and-blood person sitting across a desk when you negotiate a student loan to your "friends" on social media, to the "ideal" reader you imagine for whatever you are writing. The figure on the next page suggests just how many dimensions an audience can have as writers and readers negotiate their relationships with a text, whether it be oral, written, or digital.

As you see there, texts usually have **intended readers**, the people writers hope and expect to address—let's say, routine browsers of a

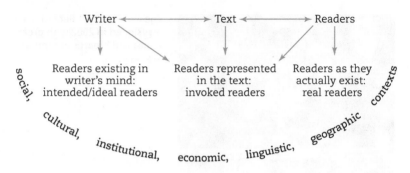

Readers and writers in context

newspaper's op-ed page. But writers also shape the responses of these actual readers in ways they imagine as appropriate or desirable—for example, maneuvering readers of editorials into making focused and knowledgeable judgments about politics and culture. Such audiences, as imagined and fashioned by writers within their texts, are called **invoked readers**.

Making matters even more complicated, readers can respond to writers' maneuvers by choosing to join the invoked audiences, to resist them, or maybe even to ignore them. Arguments may also attract "real" readers from groups not among those that writers originally imagined or expected to reach. You may post something on the Web, for instance, and discover that people you did not intend to address are commenting on it. (For them, the experience may be like reading private email intended for someone else: they find themselves drawn to and fascinated by your ideas!) As authors of this book, we think about students like you whenever we write: you are our intended readers. But notice how in dozens of ways, from the images we choose to the tone of our language, we also invoke an audience of people who take writing arguments seriously. We want you to become that kind of reader.

So audiences are *very* complicated and subtle and challenging, and yet you somehow have to attract and even persuade them. As always, Aristotle offers an answer. He identified three time-tested appeals that speakers and writers can use to reach almost any audience, labeling them *pathos*, *ethos*, and *logos*—strategies as effective today as they were in ancient times, though we usually think of them in slightly different terms. Used in the right way and deployed at the right moment, emotional, ethical, and logical appeals have enormous power, as we'll see in subsequent chapters.

RESPOND•

You can probably provide concise descriptions of the intended audience for most textbooks you have encountered. But can you detect their invoked audiences—that is, the way their authors are imagining (and perhaps shaping) the readers they would like to have? Carefully review this entire first chapter, looking for signals and strategies that might identify the audience and readers invoked by the authors of *Everything's an Argument*.

Emotional Appeals: Pathos

Emotional appeals, or **pathos**, generate emotions (fear, pity, love, anger, jealousy) that the writer hopes will lead the audience to accept a claim. Here is an alarming sentence from a book by Barry B. LePatner arguing that Americans need to make hard decisions about repairing the country's failing infrastructure:

> When the I-35W Bridge in Minneapolis shuddered, buckled, and collapsed during the evening rush hour on Wednesday, August 1, 2007, plunging 111 vehicles into the Mississippi River and sending thirteen people to their deaths, the sudden, apparently inexplicable nature of the event at first gave the appearance of an act of God.
> —*Too Big to Fall: America's Failing Infrastructure and the Way Forward*

If you ever drive across a bridge, LePatner has probably gotten your attention. His sober and yet descriptive language helps readers imagine the dire consequence of neglected road maintenance and bad design decisions. Making an emotional appeal like this can dramatize an issue and sometimes even create a bond between writer and readers. (For more about emotional appeals, see Chapter 2.)

Ethical Appeals: Ethos

When writers or speakers come across as trustworthy, audiences are likely to listen to and accept their arguments. That trustworthiness (along with fairness and respect) is a mark of **ethos**, or credibility. Showing that you know what you are talking about exerts an ethical appeal, as does emphasizing that you share values with and respect your audience. Once again, here's Barry LePatner from *Too Big to Fall*, shoring up his authority for writing about problems with America's roads and bridges by invoking the ethos of people even more credible:

> For those who would seek to dismiss the facts that support the thesis of this book, I ask them to consult the many professional engineers in state transportation departments who face these problems on a daily basis. These professionals understand the physics of bridge and road design, and the real problems of ignoring what happens to steel and concrete when they are exposed to the elements without a strict regimen of ongoing maintenance.

It's a sound rhetorical move to enhance credibility this way. For more about ethical appeals, see Chapter 3.

Logical Appeals: Logos

Appeals to logic, or **logos**, are often given prominence and authority in U.S. culture: "Just the facts, ma'am," a famous early TV detective on *Dragnet* used to say. Indeed, audiences respond well to the use of reasons and evidence—to the presentation of facts, statistics, credible testimony, cogent examples, or even a narrative or story that embodies a sound reason in support of an argument. Following almost two hundred pages of facts, statistics, case studies, and arguments about the sad state of American bridges, LePatner can offer this sober, logical, and inevitable conclusion:

> We can no longer afford to ignore the fact that we are in the midst of a transportation funding crisis, which has been exacerbated by an even larger and longer-term problem: how we choose to invest in our infrastructure. It is not difficult to imagine the serious consequences that will unfold if we fail to address the deplorable conditions of our bridges and roads, including the increasingly higher costs we will pay for goods and services that rely on that transportation network, and a concomitant reduction in our standard of living.

For more about logical appeals, see Chapter 4.

Bringing It Home: *Kairos* and the Rhetorical Situation

In Greek mythology, Kairos—the youngest son of Zeus—was the god of opportunity. In images, he is most often depicted as running, and his most unusual characteristic is a shock of hair on his forehead. As Kairos dashes by, you have a chance to seize that lock of hair, thereby seizing the opportune moment; once he passes you by, however, you have missed that chance.

Kairos is also a term used to describe the most suitable time and place for making an argument and the most opportune ways of expressing it. It is easy to point to shimmering rhetorical moments, when speakers find exactly the right words to stir an audience: Franklin Roosevelt's "We have nothing to fear but fear itself," Ronald Reagan's "Mr. Gorbachev, tear down this wall," and of course Martin Luther King Jr.'s "I have a dream . . ." But *kairos* matters just as much in less dramatic situations, whenever speakers or writers must size up the core elements of a rhetorical situation to decide how best to make their expertise and ethos work for a particular message aimed at a specific audience. The diagram below hints at the dynamic complexity of the rhetorical situation.

But rhetorical situations are embedded in contexts of enormous social complexity. The moment you find a subject, you inherit all the knowledge, history, culture, and technological significations that surround it. To lesser and greater degrees (depending on the subject), you also bring personal circumstances into the field — perhaps your gender, your race, your religion, your economic class, your habits of language. And all those issues weigh also upon the people you write to and for.

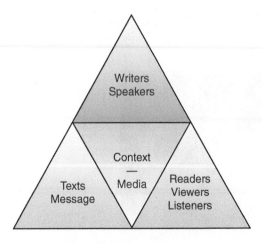

The rhetorical situation

Ronald Reagan at the Berlin Wall, June 12, 1987: "Mr. Gorbachev, tear down this wall!" © Dennis Brack/PhotoShot

So considering your rhetorical situation calls on you to think hard about the notion of *kairos*. Being aware of your rhetorical moment means being able to understand and take advantage of dynamic, shifting circumstances and to choose the best (most timely) proofs and evidence for a particular place, situation, and audience. It means seizing moments and enjoying opportunities, not being overwhelmed by them. Doing so might even lead you to challenge the title of this text: is everything an argument?

That's what makes writing arguments exciting.

RESPOND ●

Take a look at the bumper sticker below, and then analyze it. What is its purpose? What kind of argument is it? Which of the stasis questions does it most appropriately respond to? To what audiences does it appeal? What appeals does it make and how?

© Kevin Lamarque/Reuters/Corbis

CULTURAL CONTEXTS FOR ARGUMENT

Considering What's "Normal"

If you want to communicate effectively with people across cultures, then learn about the traditions in those cultures and examine the norms guiding your own behavior:

- Explore your assumptions! Most of us regard our ways of thinking as "normal" or "right." Such assumptions guide our judgments about what works in persuasive situations. But just because it may seem natural to speak bluntly in arguments, consider that others may find such aggression startling or even alarming.

- Remember: ways of arguing differ widely across cultures. Pay attention to how people from groups or cultures other than your own argue, and be sensitive to different paths of thinking you'll encounter as well as to differences in language.

- Don't assume that all people share your cultural values, ethical principles, or political assumptions. People across the world have different ways of defining *family*, *work*, or *happiness*. As you present arguments to them, consider that they may be content with their different ways of organizing their lives and societies.

- Respect the differences among individuals *within* a given group. Don't expect that every member of a community behaves—or argues—in the same way or shares the same beliefs. Avoid thinking, for instance, that there is a single Asian, African, or Hispanic culture or that Europeans are any less diverse or more predictable than Americans or Canadians in their thinking. In other words, be skeptical of stereotypes.

2
Arguments Based on Emotion: Pathos

Emotional appeals (*appeals to pathos*) are powerful tools for influencing what people think and believe. We all make decisions—even including the most important ones—based on our feelings. That's what the Food and Drug Administration hoped to capitalize on when it introduced nine tough warning labels for cigarettes, one of which you see above. One look at the stained, rotting teeth and the lip sore may arouse emotions of fear strong enough to convince people not to smoke.

In the second panel, Bob Dorigo Jones, an opponent of lawsuit abuse, takes concerns about product liability in a different direction, publishing a book entitled *Remove Child before Folding: The 101 Stupidest, Silliest, and Wackiest Warning Labels Ever* to make us laugh and thereby, perhaps, to wonder why common sense seems in such short supply. In the third panel, editorial cartoonist for the *Indianapolis Star* Gary Varvel uses the anti-smoking meme to point out a potent irony in burgeoning campaigns to legalize marijuana.

The arguments packed into these three images all appeal to emotion, and research has shown us that we often make decisions based on just such appeals. So when you hear that formal or academic arguments should rely solely on facts to convince us, remember that facts alone often won't carry the day, even for a worthy cause. The largely successful case made this decade for same-sex marriage provides a notable example of a movement that persuaded people equally by virtue of the reasonableness and the passion of its claims. Like many political and social debates, though, the issue provoked powerful emotions on every side—feelings that sometimes led to extreme words and tactics.

Of course, we don't have to look hard for arguments fueled with emotions such as hatred, envy, and greed, or for campaigns intended to drive wedges between economic or social groups, making them fearful or resentful. For that reason alone, writers should not use emotional appeals rashly or casually. (For more about emotional fallacies, see p. 72.)

Reading Critically for Pathos

On February 24, 2014, Senator Tom Harkin of Iowa, fresh from two "fact-finding" trips to Cuba, described his experiences on the Senate floor in a rambling, forty-minute speech, praising that island nation's accomplishments in health care and education and urging a normalization of Cuban–American relationships. Later that day, Florida senator Marco Rubio, expecting to speak about growing repression in Venezuela, found it impossible to ignore Harkin's rosy view of the "fascinating" socialist experiment ninety miles from the coast of the United States. Seizing a kairotic moment, the first-term senator delivered a passionate fifteen-minute rejoinder to Harkin without a script or teleprompter—though Rubio did use posters prepared originally for the Venezuelan talk. After a sarcastic taunt ("Sounded like he had a wonderful trip visiting what he described as a real paradise"), Rubio quickly turned serious, even angry, as he offered his take on the country Harkin had toured:

> I heard him also talk about these great doctors that they have in Cuba. I have no doubt they're very talented. I've met a bunch of them. You know where I met them? In the United States because they defected. Because in Cuba, doctors would rather drive a taxi cab or work in a hotel than be a doctor. I wonder if they spoke to him about the outbreak of cholera that they've been unable to control, or about the

three-tiered system of health care that exists where foreigners and government officials get health care much better than that that's available to the general population.

The speech thereafter settles into a rhythm of patterned inquiries designed to raise doubts about what Senator Harkin had seen, Rubio's informal language rippling with contempt for his colleague's naïveté:

> I heard about their [the Cubans'] wonderful literacy rate, how everyone in Cuba knows how to read. That's fantastic. Here's the problem: they can only read censored stuff. They're not allowed access to the Internet. The only newspapers they're allowed to read are *Granma* or the ones produced by the government. . . .
> He talked about these great baseball players that are coming from Cuba—and they are. But I wonder if they informed him [that] every single one of those guys playing in the Major Leagues defected. They left Cuba to play here. . . .
> So it's great to have literacy, but if you don't have access to the information, what's the point of it? So I wish somebody would have asked about that on that trip. . . .
> I wonder if anybody asked about terrorism, because Cuba is a state sponsor of terrorism. . . .

Language this heated and pointed has risks, especially when a young legislator is taking on a genial and far more experienced colleague. But Rubio, the son of Cuban immigrants, isn't shy about allowing his feelings to show. Segueing to his original topic—growing political repression in socialist Venezuela—he uses the kind of verbal repetition common in oratory to drive home his major concern about Cuba, its influence on other nations:

> Let me tell you what the Cubans are really good at, because they don't know how to run their economy, they don't know how to build, they don't know how to govern a people. What they are really good at is repression. What they are really good at is shutting off information to the Internet and to radio and television and social media. That's what they're really good at. And they're not just good at it domestically, they're good exporters of these things.

Rubio's actual audience in the U.S. Senate was very small, but today all speeches from that chamber are carried nationwide and archived by C-SPAN, and in the age of YouTube, bits and pieces of political addresses reach many listeners. Former speechwriter and *Wall Street Journal* columnist Peggy Noonan was among those who caught Rubio's remarks and

As originally aired on C-SPAN2 on February 24 2014

blogged about them: "We have pressed in these parts for American political figures to speak clearly and with moral confidence about American
sympathies in various international disputes. Rubio's speech is honest
political indignation successfully deployed." You can watch the entire
speech on C-SPAN's Web site (listed as "Rubio Speech on Venezuela") to see
if you agree. And though Cuba and the United States did re-establish diplomatic relationships roughly ten months after the Harkin/Rubio exchange,
issues raised by both senators—from health care to the immigration
status of Cuban baseball players—will likely be argued for years to come.

RESPOND●

Working with a classmate, make a list of reasons why speakers in highly
charged situations might need to use emotional appeals cautiously, even
sparingly. What consequences might heightened emotional appeals lead
to? What is at stake for the speaker in such situations, in terms of credibility and ethos? What are the advantages of evoking emotions in support of
your claims or ideas?

Using Emotions to Build Bridges

You may sometimes want to use emotions to connect with readers to
assure them that you understand their experiences or "feel their pain,"
to borrow a sentiment popularized by President Bill Clinton. Such a
bridge is especially important when you're writing about matters that
readers regard as sensitive. Before they'll trust you, they'll want

assurances that you understand the issues in depth. If you strike the right emotional note, you'll establish an important connection. That's what Apple founder Steve Jobs does in a much-admired 2005 commencement address in which he tells the audience that he doesn't have a fancy speech, just three stories from his life:

> My second story is about love and loss. I was lucky. I found what I loved to do early in life. Woz [Steve Wozniak] and I started Apple in my parents' garage when I was twenty. We worked hard and in ten years, Apple had grown from just the two of us in a garage into a $2 billion company with over four thousand employees. We'd just released our finest creation, the Macintosh, a year earlier, and I'd just turned thirty, and then I got fired. How can you get fired from a company you started? Well, as Apple grew, we hired someone who I thought was very talented to run the company with me, and for the first year or so, things went well. But then our visions of the future began to diverge, and eventually we had a falling out. When we did, our board of directors sided with him, and so at thirty, I was out, and very publicly out. . . .
>
> I didn't see it then, but it turned out that getting fired from Apple was the best thing that could have ever happened to me. The heaviness of being successful was replaced by the lightness of being a beginner again, less sure about everything. It freed me to enter one of the most creative periods in my life. During the next five years I started a company named NeXT, another company named Pixar and fell in love with an amazing woman who would become my wife. Pixar went on to create the world's first computer-animated feature film, *Toy Story*, and is now the most successful animation studio in the world.
>
> —Steve Jobs, "You've Got to Find What You Love, Jobs Says"

In no obvious way is Jobs's recollection a formal argument. But it prepares his audience to accept the advice he'll give later in his speech, at least partly because he's speaking from meaningful personal experiences.

A more obvious way to build an emotional tie is simply to help readers identify with your experiences. If, like Georgina Kleege, you were blind and wanted to argue for more sensible attitudes toward blind people, you might ask readers in the first paragraph of your argument to confront their prejudices. Here Kleege, a writer and college instructor, makes an emotional point by telling a story:

> I tell the class, "I am legally blind." There is a pause, a collective intake of breath. I feel them look away uncertainly and then look back. After all, I just said I couldn't see. Or did I? I had managed to get there on my own—no cane, no dog, none of the usual trappings of blindness.

Eyeing me askance now, they might detect that my gaze is not quite focused. . . . They watch me glance down, or towards the door where someone's coming in late. I'm just like anyone else.

—Georgina Kleege, "Call It Blindness"

Given the way she narrates the first day of class, readers are as likely to identify with the students as with Kleege, imagining themselves sitting in a classroom, facing a sightless instructor, confronting their own prejudices about the blind. Kleege wants to put her audience on the edge emotionally.

Let's consider another rhetorical situation: how do you win over an audience when the logical claims that you're making are likely to go against what many in the audience believe? Once again, a slightly risky appeal to emotions on a personal level may work. That's the tack that Michael Pollan takes in bringing readers to consider that "the great moral struggle of our time will be for the rights of animals." In introducing his lengthy exploratory argument, Pollan uses personal experience to appeal to his audience:

The first time I opened Peter Singer's *Animal Liberation*, I was dining alone at the Palm, trying to enjoy a rib-eye steak cooked medium-rare.

A visual version of Michael Pollan's rhetorical situation. © Robert Mankoff/The New Yorker Collection/The Cartoon Bank

If this sounds like a good recipe for cognitive dissonance (if not indigestion), that was sort of the idea. Preposterous as it might seem to supporters of animal rights, what I was doing was tantamount to reading *Uncle Tom's Cabin* on a plantation in the Deep South in 1852.
—Michael Pollan, "An Animal's Place"

In creating a vivid image of his first encounter with Singer's book, Pollan's opening builds a bridge between himself as a person trying to enter into the animal rights debate in a fair and open-minded, if still skeptical, way and readers who might be passionate about either side of this argument.

Using Emotions to Sustain an Argument

You can also use emotional appeals to make logical claims stronger or more memorable. That is the way that photographs and other images add power to arguments. In a TV attack ad, the scowling cell phone video of a disheveled political opponent may do as much damage as the insinuation that he bought his home on the cheap from a financier convicted of fraud. In contrast, a human face smiling or showing honest emotion can sell just about any product—that's why indicted political figures now routinely smile for their mug shots. Using emotion is tricky, however. Lay on too much feeling—especially sentiments like outrage, pity, or shame, which make people uncomfortable—and you may offend the very audiences you hoped to convince.

Still, strong emotions can add energy to a passage or an entire argument, as they do when Walter Russell Mead, editor-at-large of the *American Interest*, argues about what *really* motivates Americans to donate lavishly to many colleges and universities. As you read the following excerpt, notice how the author paints vivid pictures of people at college sporting events, describes the emotions at those games, and then argues what schools really need to do to win contributions:

But if you want to understand why so many generations of Americans have sent so much dough back to the campuses where they wasted some of the happiest years of their lives, watch the intensity of the tens of thousands of fans who attend these events. Look at the shirtless boys with faces and torsos painted in the school colors; look at the cheerleaders on the fields, the "waves" surging through the stands.

American universities, those temples of reason (at their best), are tribes. The kids bond to each other and to their schools in the heat of the intense emotions that these contests generate. Those shirtless kids covered in paint, shivering in the November weather as they cheer their team on, will be prosperous, middle-aged alumni one day—and when they are, they will still be stirred by the memory of the emotions and the loyalty that brought them out to the field.

If you want your alumni to give, you first have to make them fall in love with your school. This is not about having better chemistry programs or more faculty with higher name recognition than the school up the road. It is not about scoring higher on world indices of university quality. It is about competition, drama, intensity, about hope and fear, collective celebrations or collective disasters, seared into young and impressionable hearts where they will never be forgotten—and where they will be annually renewed as each sport in its season produces new highs and lows, new hopes and fears. Alumni watching their schools' games on TV, or celebrating or mourning their schools' results each week with friends, family and colleagues, are renewing their ties with their alma maters affirming that being an "Aggie" or a "Tar Heel" is an *identity*, not a line on the resume.

This is why most of them give. It is irrational and tribal love. It is intense emotion, not a vague sense of obligation or philanthropy. They want to beat State.

—Walter Russell Mead and *The American Interest* staff,
"It All Begins with Football"

Mead's claim, emotional in itself, may not be exactly what college and university administrators and faculty want to hear. But in using language this evocative, he makes his argument memorable, hoping perhaps to make general readers admit how they have felt and acted themselves.

Kevin C. Cox/Getty Images

It's difficult to gauge how much emotion will work in a given argument. Some issues—such as racism, immigration, abortion, and gun control—provoke strong feelings and, as a result, are often argued on emotional terms. But even issues that seem deadly dull—such as reform of federal student loan programs—can be argued passionately when proposed changes in these programs are set in human terms: reduce support for college loans and Kai, Riley, and Jayden end up in dead-end, low-paying jobs; don't reform the program and we're looking at another Wall Street–sized loan bailout and subsequent recession. Both alternatives might scare people into paying enough attention to take political action.

Using Humor

Humor has always played an important role in argument, sometimes as the sugar that makes the medicine go down. You can slip humor into an argument to put readers at ease, thereby making them more open to a proposal you have to offer. It's hard to say *no* when you're laughing. Humor also makes otherwise sober people suspend their judgment and even their prejudices, perhaps because the surprise and naughtiness of wit are combustive: they provoke laughter or smiles, not reflection. Who can resist a no-holds-barred attack on a famous personality, such as this assessment of *Twilight* star Kristen Stewart:

> The original scoffing, scowling, stammering, stuttering, gaping open mouth, temper-tantrum throwing, lip-biting, hair-flipping, plank of wood moody actress . . . A tape recorder in a mannequin could do her job.

Humor deployed cleverly may be why TV shows like *South Park* and *Modern Family* became popular with mainstream audiences, despite their willingness to explore controversial themes. Similarly, it's possible to make a point through humor that might not work in more sober writing. People argue endlessly about eating the right foods, typically defined by diet gurus who favor locally sourced, organically grown, and profoundly dull vegetables. *Wall Street Journal* columnist Ron Rosenbaum will have none of that. With new research suggesting that fatty diets may have unanticipated health benefits, Rosenbaum deploys some high-calorie humor to argue for the pleasures of dining lavishly:

> Preventing obesity is a laudable goal, but it has become the rationale for indiscriminate fat hunters. It can shade into a kind of bullying of

the overweight, a badgering of anyone who likes butter or heavy cream. To the antifat crusaders, I say: Attack fatty junk food all you want. I'm with you. But you can deny me my roasted marrow bones when you pry them from my cold, dead hands.

I'm not suggesting that we embrace these life-changing food experiences just on grounds of pure pleasure (though there's much to be said for pure pleasure). As it turns out, the science on the matter is changing as well. We are discovering that fatty delights can actually be good for you: They allow Spaniards, Italians and Greeks to live longer, and they make us satisfied with eating less. I'm speaking up not for obesity-generating fat, then, but for the kind of fatty food that leads to swooning sensual satiety.

Roast goose, for instance, is a supremely succulent, mind-alteringly flavorful fatty food. In most of America, roast goose would be viewed as the raven of cardiac mortality, hoarsely honking "never more." And listening to the doctors on cable TV, you might think that it's better to cook up a batch of meth than to cook with butter.

Eating fatty foods has become the culinary version of *Breaking Bad*: a dangerous walk on the wild side for the otherwise timid consumers of tasteless butter substitutes and Lean Cuisine.

—Ron Rosenbaum, "Let Them Eat Fat"

Our laughter testifies to what some people have thought all along: people who want us to eat tofu are the real problem. Note the pleasure Rosenbaum takes in the emotive power of words themselves: *swooning sensual satiety; the raven of cardiac mortality, hoarsely honking "never more."*

A writer or speaker can even use humor to deal with sensitive issues. For example, sports commentator Bob Costas, given the honor of eulogizing the great baseball player Mickey Mantle, couldn't ignore problems in Mantle's life. So he argues for Mantle's greatness by admitting the man's weaknesses indirectly through humor:

It brings to mind a story Mickey liked to tell on himself and maybe some of you have heard it. He pictured himself at the pearly gates, met by St. Peter, who shook his head and said, "Mick, we checked the record. We know some of what went on. Sorry, we can't let you in. But before you go, God wants to know if you'd sign these six dozen baseballs."

—Bob Costas, "Eulogy for Mickey Mantle"

Similarly, politicians may use humor to deal with issues they couldn't acknowledge in any other way. Here, for example, is former president

George W. Bush at the 2004 Radio and TV Correspondents' Dinner discussing his much-mocked intellect:

> Those stories about my intellectual capacity do get under my skin. You know, for a while I even thought my staff believed it. There on my schedule first thing every morning it said, "Intelligence briefing."
> —George W. Bush

Not all humor is well-intentioned or barb-free. In fact, among the most powerful forms of emotional argument is ridicule—humor aimed at a particular target. Eighteenth-century poet and critic Samuel Johnson was known for his stinging and humorous put-downs, such as this comment to an aspiring writer: "Your manuscript is both good and original, but the part that is good is not original and the part that is original is not good." (Expect your own writing teachers to be kinder.) In our own time, the *Onion* has earned a reputation for its mastery of both ridicule and satire, the art of using over-the-top humor to making a serious point.

But because ridicule is a double-edged sword, it requires a deft hand to wield it. Humor that reflects bad taste discredits a writer completely, as does satire that misses its mark. Unless your target deserves riposte and you can be very funny, it's usually better to steer clear of such humor.

Using Arguments Based on Emotion

You don't want to play puppet master with people's emotions when you write arguments, but it's a good idea to spend some time early in your work thinking about how you want readers to feel as they consider your persuasive claims. For example, would readers of your editorial about campus traffic policies be more inclined to agree with you if you made them envy faculty privileges, or would arousing their sense of fairness work better? What emotional appeals might persuade meat eaters to consider a vegan diet—or vice versa? Would sketches of stage props on a Web site persuade people to buy a season ticket to the theater, or would you spark more interest by featuring pictures of costumed performers?

Consider, too, the effect that a story can have on readers. Writers and journalists routinely use what are called *human-interest stories* to give presence to issues or arguments. You can do the same, using a particular incident to evoke sympathy, understanding, outrage, or amusement. Take care, though, to tell an honest story.

RESPOND●

1. To what specific emotions do the following slogans, sales pitches, and maxims appeal?

   "Just do it." (ad for Nike)

   "Think different." (ad for Apple computers)

   "Reach out and touch someone." (ad for AT&T)

   "By any means necessary." (rallying cry from Malcolm X)

   "Have it your way." (slogan for Burger King)

   "The ultimate driving machine." (slogan for BMW)

   "It's everywhere you want to be." (slogan for Visa)

   "Know what comes between me and my Calvins? Nothing!" (tag line for Calvin Klein jeans)

   "Don't mess with Texas!" (anti-litter campaign slogan)

   "American by Birth. Rebel by Choice." (slogan for Harley-Davidson)

2. Bring a magazine to class, and analyze the emotional appeals in as many full-page ads as you can. Then classify those ads by types of emotional appeal, and see whether you can connect the appeals to the subject or target audience of the magazine. Compare your results with those of your classmates, and discuss your findings. For instance, how exactly are the ads in publications such as *Cosmopolitan*, *Wired*, *Sports Illustrated*, *Motor Trend*, and *Smithsonian* adapted to their specific audiences?

3. How do arguments based on emotion work in different media? Are such arguments more or less effective in books, articles, television (both news and entertainment shows), films, brochures, magazines, email, Web sites, the theater, street protests, and so on? You might explore how a single medium handles emotional appeals or compare different media. For example, why do the comments pages of blogs seem to encourage angry outbursts? Are newspapers an emotionally colder source of information than television news programs? If so, why?

4. Spend some time looking for arguments that use ridicule or humor to make their point: check out your favorite Twitter feeds or blogs; watch for bumper stickers, posters, or advertisements; and listen to popular song lyrics. Bring one or two examples to class, and be ready to explain how the humor makes an emotional appeal and whether it's effective.

3
Arguments Based on Character: Ethos

Left to right: © Jon Arnold Images Ltd./Alamy; © Bernhard Classen/age fotostock; Richard Shotwell/Invision/AP

Whenever you read anything—whether it's a news article, an advertisement, a speech, or a text message—you no doubt subconsciously analyze the message for a sense of the character and credibility of the sender: *Is this someone I know and trust? Does the PBS reporter seem biased? Why should I believe an IRS official? Is this scholar really an authority on the subject?* Our culture teaches us to be skeptical of most messages, especially those that bombard us with slogans, and such reasonable doubt is a crucial skill in reading and evaluating arguments.

For that reason, people and institutions that hope to influence us do everything they can to establish their character and credibility, what ancient rhetors referred to as *ethos*. And sometimes slogans such as "All the News That's Fit to Print," "Fair & Balanced," or "Lean Forward" can be effective. At the very least, if a phrase is repeated often enough, it begins to sound plausible. Maybe CNN is the most trusted name in news!

But establishing character usually takes more than repetition, as marketers of all kinds know. It arises from credentials actually earned in some way. In the auto industry, for instance, companies such as Toyota, General Motors, and Nissan are hustling to present themselves as environmentally responsible producers of fuel-efficient, low-emission cars—the Prius, Volt, and Leaf. BMW, maker of "the ultimate driving machine," points to its fuel-sipping i3 and i8 cars as evidence of its commitment to "sustainable mobility." And Elon Musk (who builds rockets as well as Tesla cars) polishes his good-citizenship bona fides by sharing his electric vehicle patents with other manufacturers. All of these companies realize that their future success is linked to an ability to project a convincing ethos for themselves and their products.

If corporations and institutions can establish an ethos, consider how much character matters when we think about people in the public arena. Perhaps no individual managed a more exceptional assertion of personal ethos than Jorge Mario Bergoglio did after he became Pope Francis on March 13, 2013, following the abdication of Benedict XVI—a man many found scholarly, cold, and out of touch with the modern world. James Carroll, writing for the *New Yorker*, identifies the precise moment when the world realized that it was dealing with a new sort of pope:

> "Who am I to judge?" With those five words, spoken in late July [2013] in reply to a reporter's question about the status of gay priests in the Church, Pope Francis stepped away from the disapproving tone, the explicit moralizing typical of popes and bishops.
>
> —James Carroll, "Who Am I to Judge?"

Carroll goes on to explain that Francis quickly established his ethos with a series of specific actions, decisions, and moments of identification with ordinary people, marking him as someone even nonbelievers might listen to and respect:

> As pope, Francis has simplified the Renaissance regalia of the papacy by abandoning fur-trimmed velvet capes, choosing to live in a two-room apartment instead of the Apostolic Palace, and replacing the papal Mercedes with a Ford Focus. Instead of the traditional red slip-ons, Francis wears ordinary black shoes. . . . Yet Francis didn't criticize the choices of other prelates. "He makes changes without attacking people," a Jesuit official told me. In his interview with *La Civiltà Cattolica*, Francis said, "My choices, including those related to the day-to-day aspects of life, like the use of a modest car, are related to a spiritual discernment that responds to a need that arises from looking at things, at people, and from reading the signs of the times."

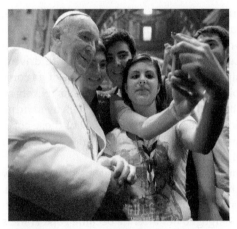

AP Photo/L'Osservatore Romano, Riccardo Aguiari

In that last sentence, Francis acknowledges that ethos is gained, in part, through identification with one's audience and era. And this man, movingly photographed embracing the sick and disfigured, also posed for selfies!

You can see, then, why Aristotle treats ethos as a powerful argumentative appeal. Ethos creates quick and sometimes almost irresistible connections between readers and arguments. We observe people, groups, or institutions making and defending claims all the time and inevitably ask ourselves, *Should we pay attention to them? Can we rely on them? Do we dare to trust them?* Consider, though, that the same questions will be asked about you and your work, especially in academic settings.

Thinking Critically about Arguments Based on Character

Put simply, arguments based on character (ethos) depend on *trust*. We tend to accept arguments from those we trust, and we trust them (whether individuals, groups, or institutions) in good part because of their reputations. Three main elements — credibility, authority, and unselfish or clear motives — add up to *ethos*.

To answer serious and important questions, we often turn to professionals (doctors, lawyers, engineers, teachers, pastors) or to experts (those with knowledge and experience) for good advice. Based on their backgrounds, such people come with their ethos already established.

Thus, appeals or arguments about character often turn on claims like these:

- A person (or group or institution) is or is not trustworthy or credible on this issue.

- A person (or group or institution) does or does not have the authority to speak to this issue.

- A person (or group or institution) does or does not have unselfish or clear motives for addressing this subject.

Establishing Trustworthiness and Credibility

Trustworthiness and credibility speak to a writer's honesty, respect for an audience and its values, and plain old likability. Sometimes a sense of humor can play an important role in getting an audience to listen to or "like" you. It's no accident that all but the most serious speeches begin with a joke or funny story: the humor puts listeners at ease and helps them identify with the speaker. Writer J. K. Rowling, for example, puts her audience (and herself) at ease early in the commencement address she delivered at Harvard in 2008 by getting real about such speeches:

> Delivering a commencement address is a great responsibility; or so I thought until I cast my mind back to my own graduation. The commencement speaker that day was the distinguished British philosopher Baroness Mary Warnock. Reflecting on her speech has helped me enormously in writing this one, because it turns out that I can't remember a single word she said. This liberating discovery enables me to proceed without any fear that I might inadvertently influence you to abandon promising careers in business, the law, or politics for the giddy delights of becoming a gay wizard.
>
> You see? If all you remember in years to come is the "gay wizard" joke, I've come out ahead of Baroness Mary Warnock. Achievable goals: the first step to self improvement.
>
> —J. K. Rowling, "The Fringe Benefits of Failure,
> and the Importance of Imagination"

In just a few sentences, Rowling pokes fun at herself, undercuts the expectation that graduation addresses change people's lives, slides in an allusion from her Harry Potter series, and then even offers a smidgen of advice. For an audience well disposed toward her already, Rowling has likely lived up to expectations.

But using humor to enhance your credibility may be more common in oratory than in the kind of writing you'll do in school. Fortunately, you have many options, one being simply to make plausible claims and then back them up with evidence. Academic audiences appreciate a reasonable disposition; we will discuss this approach at greater length in the next chapter.

You can also establish trustworthiness by connecting your own beliefs to core principles that are well established and widely respected. This strategy is particularly effective when your position seems to be—at first glance, at least—a threat to traditional values. For example, when former Smith College president Ruth J. Simmons describes her professional self to a commencement audience she is addressing (see Chapter 1), she presents her acquired reputation in terms that align perfectly with contemporary values:

> For my part, I was cast as a troublemaker in my early career and accepted the disapproval that accompanies the expression of unpopular views: unpopular views about disparate pay for women and minorities; unpopular views about sexual harassment; unpopular views about exclusionary practices in our universities.
>
> —Ruth J. Simmons

It's fine to be a rebel when you are on the right side of history.

Writers who establish their credibility seem trustworthy. But sometimes, to be credible, you have to admit limitations, too, as *New York Times* columnist David Brooks does as he wrestles with a problem common in our time, an inability to focus on things that matter:

> Like everyone else, I am losing the attention war. I toggle over to my emails when I should be working. I text when I should be paying attention to the people in front of me. I spend hours looking at mildly diverting stuff on YouTube. ("Look, there's a bunch of guys who can play 'Billie Jean' on beer bottles!")
>
> And, like everyone else, I've nodded along with the prohibition sermons imploring me to limit my information diet. Stop multitasking! Turn off the devices at least once a week!
>
> And, like everyone else, these sermons have had no effect. Many of us lead lives of distraction, unable to focus on what we know we should focus on.
>
> —David Brooks, "The Art of Focus"

Making such concessions to readers sends a strong signal that you've looked critically at your own position and can therefore be trusted when you turn to arguing its merits. Speaking to readers directly, using I or you or us, can also help you connect with them, as can using contractions and everyday or colloquial language — both strategies employed by Brooks. In other situations, you may find that a more formal tone gives your claims greater credibility. You'll be making such choices as you search for the ethos that represents you best.

In fact, whenever you write a paper or present an idea, you are sending signals about your credibility, whether you intend to or not. If your ideas are reasonable, your sources are reliable, and your language is appropriate to the project, you suggest to academic readers that you're someone whose ideas *might* deserve attention. Details matter: helpful graphs, tables, charts, or illustrations may carry weight with readers, as will the visual attractiveness of your text, whether in print or digital form. Obviously, correct spelling, grammar, and mechanics are important too. And though you might not worry about it now, at some point you may need letters of recommendation from instructors or supervisors. How will they remember you? Often chiefly from the ethos you have established in your work. Think about that.

Claiming Authority

When you read or listen to an argument, you have every right to ask about the writer's authority: *What does he know about the subject? What experiences does she have that make her especially knowledgeable? Why should I pay attention to this person?* When you offer an argument yourself, you have to anticipate and be prepared to answer questions like these, either directly or indirectly.

How does someone construct an authoritative ethos? In examining what he describes as "the fundamental problem with President Obama's communications ethos," Ron Fournier, editorial director of *National Journal*, explains that authority cannot be taken for granted:

> He and his advisers are so certain about their moral and political standing that they believe it's enough to make a declaration. *If we say it, the public should believe it.*
>
> That's not how it works. A president must earn the public's trust. He must teach and persuade; speak clearly, and follow word with action; show empathy toward his rivals, and acknowledge the merits of a critique. A successful president pays careful attention to how his image is projected both to U.S. voters and to the people of the world.

He knows that to be strong, a leader must look strong. Image matters, especially in an era so dominated by them.

—Ron Fournier, "Is the White House Lying, or Just Bad at Crisis Communications?"

Of course, writers establish their authority in various ways. Sometimes the assertion of ethos will be bold and personal, as it is when writer and activist Terry Tempest Williams attacks those who poisoned the Utah deserts with nuclear radiation. What gives her the right to speak on this subject? Not scientific expertise, but gut-wrenching personal experience:

> I belong to the Clan of One-Breasted Women. My mother, my grandmothers, and six aunts have all had mastectomies. Seven are dead. The two who survive have just completed rounds of chemotherapy and radiation.
>
> I've had my own problems: two biopsies for breast cancer and a small tumor between my ribs diagnosed as a "borderline malignancy."
>
> —Terry Tempest Williams, "The Clan of One-Breasted Women"

We are willing to listen to Williams because she has lived with the nuclear peril she will deal with in the remainder of her essay.

Other means of claiming authority are less dramatic. By simply attaching titles to their names, writers assert that they hold medical or legal or engineering degrees, or some other important credentials. Or they may mention the number of years they've worked in a given field or the distinguished positions they have held. As a reader, you'll pay more attention to an argument about global warming offered by a professor of atmospheric and oceanic science at the University of Minnesota than one by your Uncle Sid, who sells tools. But you'll prefer your uncle to the professor when you need advice about a reliable rotary saw.

When readers might be skeptical of both you and your claims, you may have to be even more specific about your credentials. That's exactly the strategy Richard Bernstein uses to establish his right to speak on the subject of "Asian culture." What gives a New York writer named Bernstein the authority to write about Asian peoples? Bernstein tells us in a sparkling example of an argument based on character:

> The Asian culture, as it happens, is something I know a bit about, having spent five years at Harvard striving for a Ph.D. in a joint program called History and East Asian Languages and, after that, living either as a student (for one year) or a journalist (six years) in China and Southeast Asia. At least I know enough to know there is no such thing as the "Asian culture."   —Richard Bernstein, *Dictatorship of Virtue*

When you write for readers who trust you and your work, you may not have to make such an open claim to authority. But making this type of appeal is always an option.

Coming Clean about Motives

When people are trying to convince you of something, it's important (and natural) to ask: *Whose interests are they serving? How will they profit from their proposal?* Such suspicions go to the heart of ethical arguments.

In a hugely controversial essay published in the *Princeton Tory*, Tal Fortgang, a first-year student at the Ivy League school, argues that those on campus who used the phrase "Check your privilege" to berate white male students like him for the advantages they enjoy are, in fact, judging him according to gender and race, and not for "all the hard work I have done in my life." To challenge stereotypical assumptions about the "racist patriarchy" that supposedly paved his way to Princeton, Fortgang writes about the experiences of his ancestors, opening the paragraphs with a striking parallel structure:

> Perhaps it's the privilege my grandfather and his brother had to flee their home as teenagers when the Nazis invaded Poland, leaving their mother and five younger siblings behind, running and running. . . .
>
> Or maybe it's the privilege my grandmother had of spending weeks upon weeks on a death march through Polish forests in subzero temperatures, one of just a handful to survive. . . .
>
> Perhaps my privilege is that those two resilient individuals came to America with no money and no English, obtained citizenship, learned the language and met each other. . . .
>
> Perhaps it was my privilege that my own father worked hard enough in City College to earn a spot at a top graduate school, got a good job, and for 25 years got up well before the crack of dawn, sacrificing precious time he wanted to spend with those he valued most—his wife and kids—to earn that living.
>
> —Tal Fortgang, "Checking My Privilege:
> Character as the Basis of Privilege"

Fortgang thus attempts to establish his own ethos and win the argument against those who make assumptions about his roots by dramatizing the ethos of his ancestors:

> That's the problem with calling someone out for the "privilege" which you assume has defined their narrative. You don't know what their

struggles have been, what they may have gone through to be where they are. Assuming they've benefitted from "power systems" or other conspiratorial imaginary institutions denies them credit for all they've done, things of which you may not even conceive. You don't know whose father died defending your freedom. You don't know whose mother escaped oppression. You don't know who conquered their demons, or may still [be] conquering them now.

As you might imagine, the pushback to "Checking My Privilege" was enormous, some of the hundreds of comments posted to an online version accusing Fortgang himself of assuming the very ethos of victimhood against which he inveighs. Peter Finocchiaro, a reviewer on *Slate*, is especially brutal: "Only a few short months ago he was living at home with his parents. His life experience, one presumes, is fairly limited. So in that sense, he doesn't really know any better. . . . He is an ignorant 19-year-old white guy from Westchester." You can see in this debate how ethos quickly raises issues of knowledge and motives. Fortgang tries to resist the stereotype others would impose on his character, but others regard the very ethos he fashions in his essay as evidence of his naïveté about race, discrimination, and, yes, privilege.

We all, of course, have connections and interests that bind us to other human beings. It makes sense that a young man would explore his social identity, that a woman might be concerned with women's issues, that members of minority groups might define social and cultural conditions on their own terms — or even that investors might look out for their investments. It's simply good strategy to let your audiences know where your loyalties lie when such information does, in fact, shape your work.

Using Ethos in Your Own Writing

- Establish your credibility by acknowledging your audience's values, showing respect for them, and establishing common ground where (and if) possible. How will you convince your audience you are trustworthy? What will you admit about your own limitations?

- Establish your authority by showing you have done your homework and know your topic well. How will you show that you know your topic well? What appropriate personal experience can you draw on?

- Examine your motives for writing. What, if anything, do you stand to gain from your argument? How can you explain those advantages to your audience?

CULTURAL CONTEXTS FOR ARGUMENT

Ethos

In the United States, students are often asked to establish authority by drawing on personal experiences, by reporting on research they or others have conducted, and by taking a position for which they can offer strong evidence. But this expectation about student authority is by no means universal.

Some cultures regard student writers as novices who can most effectively make arguments by reflecting on what they've learned from their teachers and elders—those who hold the most important knowledge and, hence, authority. When you're arguing a point with people from cultures other than your own, ask questions like:

- Whom are you addressing, and what is your relationship with that person?
- What knowledge are you expected to have? Is it appropriate or expected for you to demonstrate that knowledge—and if so, how?
- What tone is appropriate? And remember: politeness is rarely, if ever, inappropriate.

RESPOND•

1. Consider the ethos of these public figures. Then describe one or two products that might benefit from their endorsements as well as several that would not.

   Edward Snowden—whistleblower

   Kaley Cuoco-Sweeting—actress

   James Earl Jones—actor

   Michael Sam—athlete

   Megyn Kelly—TV news commentator

   Miley Cyrus—singer

   Seth Meyers—late-night TV host

   Cristiano Ronaldo—soccer player

2. Opponents of Richard Nixon, the thirty-seventh president of the United States, once raised doubts about his integrity by asking a single

ruinous question: *Would you buy a used car from this man?* Create your own version of the argument of character. Begin by choosing an intriguing or controversial person or group and finding an image online. Then download the image into a word-processing file. Create a caption for the photo that is modeled after the question asked about Nixon: *Would you give this woman your email password? Would you share a campsite with this couple? Would you eat lasagna that this guy fixed?* Finally, write a serious 300-word argument that explores the character flaws or strengths of your subject(s).

3. Take a close look at your Facebook page (or your page on any other social media site). What are some aspects of your character, true or not, that might be conveyed by the photos, videos, and messages you have posted online? Analyze the ethos or character you see projected there, using the advice in this chapter to guide your analysis.

4

Arguments Based on Facts and Reason: Logos

"And it's recommended by nine out of ten people we believe to be doctors."

Left to right: Yui Mok/Press Association via AP Images; © NBC/Photofest, Inc.; © Frank Cotham/The New Yorker/The Cartoon Bank

These three images say a lot about the use and place of logic (*logos*) in Western and American culture. The first shows Benedict Cumberbatch from the BBC TV series *Sherlock*, just one of many actors to play Arthur Conan Doyle's much-loved fictional detective Sherlock Holmes, who solves perplexing crimes by using precise observation and impeccable logic. The second refers to an equally popular TV (and film) series character, Spock, the Vulcan officer in *Star Trek* who tries to live a life guided by reason alone—his most predicable observation being some version of "that would not be logical." The third is a cartoon spoofing a pseudo-logical argument (nine out of ten prefer X) made so often in advertising that it has become something of a joke.

These images attest to the prominent place that logic holds for most people: like Holmes, we want to know the facts on the assumption that they will help us make sound judgments. We admire those whose logic is, like Spock's, impeccable. So when arguments begin, "Nine out of ten authorities recommend," we respond favorably: those are good odds. But the three images also challenge reliance on logic alone: Sherlock Holmes and Spock are characters drawn in broad and often parodic strokes; the "nine out of ten" cartoon itself spoofs abuses of reason. Given a choice, however, most of us profess to respect and even prefer *appeals to logos*—that is, claims based on facts, evidence, and reason—but we're also inclined to read factual arguments within the context of our feelings and the ethos of people making the appeals.

Thinking Critically about Hard Evidence

Aristotle helps us out in classifying arguments by distinguishing two kinds:

Artistic Proofs	Arguments the writer/ speaker creates	Constructed arguments	Appeals to reason; common sense
Inartistic Proofs	Arguments the writer/ speaker is given	Hard evidence	Facts, statistics, testimonies, witnesses, contracts, documents

We can see these different kinds of logical appeals at work in a single paragraph from President Barack Obama's 2014 State of the Union address. Typically in such speeches—nationally televised and closely reviewed—the president assesses the current condition of the United States and then lays out an agenda for the coming years, a laundry list of commitments and goals. One of those items mentioned about halfway through the 2014 address focuses on the admirable objective of improving the conditions of working women:

> Today, women make up about half our workforce. But they still make 77 cents for every dollar a man earns. That is wrong, and in 2014, it's an embarrassment. A woman deserves equal pay for equal work. She deserves to have a baby without sacrificing her job. A mother deserves a day off to care for a sick child or sick parent without running into hardship—and you know what, a father does, too. It's time to do away with workplace policies that belong in a *Mad Men* episode. This year, let's all come together—Congress, the White House, and businesses from Wall Street to Main Street—to give every woman the opportunity she deserves. Because I firmly believe when women succeed, America succeeds.
>
> —Barack Obama, State of the Union address

As you see, Obama opens the paragraph with an important "inartistic" proof, that ratio of just 77 cents to a dollar representing what women earn in the United States compared to men. Beginning with that fact, he then offers a series of reasonable "artistic" appeals phrased as applause lines: *that is wrong; a woman deserves equal pay; a mother deserves a day off . . . a father does, too.*" Obama then concludes the paragraph by stating the core principle behind all these claims, what we'll later describe as the *warrant* in an argument (see Chapter 7): *when women succeed, America succeeds.*

Note, then, the importance of that single number the president puts forward. It is evidence that, despite decades of political commitment to pay equity and even federal laws banning gender discrimination in employment and compensation, much work remains to be done. Who can be satisfied with the status quo in the face of that damning number? But where did that statistic come from, and *what if it is wrong?*

Now, no one expects footnotes and documentation in a presidential address. The ethos of the office itself makes the public (at least some portion of it) willing to accept a president's factual claims, if only because his remarks have surely been vetted by legions of staffers. Yet some statistics and claims assume a life of their own, repeated so often that most people—even presidents and their speechwriters—assume that they are true. Add the problem of "confirmation bias," the tendency of most people to believe evidence that confirms their views of the world, and you have numbers that will not die.

We live, however, in an age of critics and fact-checkers. Writing for the *Daily Beast*, Christina Hoff Sommers, a former professor of philosophy and no fan of contemporary feminism, complains that the president is perpetuating an error: "What is wrong and embarrassing is the President of the United States reciting a massively discredited factoid." And in case you won't believe Sommers (and most feminists and those in the president's camp wouldn't), she directs skeptics to a more objective source, the *Washington Post*, which routinely fact-checks the State of the Union and other major addresses.

Like Sommers, that paper does raise questions about the 77/100 earnings ratio, and its detailed analysis of that number suggests just how complicated evidential claims can be. Here's a shortened version of the *Post*'s statement, which you'll note cites several government sources:

> There is clearly a wage gap, but differences in the life choices of men and women—such as women tending to leave the workforce when they have children—make it difficult to make simple comparisons.

Obama is using a figure (annual wages, from the Census Bureau) that makes the disparity appear the greatest. The Bureau of Labor Statistics, for instance, shows that the gap is 19 cents when looking at weekly wages. The gap is even smaller when you look at hourly wages — it is 14 cents — but then not every wage earner is paid on an hourly basis, so that statistic excludes salaried workers. . . .

Economists at the Federal Reserve Bank of St. Louis surveyed economic literature and concluded that "research suggests that the actual gender wage gap (when female workers are compared with male workers who have similar characteristics) is much lower than the raw

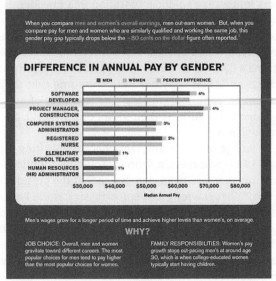

Factual arguments are often made or enhanced by charts, graphs, and infographics. Here PayScale, an online salary and wage information site, presents numbers to explain the pay equity issue: "Yes, men do earn more than women on average, but not that much more when they work the same job and they have similar experience and abilities." We reproduce here just a portion of the full infographic. PayScale, Inc., by permission

wage gap." They cited one survey, prepared for the Labor Department, which concluded that when such differences are accounted for, much of the hourly wage gap dwindled, to about 5 cents on the dollar.

Is the entire paragraph of the president's address discredited because his hard evidence seems overstated or oversimplified? Not if we accept the *constructed* arguments he makes on the general principle of fairness for offering women—and men—more support as laborers in the job force. But he might have been more convincing at this point in a very lengthy speech if someone in the White House had taken a moment to check the government's own numbers, as the *Washington Post* did. This ongoing controversy over wage equity does, however, illustrate how closely logical arguments—whether artistic or inartistic—will be read and criticized. And so the connections between them matter.

RESPOND●

Discuss whether the following statements are examples of hard evidence or constructed arguments. Not all cases are clear-cut.

1. Drunk drivers are involved in more than 50 percent of traffic deaths.
2. DNA tests of skin found under the victim's fingernails suggest that the defendant was responsible for the assault.
3. A psychologist testified that teenage violence could not be blamed on video games.
4. An apple a day keeps the doctor away.
5. "The only thing we have to fear is fear itself."
6. Air bags ought to be removed from vehicles because they can kill young children and small-framed adults.

Facts

Gathering factual information and transmitting it faithfully practically define what we mean by professional journalism and scholarship. We'll even listen to people we don't agree with if their evidence is really good. Below, a reviewer for the conservative *National Review* praises William Julius Wilson, a liberal sociologist, because of how well he presents his case:

> In his eagerly awaited new book, Wilson argues that ghetto blacks are worse off than ever, victimized by a near-total loss of low-skill jobs in and around inner-city neighborhoods. In support of this thesis, he

> *musters mountains of data, plus excerpts from some of the thousands of surveys and face-to-face interviews that he and his research team conducted among inner-city Chicagoans.* It is a book that deserves a wide audience among thinking conservatives.
>
> —John J. DiIulio Jr., "When Decency Disappears" (emphasis added)

When your facts are compelling, they may stand on their own in a low-stakes argument, supported by little more than saying where they come from. Consider the power of phrases such as "reported by the *Wall Street Journal*" or "according to FactCheck.org." Such sources gain credibility if they have reported facts accurately and reliably over time. Using such credible sources in an argument can also reflect positively on you.

In scholarly arguments, which have higher expectations for accuracy, what counts is drawing sober conclusions from the evidence turned up through detailed research or empirical studies. The language of such material may seem dryly factual to you, even when the content is inherently interesting. But presenting new knowledge dispassionately is (ideally at least) the whole point of scholarly writing, marking a contrast between it and the kind of intellectual warfare that occurs in many media forums, especially news programs and blogs. Here for example is a portion of a lengthy opening paragraph in the "Discussion and Conclusions" section of a scholarly paper arguing that people who spend a great deal of time on Facebook often frame their lives by what they observe there:

> The results of this research support the argument that using Facebook affects people's perceptions of others. For those that have used Facebook longer, it is easier to remember positive messages and happy pictures posted on Facebook; these readily available examples give users an impression that others are happier. As expected in the first hypothesis, the results show that the longer people have used Facebook, the stronger was their belief that others were happier than themselves, and the less they agreed that life is fair. Furthermore, as predicted in the second hypothesis, this research found that the more "friends" people included on their Facebook whom they did not know personally, the stronger they believed that others had better lives than themselves. In other words, looking at happy pictures of others on Facebook gives people an impression that others are "always" happy and having good lives, as evident from these pictures of happy moments. In contrast to their own experiences of life events, which

are not always positive, people are very likely to conclude that others have better lives than themselves and that life is not fair.

—Hui-Tzu Grace Chou, PhD, and Nicholas Edge, BS,
"'They Are Happier and Having Better Lives Than I Am':
The Impact of Using Facebook on Perceptions of Others' Lives"

There are no fireworks in this conclusion, no slanted or hot language, no unfair or selective reporting of data, just a faithful attention to the facts and behaviors uncovered by the study. But one can easily imagine these facts being subsequently used to support overdramatized claims about the dangers of social networks. That's often what happens to scholarly studies when they are read and interpreted in the popular media.

Of course, arguing with facts can involve challenging even the most reputable sources if they lead to unfair or selective reporting or if the stories are presented or "framed" unfairly.

In an ideal world, good information — no matter where it comes from — would always drive out bad. But you already know that we don't live in an ideal world, so sometimes bad information gets repeated in an echo chamber that amplifies the errors.

Statistics

You've probably heard the old saying "There are three kinds of lies: lies, damned lies, and statistics," and, to be sure, it is possible to lie with numbers, even those that are accurate, because numbers rarely speak for themselves. They need to be interpreted by writers — and writers almost always have agendas that shape the interpretations.

Of course, just because they are often misused doesn't mean that statistics are meaningless, but it does suggest that you need to use them carefully and to remember that your careful reading of numbers is essential. Consider the attention-grabbing map on the next page that went viral in June 2014. Created by Mark Gongloff of the *Huffington Post* in the wake of a school shooting in Oregon, it plotted the location of all seventy-four school shootings that had occurred in the United States since the Sandy Hook tragedy in December 2012, when twenty elementary school children and six adults were gunned down by a rifle-wielding killer. For the graphic, Gongloff drew on a list assembled by the group Everytown for Gun Safety, an organization formed by former New York City mayor and billionaire Michael Bloomberg to counter the influence of the National Rifle Association (NRA). Both the map and Everytown's

Everytown for Gun Safety Action

sobering list of shootings received wide attention in the media, given the startling number of incidents it recorded.

It didn't take long before questions were raised about their accuracy. Were American elementary and secondary school children under such frequent assault as the map based on Everytown's list suggested? Well, yes and no. Guns were going off on and around school campuses, but the firearms weren't always aimed at children. The *Washington Post*, CNN, and other news outlets soon found themselves pulling back on their initial reporting, offering a more nuanced view of the controversial number. To do that, the *Washington Post* began by posing an important question:

> What constitutes a school shooting?
>
> That five-word question has no simple answer, a fact underscored by the backlash to an advocacy group's recent list of school shootings. The list, maintained by Everytown, a group that backs policies to limit gun violence, was updated last week to reflect what it identified as the 74 school shootings since the massacre in Newtown, Conn., a massacre that sparked a national debate over gun control.
>
> Multiple news outlets, including this one, reported on Everytown's data, prompting a backlash over the broad methodology used. As we wrote in our original post, the group considered any instance of a firearm discharging on school property as a shooting—thus casting a broad net that includes homicides, suicides, accidental discharges

and, in a handful of cases, shootings that had no relation to the schools themselves and occurred with no students apparently present.

—Niraj Chokshi, "Fight over School Shooting List
Underscores Difficulty in Quantifying Gun Violence"

CNN followed the same path, re-evaluating its original reporting in light of criticism from groups not on the same page as Everytown for Gun Safety:

Without a doubt, that number is startling.

So . . . CNN took a closer look at the list, delving into the circumstances of each incident Everytown included. . . .

CNN determined that 15 of the incidents Everytown included were situations similar to the violence in Newtown or Oregon—a minor or adult actively shooting inside or near a school. That works out to about one such shooting every five weeks, a startling figure in its own right.

Some of the other incidents on Everytown's list included personal arguments, accidents and alleged gang activities and drug deals.

—Ashley Fantz, Lindsey Knight, and Kevin Wang,
"A Closer Look: How Many Newtown-like
School Shootings since Sandy Hook?"

Other news organizations came up with their own revised numbers, but clearly the interpretation of a number can be as important as the statistic itself. And what were Mark Gongloff's Twitter reactions to these reassessments? They made an argument as well:

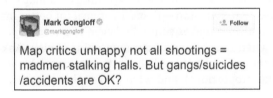

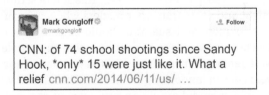

One lesson, surely, is that when you rely on statistics in your arguments, make sure you understand where they come from, what they mean, and what their limitations might be. Check and double-check them or get help in doing so: you don't want to be accused of using fictitious data based on questionable assumptions.

RESPOND•

Statistical evidence becomes useful only when interpreted fairly and reasonably. Go to the *USA Today* Web site and look for the daily graph, chart, or table called the "USA Today Snapshot." Pick a snapshot, and use the information in it to support three different claims, at least two of which make very different points. Share your claims with classmates. (The point is not to learn to use data dishonestly but to see firsthand how the same statistics can serve a variety of arguments.)

Surveys and Polls

When they verify the popularity of an idea or a proposal, surveys and polls provide strong persuasive appeals because they come as close to expressing the will of the people as anything short of an election—the most decisive poll of all. However, surveys and polls can do much more than help politicians make decisions. They can be important elements in scientific research, documenting the complexities of human behavior. They can also provide persuasive reasons for action or intervention. When surveys show, for example, that most American sixth-graders can't locate France or Wyoming on a map—not to mention Ukraine or Afghanistan—that's an appeal for better instruction in geography. It always makes sense, however, to question poll numbers, especially when they support your own point of view. Ask who commissioned the poll, who is publishing its outcome, who was surveyed (and in what proportions), and what stakes these parties might have in its outcome.

Are we being too suspicious? No. In fact, this sort of scrutiny is exactly what you might anticipate from your readers whenever you use (or create) surveys to explore an issue. You should be confident that enough subjects have been surveyed to be accurate, that the people chosen for the study were representative of the selected population as a whole, and that they were chosen randomly—not selected because of what they are likely to say. In a splendid article on how women can make research-based choices during their pregnancy, economist Emily Oster explores, for example, whether an expectant mother might in fact be able to drink responsibly. She researches not only the results of the data, but also who was surveyed, and how their participation might have influenced the results:

> It is possible to unearth research that points to light drinking as a problem, but this work is deeply flawed. One frequently cited study from the journal *Pediatrics*, published in 2001, interviewed women about their drinking while they were pregnant and then contacted them for a child behavior assessment when their children were about 6. The researchers found some evidence that lighter drinking had an impact on behavior and concluded that even one drink a day could cause behavior problems.
>
> So what's wrong with this finding?
>
> In the study, 18% of the women who didn't drink at all and 45% of the women who had one drink a day reported using cocaine during pregnancy. Presumably your first thought is, really? Cocaine? Perhaps the problem is that cocaine, not the occasional glass of Chardonnay, makes your child more likely to have behavior problems.
>
> —Emily Oster, "Take Back Your Pregnancy"

Clearly, polls, surveys, and studies need to be examined critically. You can't take even academic research at face value until you have explored its details.

The meaning of polls and surveys is also affected by the way that questions are posed. In the recent past, research revealed, for example, that polling about same-sex unions got differing responses according to how questions are worded. When people were asked whether gay and lesbian couples should be eligible for the same inheritance and partner health benefits that heterosexual couples receive, a majority of those polled said yes—unless the word *marriage* appeared in the question; then the responses are primarily negative. If anything, the differences here reveal how conflicted people may have been about the issue and how quickly opinions might shift—as they did. Remember, then, to be very careful in reviewing the wording of survey or poll questions.

Finally, always keep in mind that the date of a poll may strongly affect the results—and their usefulness in an argument. In 2010, for example, nearly 50 percent of California voters supported building more nuclear power plants. Less than a year later, that percentage had dropped to 37 percent after the meltdown of Japanese nuclear power plants in the wake of the March 2011 earthquake and tsunami. On public and political issues, you need to be sure that you are using timely information.

RESPOND●

Choose an important issue and design a series of questions to evoke a range of responses in a poll. Try to design a question that would make people strongly inclined to agree, another question that would lead them to oppose the same proposition, and a third that tries to be more neutral. Then try out your questions on your classmates.

Testimonies and Narratives

Writers can support arguments by presenting human experiences in the form of narrative or testimony—particularly if those experiences are their own. In courts, judges and juries often take into consideration detailed descriptions and narratives of exactly what occurred. Look at this reporter's account of a court case in which a panel of judges decided, based on the testimony presented, that a man had been sexually harassed by another man. The narrative, in this case, supplies the evidence:

> The Seventh Circuit, in a 1997 case known as *Doe v. City of Belleville*, drew a sweeping conclusion allowing for same-sex harassment cases of many kinds. . . . This case, for example, centered on teenage twin brothers working a summer job cutting grass in the city cemetery of Belleville, Ill. One boy wore an earring, which caused him no end of grief that particular summer—including a lot of menacing talk among his coworkers about sexually assaulting him in the woods and sending him "back to San Francisco." One of his harassers, identified in court documents as a large former marine, culminated a verbal campaign by backing the earring-wearer against a wall and grabbing him by the testicles to see "if he was a girl or a guy." The teenager had been "singled out for this abuse," the court ruled, "because the way in which he projected the sexual aspect of his personality"—meaning his gender—"did not conform to his coworkers' view of appropriate masculine behavior."
>
> —Margaret Talbot, "Men Behaving Badly"

Personal perspectives can support a claim convincingly and logically, especially if a writer has earned the trust of readers. In arguing that Tea Party supporters of a government shutdown in 2011 had no business being offended when some opponents described them as "terrorists," Froma Harrop, one of the writers who used the term, argued logically and from experience why the characterization was appropriate:

> [T]he hurt the tea party writers most complained of was to their feelings. I had engaged in name-calling, they kept saying. One professing to want more civility in our national conversation, as I do, should not be flinging around the *terrorist* word.

May I presume to disagree? Civility is a subjective concept, to be sure, but hurting people's feelings in the course of making solid arguments is fair and square. The decline in the quality of our public discourse results not so much from an excess of spleen, but a deficit of well-constructed arguments. Few things upset partisans more than when the other side makes a case that bats home.

"Most of us know that effectively scoring on a point of argument opens us to the accusation of mean-spiritedness," writes Frank Partsch, who leads the National Conference of Editorial Writers' Civility Project. "It comes with the territory, and a commitment to civility should not suggest that punches will be pulled in order to avoid such accusations."

—Froma Harrop, "Hurt Feelings Can
Be a Consequence of Strong Arguments"

This narrative introduction gives a rationale for supporting the claim Harrop is making: we can expect consequences when we argue ineffectively. (For more on establishing credibility with readers, see Chapter 3.)

RESPOND●

Bring to class a full review of a recent film that you either enjoyed or did not enjoy. Using testimony from that review, write a brief argument to your classmates explaining why they should see that movie (or why they should avoid it), being sure to use evidence from the review fairly and reasonably. Then exchange arguments with a classmate, and decide whether the evidence in your peer's argument helps to change your opinion about the movie. What's convincing about the evidence? If it doesn't convince you, why doesn't it?

Using Reason and Common Sense

If you don't have "hard facts," you can turn to those arguments Aristotle describes as "constructed" from reason and common sense. The formal study of such reasoning is called *logic*, and you probably recognize a famous example of deductive reasoning, called a **syllogism**:

All human beings are mortal.

Socrates is a human being.

Therefore, Socrates is mortal.

Logic: another thing that penguins aren't very good at.

© Randy Glasbergen/glasbergen.com

In valid syllogisms, the conclusion follows logically—and technically—from the premises that lead up to it. Many have criticized syllogistic reasoning for being limited, and others have poked fun at it, as in the cartoon above.

But we routinely see something like syllogistic reasoning operating in public arguments, particularly when writers take the time to explain key principles. Consider the step-by-step reasoning Michael Gerson uses to explain why exactly it was wrong for the Internal Revenue Service in 2010–2011 to target specific political groups, making it more difficult for them to organize politically:

> Why does this matter deserve heightened scrutiny from the rest of us? Because crimes against democracy are particularly insidious. Representative government involves a type of trade. As citizens, we cede power to public officials for important purposes that require centralized power: defending the country, imposing order, collecting taxes to promote the common good. In exchange, we expect public institutions to be even-handed and disinterested. When the stewards of power—biased judges

or corrupt policemen or politically motivated IRS officials—act unfairly, it undermines trust in the whole system.

—Michael Gerson, "An Arrogant and Lawless IRS"

Gerson's criticism of the IRS actions might be mapped out by the following sequence of statements.

Crimes against democracy undermine trust in the system.

Treating taxpayers differently because of their political beliefs is a crime against democracy.

Therefore, IRS actions that target political groups undermine the American system.

Few writers, of course, think about formal deductive reasoning when they support their claims. Even Aristotle recognized that most people argue perfectly well using informal logic. To do so, they rely mostly on habits of mind and assumptions that they share with their readers or listeners—as Gerson essentially does in his paragraph.

In Chapter 7, we describe a system of informal logic that you may find useful in shaping credible appeals to reason—Toulmin argument. Here, we briefly examine some ways that people use informal logic in their everyday lives. Once again, we begin with Aristotle, who used the term **enthymeme** to describe an ordinary kind of sentence that includes both a claim and a reason but depends on the audience's agreement with an assumption that is left implicit rather than spelled out. Enthymemes can be very persuasive when most people agree with the assumptions they rest on. The following sentences are all enthymemes:

We'd better cancel the picnic because it's going to rain.

Flat taxes are fair because they treat everyone the same.

I'll buy a PC instead of a Mac because it's cheaper.

Sometimes enthymemes seem so obvious that readers don't realize that they're drawing inferences when they agree with them. Consider the first example:

We'd better cancel the picnic because it's going to rain.

Let's expand the enthymeme a bit to say more of what the speaker may mean:

We'd better cancel the picnic this afternoon because the weather bureau is predicting a 70 percent chance of rain for the remainder of the day.

Embedded in this brief argument are all sorts of assumptions and fragments of cultural information that are left implicit but that help to make it persuasive:

> Picnics are ordinarily held outdoors.
>
> When the weather is bad, it's best to cancel picnics.
>
> Rain is bad weather for picnics.
>
> A 70 percent chance of rain means that rain is more likely to occur than not.
>
> When rain is more likely to occur than not, it makes sense to cancel picnics.

For most people, the original statement carries all this information on its own; the enthymeme is a compressed argument, based on what audiences know and will accept.

CULTURAL CONTEXTS FOR ARGUMENT

Logos

In the United States, student writers are expected to draw on "hard facts" and evidence as often as possible in supporting their claims: while ethical and emotional appeals are important, logical appeals tend to hold sway in academic writing. So statistics and facts speak volumes, as does reasoning based on time-honored values such as fairness and equity. In writing to global audiences, you need to remember that not all cultures value the same kinds of appeals. If you want to write to audiences across cultures, you need to know about the norms and values in those cultures. Chinese culture, for example, values authority and often indirect allusion over "facts" alone. Some African cultures value cooperation and community over individualism, and still other cultures value religious texts as providing compelling evidence. So think carefully about what you consider strong evidence, and pay attention to what counts as evidence to others. You can begin by asking yourself questions like:

- What evidence is most valued by your audience: Facts? Concrete examples? Firsthand experience? Religious or philosophical texts? Something else?
- Will analogies count as support? How about precedents?
- Will the testimony of experts count? If so, what kinds of experts are valued most?

But sometimes enthymemes aren't self-evident:

> Be wary of environmentalism because it's religion disguised as science.

> iPhones are undermining civil society by making us even more focused on ourselves.

> It's time to make all public toilets unisex because to do otherwise is discriminatory.

In these cases, you'll have to work much harder to defend both the claim and the implicit assumptions that it's based on by drawing out the inferences that seem self-evident in other enthymemes. And you'll likely also have to supply credible evidence; a simple declaration of fact won't suffice.

Providing Logical Structures for Argument

Some arguments depend on particular logical structures to make their points. In the following pages, we identify a few of these logical structures.

Degree

Arguments based on degree are so common that people barely notice them, nor do they pay much attention to how they work because they seem self-evident. Most audiences will readily accept that *more of a good thing* or *less of a bad thing* is good. In her novel *The Fountainhead*, Ayn Rand asks: "If physical slavery is repulsive, how much more repulsive is the concept of servility of the spirit?" Most readers immediately comprehend the point Rand intends to make about slavery of the spirit because they already know that physical slavery is cruel and would reject any forms of slavery that were even crueler on the principle that *more of a bad thing is bad*. Rand still needs to offer evidence that "servility of the spirit" is, in fact, worse than bodily servitude, but she has begun with a logical structure readers can grasp. Here are other arguments that work similarly:

> If I can get a ten-year warranty on an inexpensive Kia, shouldn't I get the same or better warranty from a more expensive Lexus?

> The health benefits from using stem cells in research will surely outweigh the ethical risks.

> Better a conventional war now than a nuclear confrontation later.

A demonstrator at an immigrants' rights rally in New York City in 2007. Arguments based on values that are widely shared within a society—such as the idea of equal rights in American culture—have an automatic advantage with audiences. AP Photo/Seth Wenig

Analogies

Analogies, typically complex or extended comparisons, explain one idea or concept by comparing it to something else.

Here, writer and founder of literacy project 826 Valencia, Dave Eggers, uses an analogy in arguing that we do not value teachers as much as we should:

> When we don't get the results we want in our military endeavors, we don't blame the soldiers. We don't say, "It's these lazy soldiers and their bloated benefits plans! That's why we haven't done better in Afghanistan!" No, if the results aren't there, we blame the planners. . . . No one contemplates blaming the men and women fighting every day in the trenches for little pay and scant recognition. And yet in education we do just that. When we don't like the way our students score on international standardized tests, we blame the teachers.
>
> —Dave Eggers and Nínive Calegari, "The High Cost of Low Teacher Salaries"

Precedent

Arguments from **precedent** and arguments of analogy both involve comparisons. Consider an assertion like this one, which uses a comparison as a precedent:

> If motorists in most other states can pump their own gas safely, surely the state of Oregon can trust its own drivers to be as capable. It's time for Oregon to permit self-service gas stations.

You could tease out several inferences from this claim to explain its reasonableness: people in Oregon are as capable as people in other states; people with equivalent capabilities can do the same thing; pumping gas is not hard; and so forth. But you don't have to because most readers get the argument simply because of the way it is put together.

Here is an excerpt from an extended argument by blogger Abby Phillip, in which she argues that the Ebola outbreak that began in 2014 may not follow the same pattern as past outbreaks:

> An idea long viewed as an unlikely possibility is now becoming increasingly real: Ebola might not go away for a very long time.
>
> It has never happened before in the thirty-eight-year history of the virus. Every other time Ebola has made the unlikely jump from the animal world to the human one, it has been snuffed out within days, weeks or, at most, months.
>
> This time, though, in Guinea, Sierra Leone and Liberia, the Ebola virus is raging like a forest fire, in the words of several public health officials. And some of them are raising the possibility that the outbreak-turned-full-fledged-epidemic could become fundamentally different from any other Ebola outbreak on record, in that it might stick around.
>
> "What's always worked before—contact tracing, isolation and quarantine—is not going to work, and it's not working now," said Daniel Lucey, a professor of microbiology and immunology at Georgetown University Medical Center, who spent three weeks treating Ebola patients in Sierra Leone and will soon travel to the Liberian capital of Monrovia for another five-week stint.
>
> "In my opinion," Lucey added, "a year from now, we won't have one or two cases; we'll have many cases of Ebola."
>
> Unlike past outbreaks, in which Ebola emerged in the sparsely populated countryside of central Africa, this outbreak has become an exponentially spreading urban menace.
>
> —Abby Phillip, "This Ebola Outbreak Could Be Here to Stay"

Unfortunately, the prediction proved to be more accurate than Phillip might have preferred.

You'll encounter additional kinds of logical structures as you create your own arguments. You'll find some of them in Chapter 5, "Fallacies of Argument," and still more in Chapter 7 on Toulmin argument.

5

Fallacies of Argument

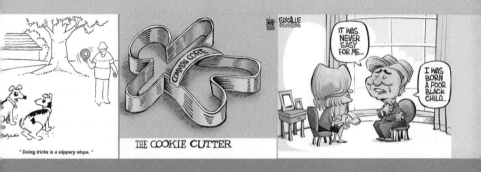

Left to right: Roy Delgado/www.Cartoonstock.com; © Bish/Cagle Cartoons, Inc.; © Eric Allie/Cagle Cartoons, Inc.

Do these editorial cartoons strike a chord with you? All three are compli-cated. The first panel pokes fun at slippery slope arguments, which aim to thwart action by predicting dire consequences: chase that Frisbee and you'll soon be pulling milk carts. The second item uses a scare tactic (a potential fallacy of argument) to raise opposition to the educational reform called "Common Core," suggesting ominously that the program's cookie-cutter approach will produce children who all think alike. And the third cartoon points to a fallacy of argument that a prominent politi-cian has perhaps slipped into—the sentimental appeal; it alludes to Hillary Clinton's comment in a 2014 interview with Diane Sawyer that she and husband Bill "came out of the White House not only dead broke but in debt."

Fallacies are argumentative moves flawed by their very nature or structure. Because such tactics can make productive principled argu-ment more difficult, they potentially hurt everyone involved, including the people responsible for them. The worst sorts of fallacies muck up the frank but civil conversations that people should be able to have, regardless of their differences.

Yet it's hard to deny the power in offering audiences a compelling either/or choice or a vulnerable straw man in an argument. For exactly that reason, it's important that you can recognize and point out fallacies in the work of others—and avoid them in your own writing. This chapter aims to help you meet these goals: here we'll introduce you to fallacies of argument classified according to the emotional, ethical, and logical appeals we've discussed earlier (see Chapters 2, 3, and 4).

Fallacies of Emotional Argument

Emotional arguments can be powerful and suitable in many circumstances, and most writers use them frequently. However, writers who pull on their readers' heartstrings or raise their blood pressure too often can violate the good faith on which legitimate argument depends.

Scare Tactics

Politicians, advertisers, and public figures sometimes peddle their ideas by frightening people and exaggerating possible dangers well beyond their statistical likelihood. Such ploys work because it's easier to imagine something terrible happening than to appreciate its rarity.

Scare tactics can also be used to stampede legitimate fears into panic or prejudice. Laborers who genuinely worry about losing their jobs can be persuaded to fear immigrants who might work for less money. Seniors living on fixed incomes can be convinced that minor changes to entitlement programs represent dire threats to their well-being. Such tactics have the effect of closing off thinking because people who are scared often act irrationally. Even well-intended fear campaigns—like those directed against smoking, unprotected sex, or the use of illegal drugs—can misfire if their warnings prove too shrill. People just stop listening.

Either/Or Choices

Either/or choices can be well-intentioned strategies to get something accomplished. Parents use them all the time ("Eat your broccoli, or you won't get dessert"). But they become fallacious arguments when they

A false choice? © Adam Zyglis/Cagle Cartoons, Inc.

reduce a complicated issue to excessively simple terms or when they're designed to obscure legitimate alternatives. Here, for example, is Riyad Mansour, the Palestinian representative to the United Nations, offering the nation of Israel just such a choice in an interview with Charlie Rose in January 2014:

> It is up to them [the Israelis] to decide what kind of a state they want to be. Do they want to be a democratic state where Israel will be the state for all of its citizens? Or do they want to be a state for the Jewish people, therefore excluding 1.6 million Palestinian Arabs who are Israelis from their society? That debate is not our debate. That debate is their debate.

But Joel B. Pollak, writing for Breitbart News Network, describes Mansour's claim as a "false choice" since Israel already is a Jewish state that nonetheless allows Muslims to be full citizens. The either/or argument Mansour presents, according to Pollack, does not describe the realities of this complex political situation.

Slippery Slope

The **slippery slope** fallacy portrays today's tiny misstep as tomorrow's slide into disaster. Some arguments that aim at preventing dire consequences do not take the slippery slope approach (for example, the parent who corrects a child for misbehavior now is acting sensibly to prevent more serious problems as the child grows older). A slippery slope argument becomes wrongheaded when a writer exaggerates the likely consequences of an action, usually to frighten readers. As such, slippery slope arguments are also scare tactics. In recent years, the issue of gun ownership in America has evoked many slippery slope arguments. Here's one perspective on the tactic:

> The leadership of the NRA is exceptionally fond of the Slippery Slope argument. "Universal background checks will inevitably be followed by a national registry of gun-owners which will inevitably be followed by confiscation of all their guns." Or, "A ban on assault-style weapons and thirty+ round magazines will inevitably be followed by a ban on hand guns with ten-round magazines, that will inevitably be followed by bans on all guns, including antique dueling pistols inherited from our Founding Fathers."
>
> Problem number one with this slide down the fearsome slope is how much weaponry has changed since the days of militias with muskets. Even the NRA agrees that lines have to be drawn somewhere. They do not favor legalization of civilian use of rocket-propelled grenades, bazookas or stinger missiles. If there is a slippery slope we are starting approximately half-way down.
>
> —Michael Wolkowitz, "Slippery Slopes, Imagined and Real"

Social and political ideas and proposals do have consequences, but they aren't always as dire as writers fond of slippery slope tactics would have you believe.

Overly Sentimental Appeals

Overly **sentimental appeals** use tender emotions excessively to distract readers from facts. Often, such appeals are highly personal and individual and focus attention on heartwarming or heartrending situations that make readers feel guilty if they challenge an idea, a policy, or a proposal. Emotions become an impediment to civil discourse when they keep people from thinking clearly.

Such sentimental appeals are a major vehicle of television news, where tugging at viewers' heartstrings can mean high ratings. For example,

This image, taken from a gun control protest, is designed to elicit sympathy by causing the viewer to think about the dangers guns pose to innocent children and, thus, support the cause. Tim Boyle/Getty Images

when a camera documents the day-to-day sacrifices of a single parent trying to meet mortgage payments and keep her kids in college, the woman's on-screen struggles can seem to represent the plight of an entire class of people threatened by callous bankers and college administrators. But while such human interest stories stir genuine emotions, they seldom give a complete picture of complex social or economic issues.

Bandwagon Appeals

Bandwagon appeals urge people to follow the same path everyone else is taking. Such arguments can be relatively benign and seem harmless. But they do push people to take the easier path rather than think independently about what choices to make or where to go.

Many American parents seem to have an innate ability to refute bandwagon appeals. When their kids whine, *Everyone else is going camping without chaperones,* the parents reply, *And if everyone else jumps off a cliff (or a railroad bridge or the Empire State Building), you will too?* The children groan—and then try a different line of argument.

Wear pajamas.
Drink hot chocolate.
**Talk about getting
health insurance.**

_____

#GetTalking
barackobama.com/talk

Some bandwagon appeals work better than others.

Unfortunately, not all bandwagon approaches are so transparent. In recent decades, bandwagon issues have included a war on drugs, the nuclear freeze movement, campaigns against drunk driving, campaigns for immigration reform, bailouts for banks and businesses, and *many* fads in education from high-stakes testing to MOOCs. All these issues are too complex to permit the suspension of judgment that bandwagon tactics require.

Fallacies of Ethical Argument

Because readers give their closest attention to authors they respect or trust, writers usually want to present themselves as honest, well-informed, likable, or sympathetic. But not all the devices that writers use to gain the attention and confidence of readers are admirable. (For more on appeals based on character, see Chapter 3.)

Appeals to False Authority

Many academic research papers find and reflect on the work of reputable authorities and introduce these authorities through direct quotations or citations as credible evidence. (For more on assessing the reliability of sources, see Chapter 19.) **False authority**, however, occurs when writers offer themselves or other authorities as sufficient warrant for believing a claim:

Claim	X is true because I say so.
Warrant	What I say must be true.
Claim	X is true because Y says so.
Warrant	What Y says must be true.

Though they are seldom stated so baldly, claims of authority drive many political campaigns. American pundits and politicians are fond of citing the U.S. Constitution and its Bill of Rights (Canadians have their Charter of Rights and Freedoms) as ultimate authorities, a reasonable practice when the documents are interpreted respectfully. However, the rights claimed sometimes aren't in the texts themselves or don't mean what the speakers think they do. And most constitutional matters are debatable—as volumes of court records prove. Likewise, religious believers often base arguments on books or traditions that wield great authority in a particular religious community. But the power of such texts is usually limited to that group and less capable of persuading others solely on the grounds of authority.

In short, you should pay serious attention to claims supported by respected authorities, such as the Centers for Disease Control, the National Science Foundation, or the *Globe and Mail*. But don't accept information simply because it is put forth by such offices and agencies. To quote a Russian proverb made famous by Ronald Reagan, "Trust, but verify."

Dogmatism

A writer who asserts or assumes that a particular position is the *only one* that is conceivably acceptable is expressing **dogmatism**, a fallacy of character that undermines the trust that must exist between those who make and listen to arguments. When people or organizations write dogmatically, they imply that no arguments are necessary: the truth is self-evident and needs no support. Here is an extreme example of such an appeal, quoted in an *Atlantic* story by Tracy Brown

Hamilton and describing an anti-smoking appeal made by the Third Reich:

> "Brother national socialist, do you know that your Fuhrer is against smoking and thinks that every German is responsible to the whole people for all his deeds and omissions, and does not have the right to damage his body with drugs?"
>
> —From Tracy Brown Hamilton, "The Nazis' Forgotten Anti-Smoking Campaign"

Subjects or ideas that can be defended with facts, testimony, and good reasons ought not to be off the table in a free society. In general, whenever someone suggests that even raising an issue for debate is totally unacceptable—whether on the grounds that it's racist, sexist, unpatriotic, blasphemous, insensitive, or offensive in some other way—you should be suspicious.

Ad Hominem Arguments

Ad hominem (Latin for "to the man") **arguments** attack the character of a person rather than the claims he or she makes: when you destroy the credibility of your opponents, you either destroy their ability to present reasonable appeals or distract from the successful arguments they may be offering. Such attacks, of course, aren't aimed at men only, as columnist Jamie Stiehm proved when she criticized Supreme Court Justice Sonia Sotomayor for delaying an Obamacare mandate objected to by the Little Sisters of the Poor, a Catholic religious order. Stiehm directly targets Sotomayor's religious beliefs:

> Et tu, Justice Sonia Sotomayor? Really, we can't trust you on women's health and human rights? The lady from the Bronx just dropped the ball on American women and girls as surely as she did the sparkling ball at midnight on New Year's Eve in Times Square. Or maybe she's just a good Catholic girl.
>
> —Jamie Stiehm, "The Catholic Supreme Court's War on Women"

Stiehm then widens her *ad hominem* assault to include Catholics in general:

> Sotomayor's blow brings us to confront an uncomfortable reality. More than WASPs, Methodists, Jews, Quakers or Baptists, Catholics often try to impose their beliefs on you, me, public discourse and institutions. Especially if "you" are female.

Arguably, *ad hominem* tactics like this turn arguments into two-sided affairs with good guys and bad guys (or gals), and that's unfortunate, since character often really *does* matter in argument. People expect the proponent of peace to be civil, a secretary of the treasury to pay his or her taxes, and the champion of family values to be a faithful spouse. But it's fallacious to attack an idea by uncovering the foibles of its advocates or by attacking their motives, backgrounds, or unchangeable traits.

Stacking the Deck

Just as gamblers try to stack the deck by arranging cards so they are sure to win, writers **stack the deck** when they show only one side of the story—the one in their favor. In a Facebook forum on the documentary film *Super Size Me* (which followed a 32-year-old man who ate three meals a day at McDonald's for thirty days with drastic health consequences), one student points out an example of stacking the deck:

> One of the fallacies was stacking the deck. Spurlock stated many facts and gave plenty of evidence of what can happen if you eat fast food in abundance. Weight gain, decline in health, habit forming, and a toll on your daily life. But he failed to show what could happen if you ate the fast food and participated in daily exercise and took vitamins. The fallacy is that he does not show us both sides of what can happen. Possibly you could eat McDonald's for three meals a day for thirty days and if you engaged in daily exercise and took vitamins maybe your health would be just fine. But we were not ever shown that side of the experiment.
>
> —Heather Tew Alleman, on a Facebook forum

In the same way, reviewers have been critical of documentaries by Michael Moore and Dinesh D'Souza that resolutely show only one side of a story or prove highly selective in their coverage. When you stack the deck, you take a big chance that your readers will react like Alleman and decide not to trust you: that's one reason it's so important to show that you have considered alternatives in making any argument.

Fallacies of Logical Argument

You'll encounter a problem in any argument when the claims, warrants, or proofs in it are invalid, insufficient, or disconnected. In theory, such problems seem easy enough to spot, but in practice, they can be camouflaged by a skillful use of words or images. Indeed, logical fallacies pose a challenge to civil argument because they often seem reasonable and natural, especially when they appeal to people's self-interests.

Hasty Generalization

A **hasty generalization** is an inference drawn from insufficient evidence: because *my* Fiat broke down, then *all* Fiats must be junk. It also forms the basis for most stereotypes about people or institutions: because *a few* people in a large group are observed to act in a certain way, *all* members of that group are inferred to behave similarly. The resulting conclusions are usually sweeping claims of little merit: *women are bad drivers; men are slobs; English teachers are nitpicky; computer jocks are* . . . , and on and on.

To draw valid inferences, you must always have sufficient evidence (see Chapter 18) and you must qualify your claims appropriately. After all, people do need generalizations to make reasonable decisions in life. Such claims can be offered legitimately if placed in context and tagged with sensible qualifiers—*some, a few, many, most, occasionally, rarely, possibly, in some cases, under certain circumstances, in my limited experience.*

Faulty Causality

In Latin, **faulty causality** is known as *post hoc, ergo propter hoc*, which translates as "after this, therefore because of this"—the faulty assumption that because one event or action follows another, the first causes the second. Consider a lawsuit commented on in the *Wall Street Journal* in which a writer sued Coors (unsuccessfully), claiming that drinking copious amounts of the company's beer had kept him from writing a novel.

Some actions do produce reactions. Step on the brake pedal in your car, and you move hydraulic fluid that pushes calipers against disks to create friction that stops the vehicle. In other cases, however, a supposed connection between cause and effect turns out to be completely wrong. For example, doctors now believe that when an elderly person falls and breaks a hip or leg, the injury usually caused the fall rather than the other way around.

That's why overly simple causal claims should always be subject to scrutiny. In summer 2008, writer Nicholas Carr posed a simple causal question in a cover story for the *Atlantic*: "Is Google Making Us Stupid?" Carr essentially answered yes, arguing that "as we come to rely on computers to mediate our understanding of the world, it is our own intelligence that flattens" and that the more one is online the less he or she is able to concentrate or read deeply.

But others, like Jamais Cascio (senior fellow at the Institute for Ethics and Emerging Technologies), soon challenged that causal connection: rather than making us stupid, Cascio argues, Internet tools like Google will lead to the development of "'fluid intelligence'—the ability to find meaning in confusion and to solve new problems, independent of acquired knowledge." The final word on this contentious causal relationship—the effects on the human brain caused by new technology—has yet to be written, and will probably be available only after decades of complicated research.

Begging the Question

Most teachers have heard some version of the following argument: *You can't give me a C in this course; I'm an A student.* A member of Congress accused of taking kickbacks can make much the same argument: *I can't be guilty of accepting such bribes; I'm an honest person.* In both cases, the claim is made on grounds that can't be accepted as true because those grounds themselves are in question. How can the accused bribe-taker defend herself on grounds of honesty when that honesty is in doubt? Looking at the arguments in Toulmin terms helps to see the fallacy:

Claim	You can't give me a C in this course . . .
Reason	. . . because I'm an A student.
Warrant	An A student is someone who can't receive Cs.

Claim	Representative X can't be guilty of accepting bribes . . .
Reason	. . . because she's an honest person.
Warrant	An honest person cannot be guilty of accepting bribes.

With the warrants stated, you can see why **begging the question**—assuming as true the very claim that's disputed—is a form of circular argument that goes nowhere. (For more on Toulmin argument, see Chapter 7.)

Equivocation

Equivocations—half truths or arguments that give lies an honest appearance—are usually based on tricks of language. Consider the plagiarist who copies a paper word for word from a source and then declares that "I wrote the entire paper myself"—meaning that she physically copied the piece on her own. But the plagiarist is using *wrote* equivocally and knows that most people understand the word to mean composing and not merely copying words.

Parsing words carefully can sometimes look like equivocation or be the thing itself. For example, early in 2014 Internal Revenue Service Commissioner John Koskinen promised to turn over to a committee of the House of Representatives all the relevant emails in a scandal involving the agency. Subsequently, the agency revealed that some of those requested emails had been destroyed by the failure of a computer's hard drive. But Koskinen defended his earlier promise by telling the chair of the committee, "I never said I would provide you emails we didn't have." A simple statement of fact or a slick equivocation?

Non Sequitur

A **non sequitur** is an argument whose claims, reasons, or warrants don't connect logically. You've probably detected a non sequitur when you react to an argument with a puzzled, "Wait, that doesn't follow." Children are adept at framing non sequiturs like this one: *You don't love me or you'd buy me a new bicycle!* It doesn't take a parental genius to realize that love has little connection with buying children toys.

Non sequiturs often occur when writers omit steps in an otherwise logical chain of reasoning. For example, it might be a non sequitur to argue that since postsecondary education now costs so much, it's time to move colleges and university instruction online. Such a suggestion *may* have merit, but a leap from brick-and-mortar schools to virtual ones is extreme. Numerous issues and questions must be addressed step-by-step before the proposal can be taken seriously.

Politicians sometimes resort to non sequiturs to evade thorny issues or questions. Here for example is presidential candidate Mitt Romney in a 2011 CNBC Republican primary debate turning moderator John Harwood's question about changing political positions into one about demonstrating personal integrity:

> *Harwood:* . . . Your opponents have said you switched positions on
> many issues. . . . What can you say to Republicans to persuade them

that the things you say in the campaign are rooted in something deeper than the fact that you are running for office?

Romney: John, I think people know me pretty well. . . . I think people understand that I'm a man of steadiness and constancy. I don't think you are going to find somebody who has more of those attributes than I do. I have been married to the same woman for . . . 42 years. . . . I have been in the same church my entire life.

Conservative writer Matt K. Lewis took Romney to task for this move, pointing out that a steady personal life is no guarantor of a consistent political philosophy:

This, of course, is not to say that values and character do not matter—they *do*—but it is to say that Romney's answer was a non sequitur. Everyone knows Mitt Romney is a decent, respectable person. The question is whether or not he can be trusted to advance conservatism as president.

Straw Man

Those who resort to the **straw man** fallacy attack arguments that no one is really making or portray opponents' positions as more extreme or far less coherent than they actually are. The speaker or writer thus sets up an argument that is conveniently easy to knock down (like a man of straw), proceeds to do so, and then claims victory over an opponent who may not even exist.

Straw men are especially convenient devices for politicians who want to characterize the positions of their opponents as more extreme than they actually are: consider obvious memes such as "war on women" and "war on Christmas." But straw man arguments are often more subtle. For instance, Steven Novella of Yale University argues that political commentator Charles Krauthammer slips into the fallacy when he misconstrues the meaning of "settled science" in a column on climate change. Novella rebuts Krauthammer's assertion that "There is nothing more anti-scientific than the very idea that science is settled, static, impervious to challenge" by explaining why such a claim is deceptive:

Calling something an established scientific fact means that it is reasonable to proceed with that fact as a premise, for further research or for policy. It does not mean "static, impervious to challenge." That is the straw man. Both evolution deniers and climate change deniers use this tactic to misinterpret scientific confidence as an anti-scientific resistance to new evidence or arguments. It isn't. It does mean that the burden of proof has shifted to those opposing the theory that is now well-established (because it has already met a significant burden of proof).

—Steven Novella, *NeuroLogica Blog*, February 25, 2014

In other words, Krauthammer's definition of science is not one that most scientists use.

Red Herring

This fallacy gets its name from the old British hunting practice of dragging a dried herring across the path of the fox in order to throw the hounds off the trail. A **red herring** fallacy does just that: it changes the subject abruptly or introduces an irrelevant claim or fact to throw readers or listeners off the trail. For example, people skeptical about climate change will routinely note that weather is always changing and point to the fact that Vikings settled in Greenland one thousand years ago before harsher conditions drove them away. True, scientists will say, but the point is irrelevant to arguments about worldwide global warming caused by human activity.

The red herring is not only a device writers and speakers use in the arguments they create, but it's also a charge used frequently to undermine someone else's arguments. Couple the term "red herring" in a Web search to just about any political or social cause and you'll come up with numerous articles complaining of someone's use of the device.

climate change + red herring

common core + red herring

immigration reform + red herring

"Red herring" has become a convenient way of saying "I disagree with your argument" or "your point is irrelevant." And perhaps making a too-easy rebuttal like that can itself be a fallacy?

Faulty Analogy

Comparisons can help to clarify one concept by measuring it against another that is more familiar. Consider the power and humor of this comparison attributed to Mark Twain, an implicit argument for term limits in politics:

Politicians and diapers must be changed often, and for the same reason.

When comparisons such as this one are extended, they become *analogies* — ways of understanding unfamiliar ideas by comparing them with something that's better known (see p. 68). But useful as such comparisons are, they may prove false if either taken on their own and pushed too far, or taken too seriously. At this point, they turn into **faulty analogies** — inaccurate or inconsequential comparisons between objects or concepts. Economist Paul Krugman provides an eye-opening analysis of a familiar but, as he sees it, false analogy between personal and government debt:

> Deficit-worriers portray a future in which we're impoverished by the need to pay back money we've been borrowing. They see America as being like a family that took out too large a mortgage, and will have a hard time making the monthly payments.
>
> This is, however, a really bad analogy in at least two ways.
>
> First, families have to pay back their debt. Governments don't — all they need to do is ensure that debt grows more slowly than their tax base. The debt from World War II was never repaid; it just became increasingly irrelevant as the U.S. economy grew, and with it the income subject to taxation.
>
> Second — and this is the point almost nobody seems to get — an overborrowed family owes money to someone else; U.S. debt is, to a large extent, money we owe to ourselves.

Whether you agree with the Nobel laureate or not, his explanation offers insight into how analogies work (or fail) and how to think about them critically.

RESPOND●

1. Examine each of the following political slogans or phrases for logical fallacies.

   "Resistance is futile." (Borg message on *Star Trek: The Next Generation*)

   "It's the economy, stupid." (sign on the wall at Bill Clinton's campaign headquarters)

   "Make love, not war." (antiwar slogan popularized during the Vietnam War)

   "A chicken in every pot." (campaign slogan)

   "Guns don't kill, people do." (NRA slogan)

"Dog Fighters Are Cowardly Scum." (PETA T-shirt)

"If you can't stand the heat, get out of the kitchen." (attributed to Harry S Truman)

2. Choose a paper you've written for a college class and analyze it for signs of fallacious reasoning. Then find an editorial, a syndicated column, and a news report on the same topic and look for fallacies in them. Which has the most fallacies—and what kind? What may be the role of the audience in determining when a statement is fallacious?

3. Find a Web site that is sponsored by an organization (the Future of Music Coalition, perhaps), a business (Coca-Cola, Pepsi), or another group (the Democratic or Republican National Committee), and analyze the site for fallacious reasoning. Among other considerations, look at the relationship between text and graphics and between individual pages and the pages that surround or are linked to them.

4. Political blogs such as *Mother Jones* and *InstaPundit* typically provide quick responses to daily events and detailed critiques of material in other media sites, including national newspapers. Study one such blog for a few days to see whether and how the site critiques the articles, political commentary, or writers it links to. Does the blog ever point out fallacies of argument? If so, does it explain the problems with such reasoning or just assume readers will understand the fallacies? Summarize your findings in a brief oral report to your class.

6

Rhetorical Analysis

All images © Andy Anderson, Lone River Productions

If you watched the 2013 Super Bowl between the Baltimore Ravens and the San Francisco 49ers, you may remember the commercial. For two solemn minutes, still photographs of rural America and the people who work there moved across the screen accompanied by the unmistakable voice of the late Paul Harvey reading words he had first delivered in 1978. Maria Godoy of NPR described it this way: "It may not have been as dramatic as the stadium blackout that halted play for more than a half-hour, or as extravagant as Beyonce's halftime show. But for many viewers of Super Bowl XLVII, one of the standout moments was a deceptively simple ad for the Dodge Ram called 'God Made a Farmer.'" It was a fourth quarter interrupted by cattle, churches, snowy farmyards, bales of hay, plowed fields, hardworking men, and a few sturdy women. Occasionally, a slide discreetly showed a Ram truck, sponsor of the video, but there were no overt sales pitches—only a product logo in the final frame. Yet visits to the Ram Web site spiked immediately, and sales of Ram pickups did too. (The official video has been viewed on YouTube more than 17 million times.)

So how to account for the appeal of such an unconventional and unexpected commercial? That would be the work of a **rhetorical analysis**, the close reading of a text or, in this case, a video commercial, to figure out exactly how it functions. Certainly, the creators of "God Made a Farmer" counted on the strong emotional appeal of the photographs they'd commissioned, guessing perhaps that the expert images and Harvey's spellbinding words would contrast powerfully with the frivolity and emptiness of much Super Bowl ad fare:

> God said, "I need somebody willing to sit up all night with a newborn colt. And watch it die. Then dry his eyes and say, 'Maybe next year.'"

They pushed convention, too, by the length of the spot and the muted product connection, doubtless hoping to win the goodwill of a huge audience suddenly all teary-eyed in the midst of a football game. And they surely gained the respect of a great many truck-buying farmers.

Rhetorical analyses can also probe the contexts that surround any argument or text—its impact on a society, its deeper implications, or even what it lacks or whom it excludes. Predictably, the widely admired Ram commercial (selected #1 Super Bowl XLVII spot by *Adweek*) acquired its share of critics, some attacking it for romanticizing farm life, others for ignoring the realities of industrial agriculture. And not a few writers noted what they regarded as glaring absences in its representation of farmers. Here, for instance, is copywriter and blogger Edye Deloch-Hughes, offering a highly personal and conflicted view of the spot in what amounts to an informal rhetorical analysis:

> . . . I was riveted by the still photography and stirring thirty-five-year-old delivery of legendary radio broadcaster Paul Harvey. But as I sat mesmerized, I waited to see an image that spoke to my heritage. What flashed before me were close-ups of stoic white men whose faces drowned out the obligatory medium shots of a minority token or two; their images minimized against the amber waves of grain.
>
> God made a Black farmer too. Where was my Grandpa, Grandma and Great Granny? My Auntie and Uncle Bolden? And didn't God make Hispanic and Native American farmers? They too were under-represented.
>
> I am the offspring of a century and a half of African-American care-takers of the land, from Arkansas, Mississippi and Louisiana, who experienced their toils and troubles, their sun ups and sun downs. Their injustices and beat-downs. I wrestled with my mixed emotions; loving the commercial and feeling dejected at the same time.

. . . Minimizing positive Black imagery and accomplishments is as American as wrestling cattle. We're often footnotes or accessories in history books, TV shows, movies and magazines as well as TV commercials. When content is exceptional, the omission is harder to recognize or criticize. Some friends of mine saw—or rather *felt*—the omission as I did. Others did not. I say be aware and vocal about how you are represented—if represented at all, otherwise your importance and relevance will be lost.

—Edye Deloch-Hughes, "So God Made a Black Farmer Too"

As this example suggests, whenever you undertake a rhetorical analysis, follow your instincts and look closely. Why does an ad for a cell phone or breakfast sandwich make people want one immediately? How does an op-ed piece in the *Washington Post* suddenly change your long-held position on immigration? A rhetorical analysis might help you understand. Dig as deep as you can into the context of the item you are analyzing, especially when you encounter puzzling, troubling, or unusually successful appeals—ethical, emotional, or logical. Ask yourself what strategies a speech, editorial, opinion column, film, or ad spot employs to move your heart, win your trust, and change your mind—or why, maybe, it fails to do so.

Composing a Rhetorical Analysis

You perform a rhetorical analysis by analyzing how well the components of an argument work together to persuade or move an audience. You can study arguments of any kind—advertisements (as we've seen), editorials, political cartoons, and even songs, movies, or photographs. In every case, you'll need to focus your rhetorical analysis on elements that stand out or make the piece intriguing or problematic. You could begin by exploring *some* of the following issues:

- What is the purpose of this argument? What does it hope to achieve?
- Who is the audience for this argument? Who is ignored or excluded?
- What appeals or techniques does the argument use—emotional, logical, ethical?
- What type of argument is it, and how does the genre affect the argument? (You might challenge the lack of evidence in editorials, but you wouldn't make the same complaint about bumper stickers.)

- Who is making the argument? What ethos does it create, and how does it do so? What values does the ethos evoke? How does it make the writer or creator seem trustworthy?
- What authorities does the argument rely on or appeal to?
- What facts, reasoning, and evidence are used in the argument? How are they presented?
- What claims does the argument make? What issues are raised—or ignored or evaded?
- What are the contexts—social, political, historical, cultural—for this argument? Whose interests does it serve? Who gains or loses by it?
- How is the argument organized or arranged? What media does the argument use and how effectively?
- How does the language or style of the argument persuade an audience?

In answering questions like these, try to show *how* the key devices in an argument actually make it succeed or fail. Quote freely from a written piece, or describe the elements in a visual argument. (Annotating a visual text is one option.) Let readers know where and why an argument makes sense and where it falls apart. If you believe that an argument startles, challenges, insults, or lulls audiences, explain why that is the case and provide evidence. Don't be surprised when your rhetorical analysis itself becomes an argument. That's what it should be.

Understanding the Purpose of Arguments You Are Analyzing

To understand how well any argument works, begin with its purpose: Is it to sell running shoes? To advocate for limits to college tuition? To push a political agenda? In many cases, that purpose may be obvious. A conservative blog will likely advance right-wing causes; ads from a baby food company will likely show happy infants delighted with stewed prunes.

But some projects may hide their persuasive intentions. Perhaps you've responded to a mail survey or telephone poll only to discover that the questions are leading you to switch your cable service or buy apartment insurance. Do such stealthy arguments succeed? Do consumers resent the intrusion? Answering questions like these provides material for useful rhetorical analyses that assess the strengths, risks, and ethics of such strategies.

Understanding Who Makes an Argument

Knowing *who* is claiming *what* is key to any rhetorical analysis. That's why persuasive appeals usually have a name attached to them. Remember the statements included in TV ads during the last federal election: "Hello, I'm X—and I approve this ad"? Federal law requires such statements so we can tell the difference between ads a candidate endorses and ones sponsored by groups not even affiliated with the campaigns. Their interests and motives might be very different.

But knowing a name is just a starting place for analysis. You need to dig deeper, and you could do worse than to Google such people or groups to discover more about them. What else have they produced? Who publishes them: the *Wall Street Journal*, the blog *The Daily Kos*, or even a LiveJournal celebrity gossip site such as *Oh No They Didn't*? Check out related Web sites for information about goals, policies, contributors, and funding.

Funny, offensive, or both? © Chris Maddaloni/CQ Roll Call

RESPOND•

Describe a persuasive moment that you can recall from a speech, an editorial, an advertisement, a YouTube clip, or a blog posting. Or research one of the following famous persuasive moments and describe the circumstances—the historical situation, the issues at stake, the purpose of the argument—that make it so memorable.

Abraham Lincoln's Gettysburg Address (1863)

Elizabeth Cady Stanton's Declaration of Sentiments at the Seneca Falls Convention (1848)

Chief Tecumseh's address to General William Henry Harrison (1810)

Winston Churchill's radio addresses to the British people during World War II (1940)

Martin Luther King Jr.'s "Letter from Birmingham Jail" (1963)

Ronald Reagan's tribute to the *Challenger* astronauts (1986)

Toni Morrison's speech accepting the Nobel Prize (1993)

Will.i.am's "Yes We Can" song/collage on YouTube (2008)

Identifying and Appealing to Audiences

Most arguments are composed with specific audiences in mind, and their success depends, in part, on how well their strategies, content, tone, and language meet the expectations of that audience. So your rhetorical analysis of an argumentative piece should identify its target readers or viewers (see "Appealing to Audiences," p. 21) if possible, or make an educated guess about the audience, since most arguments suggest whom they intend to reach and in what ways.

Both a flyer stapled to a bulletin board in a college dorm ("Why you shouldn't drink and drive") and a forty-foot billboard for Bud Light might be aimed at the same general population—college students. But each will adjust its appeals for the different moods of that group in different moments. For starters, the flyer will appeal to students in a serious vein, while the beer ad will probably be visually stunning and virtually text-free.

You might also examine how a writer or an argument establishes credibility with an audience. One effective means of building credibility is to show respect for your readers or viewers, especially if they may not agree with you. In introducing an article on problems facing African American women in the workplace, editor in chief of *Essence* Diane Weathers considers the problems that she faced with respecting all her potential readers:

> We spent more than a minute agonizing over the provocative cover line for our feature "White Women at Work." The countless stories we had heard from women across the country told us that this was a workplace issue we had to address. From my own experience at several major magazines, it was painfully obvious to me that Black and White women are not on the same track. Sure, we might all start out in the same place. But early in the game, most sisters I know become stuck—and the reasons have little to do with intelligence or drive. At some point we bump our heads against that ceiling. And while White women may complain of a glass ceiling, for us, the ceiling is concrete.
>
> So how do we tell this story without sounding whiny and paranoid, or turning off our White-female readers, staff members, advertisers and girlfriends? Our solution: Bring together real women (several of them highly successful senior corporate executives), put them in a room, promise them anonymity and let them speak their truth.
>
> —Diane Weathers, "Speaking Our Truth"

Retailers like Walmart build their credibility by simple "straight talk" to shoppers: our low prices make your life better. Beth Hall/Bloomberg News/Getty Images

Both paragraphs affirm Weathers's determination to treat audiences fairly *and* to deal honestly with a difficult subject. The strategy would merit attention in any rhetorical analysis.

Look, too, for signals that writers share values with readers or at least understand an audience. In the following passage, writer Jack Solomon is clear about one value that he hopes readers have in common—a preference for "straight talk":

> There are some signs in the advertising world that Americans are getting fed up with fantasy advertisements and want to hear some straight talk. Weary of extravagant product claims . . . , consumers trained by years of advertising to distrust what they hear seem to be developing an immunity to commercials.
>
> —Jack Solomon, "Masters of Desire:
> The Culture of American Advertising"

But straight talk still requires common sense. If ever a major television ad seriously misread its audience, it may have been a spot that ran during the 2014 Winter Olympics for Cadillac's pricey new plug-in hybrid, the ELR. The company seemed to go out of its way to offend a great many people, foreign and domestic. As is typical strategy in rhetorical analyses, *Huffington Post*'s Carolyn Gregoire takes care to describe in detail the item she finds offensive:

> The opening shot shows a middle-aged man, played by the actor Neal McDonough, looking out over his backyard pool, asking the question: "Why do we work so hard? For this? For stuff?"
>
> As the ad continues, it becomes clear that the answer to this rhetorical question is actually a big fat YES. And it gets worse. "Other countries, they work," he says. "They stroll home. They stop by the cafe. They take August off. Off."
>
> Then he reveals just what it is that makes Americans better than all those lazy, espresso-sipping foreigners.
>
> "Why aren't you like that?" he says. "Why aren't we like that? Because we're crazy, driven, hard-working believers, that's why."
>
> —Carolyn Gregoire, "Cadillac Made a Commercial
> about the American Dream, and It's a Nightmare"

Her conclusion then is blistering, showing how readily a rhetorical analysis becomes an argument—and subject to criticism itself:

> Cadillacs have long been a quintessentially American symbol of wealth and status. But as this commercial proves, no amount of

wealth or status is a guarantee of good taste. Now, the luxury car company is selling a vision of the American Dream at its worst: Work yourself into the ground, take as little time off as possible, and buy expensive sh*t (specifically, a 2014 Cadillac ELR).

Examining Arguments Based on Emotion: Pathos

Some emotional appeals are just ploys to win over readers with a pretty face, figurative or real. You've seen ads promising an exciting life and attractive friends if only you drink the right soda or wear a particular brand of clothes. Are you fooled by such claims? Probably not, if you pause to think about them. But that's the strategy—to distract you from thought just long enough to make a bad choice. It's a move worth commenting on in a rhetorical analysis.

How well does the emotional appeal here work?

Yet emotions can add real muscle to arguments, too, and that's worth noting. For example, persuading people not to drink and drive by making them fear death, injury, or arrest seems like a fair use of an emotional appeal. The public service announcement on page 95 uses an emotion-laden image to remind drivers to think of the consequences.

In a rhetorical analysis, you might note the juxtaposition of image with text, leading readers to connect casual notes left on windshields with the very serious consequences of drunk driving.

In analyzing emotional appeals, judge whether the emotions raised—anger, sympathy, fear, envy, joy, love, lust—advance the claims offered. Consider how columnist Ron Rosenbaum (whom we met in Chapter 2) makes the reasonable argument he offers for fatty foods all the more attractive by larding it with voluptuous language:

> The foods that best hit that sweet spot and "overwhelm the brain" with pleasure are high-quality fatty foods. They discourage us from overeating. A modest serving of short ribs or Peking duck will be both deeply pleasurable and self-limiting. As the brain swoons into insensate delight, you won't have to gorge a still-craving cortex with mediocre sensations. "Sensory-specific satiety" makes a slam-dunk case (it's science!) for eating reasonable servings of superbly satisfying fatty foods.
>
> —Ron Rosenbaum, "Let Them Eat Fat"

Does the use of evocative language ("swoons," "insensate delight," "superbly satisfying," "slam-dunk") convince you, or does it distract from considering the scientific case for "sensory-specific satiety"? Your task in a

Health food? Kittipojn Pravalpatkul/Shutterstock

rhetorical analysis is to study an author's words, the emotions they evoke, and the claims they support and then to make this kind of judgment.

RESPOND•

Browse YouTube or another Web site to find an example of a powerful emotional argument that's made visually, either alone or using words as well. In a paragraph, defend a claim about how the argument works. For example, does an image itself make a claim, or does it draw you in to consider a verbal claim? What emotion does the argument generate? How does that emotion work to persuade you?

Examining Arguments Based on Character: Ethos

It should come as no surprise: readers believe writers who seem honest, wise, and trustworthy. So in analyzing the effectiveness of an argument, look for evidence of these traits. Does the writer have the experience or authority to write on this subject? Are all claims qualified reasonably? Is evidence presented in full, not tailored to the writer's agenda? Are important objections to the author's position acknowledged and addressed? Are sources documented? Above all, does the writer sound trustworthy?

When a Norwegian anti-immigration extremist killed seventy-six innocent people in July 2011, Prime Minister Jens Stoltenberg addressed the citizens of Norway (and the world), and in doing so evoked the character or ethos of the entire nation:

> We will not let fear break us! The warmth of response from people in Norway and from the whole world makes me sure of this one thing: evil can kill a single person, but never defeat a whole people. The strongest weapon in the world—that is freedom of expression and democracy.

In analyzing this speech, you would do well to look at the way this passage deploys the deepest values of Norway—freedom of expression and democracy—to serve as a response to fear of terrorism. In doing so, Stoltenberg evokes ethical ideals to hold onto in a time of tragedy.

Or take a look at the following paragraph from a blog posting by Timothy Burke, a teacher at Swarthmore College and parent of a preschool child who is trying to think through the issue of homework for elementary school kids:

So I've been reading a bit about homework and comparing notes with parents. There is a lot of variation across districts, not just in the amount of homework that kids are being asked to do, but in the kind of homework. Some districts give kids a lot of time-consuming busywork; other districts try to concentrate on having homework assignments be substantive work that is best accomplished independently. Some give a lot from a very early point in K-12 education; some give relatively little. As both a professional educator and an individual with personal convictions, I'd tend to argue against excessive amounts of homework and against assigning busywork. But what has ultimately interested me more about reading various discussions of homework is how intense the feelings are swirling around the topic and how much that intensity strikes me as a problem in and of itself. Not just as a symptom of a kind of civic illness, an inability to collectively and democratically work through complex issues, but also in some cases as evidence of an educational failure in its own right.

Burke establishes his ethos by citing his reading and his talks with other parents.

He underscores his right to address the matter.

He expresses concern about immoderate arguments and implies that he will demonstrate an opposite approach.

In considering the role of ethos in rhetorical analyses, pay attention to the details right down to the choice of words or, in an image, the shapes and colors. The modest, tentative tone that Burke uses in his blog is an example of the kind of choice that can shape an audience's perception of ethos. But these details need your interpretation. Language that's hot and extreme can mark a writer as either passionate or loony. Work that's sober and carefully organized can paint an institution as competent or overly cautious. Technical terms and abstract phrases can make a writer seem either knowledgeable or pompous.

Examining Arguments Based on Facts and Reason: Logos

In analyzing most arguments, you'll have to decide whether an argument makes a plausible claim and offers good reasons for you to believe it. Not all arguments will package such claims in a single neat sentence, or **thesis**—nor should they. A writer may tell a story from which you have to infer the claim. Visual arguments may work the same way: viewers have to assemble the parts and draw inferences in order to get the point.

Some conventional arguments (like those on an editorial page) may be perfectly obvious: writers stake out a claim and then present reasons that you should consider, or they may first present reasons and lay out a case that leads you to accept a claim in the conclusion. Consider the following example. In a tough opinion piece in *Time*, political commentator John McWhorter argues that filmmaker Spike Lee is being racist when he rails against hipsters moving into Fort Greene, a formerly all-black neighborhood in Brooklyn, New York. Lee fears that the whites are raising housing prices, pushing out old-time residents and diminishing the African American character of Fort Greene. McWhorter, an African American like Lee, sees matters differently:

> Basically, black people are getting paid more money than they've ever seen in their lives for their houses, and a once sketchy neighborhood is now quiet and pleasant. And this is a bad thing . . . why?
>
> Lee seems to think it's somehow an injustice whenever black people pick up stakes. But I doubt many of the blacks now set to pass fat inheritances on to their kids feel that way. This is not the old story of poor blacks being pushed out of neighborhoods razed down for highway construction. Lee isn't making sense.
>
> —John McWhorter, "Spike Lee's Racism Isn't Cute"

When you encounter explicit charges like these, you analyze whether and how the claims are supported by good reasons and reliable evidence. A lengthy essay may, in fact, contain a series of claims, each developed to support an even larger point. Here's McWhorter, for instance, expanding his argument by suggesting that Lee's attitudes toward whites are irreconcilable.

> "Respect the culture" when you move in, Lee growls. But again, he isn't making sense. We can be quite sure that if whites "respected" the culture by trying to participate in it, Lee would be one of the first in line to call it "appropriation." So, no whites better open up barbecue joints or spoken word cafes or try to be rappers. Yet if whites walk on by the culture in "respectful" silence, then the word on the street becomes that they want to keep blacks at a distance.

An anti-fur protestor in London
makes a rather specific claim.
© Charles Platiau/Reuters/Corbis

Indeed, every paragraph in an argument may develop a specific and related idea. In a rhetorical analysis, you need to identify all these separate propositions and examine the relationships among them: Are they solidly linked? Are there inconsistencies that the writer should acknowledge? Does the end of the piece support what the writer said (and promised) at the beginning?

You'll also need to examine the quality of the information presented in an argument, assessing how accurately such information is reported, how conveniently it's displayed (in charts or graphs, for example), and how well the sources cited represent a range of *respected* opinions on a topic. (For more information on the use of evidence, see Chapter 4.)

Knowing how to judge the quality of sources is more important now than ever before because the digital universe is full of junk. In some ways, the computer terminal has become the equivalent of a library reference room, but the sources available online vary widely in quality and have not been evaluated by a library professional. As a consequence, you must know the difference between reliable, firsthand, or fully documented sources and those that don't meet such standards. (For using and documenting sources, see Chapters 19, 20, and 22.)

Examining the Arrangement and Media of Arguments

Aristotle carved the structure of logical argument to its bare bones when he observed that it had only two parts:

- statement
- proof

You could do worse, in examining an argument, than to make sure that every claim a writer makes is backed by sufficient evidence. Some arguments are written on the fly in the heat of the moment. Most arguments that you read and write, however, will be more than mere statements followed by proofs. Some writers will lay their cards on the table immediately; others may lead you carefully through a chain of claims toward a conclusion. Writers may even interrupt their arguments to offer background information or cultural contexts for readers. Sometimes they'll tell stories or provide anecdotes that make an argumentative point. They'll qualify the arguments they make, too, and often pause to admit that other points of view are plausible.

In other words, there are no formulas or acceptable patterns that fit all successful arguments. In writing a rhetorical analysis, you'll have to assess the organization of a persuasive text on its own merits.

It's fair, however, to complain about what may be *absent* from an argument. Most arguments of proposal (see Chapter 12), for example, include a section that defends the feasibility of a new idea, explaining how it might be funded or managed. In a rhetorical analysis, you might fault an editorial that supports a new stadium for a city without addressing feasibility issues. Similarly, analyzing a movie review that reads like an off-the-top-of-the-head opinion, you might legitimately ask what criteria of evaluation are in play (see Chapter 10).

Rhetorical analysis also calls for you to look carefully at an argument's transitions, headings and subheadings, documentation of sources, and overall tone or voice. Don't take such details for granted, since all of them contribute to the strength—or weakness—of an argument.

Nor should you ignore the way a writer or an institution uses media. Would an argument originally made in a print editorial, for instance, work better as a digital presentation (or vice versa)? Would a lengthy paper have more power if it included more images? Or do these images distract from a written argument's substance?

Finally, be open to the possibility of new or nontraditional structures of arguments. The visual arguments that you analyze may defy conventional principles of logic or arrangement—for example, making juxtapositions rather than logical transitions between elements or using quick cuts, fades, or other devices to link ideas. Quite often, these nontraditional structures will also resist the neatness of a thesis, leaving readers to construct at least a part of the argument in their heads. As we saw with the "God Made a Farmer" spot at the beginning of this chapter, advertisers are growing fond of soft-sell multimedia productions that can seem like something other than what they really are—product pitches. We may be asked not just to buy a product but also to live its lifestyle or embrace its ethos. Is that a reasonable or workable strategy for an argument? Your analysis might entertain such possibilities.

Looking at Style

Even a coherent argument full of sound evidence may not connect with readers if it's dull, off-key, or offensive. Readers naturally judge the credibility of arguments in part by how stylishly the case is made—even when they don't know exactly what style is (for more on style, see Chapter 13). Consider how these simple, blunt sentences from the opening of an argument shape your image of the author and probably determine whether you're willing to continue to read the whole piece:

> We are young, urban, and professional. We are literate, respectable, intelligent, and charming. But foremost and above all, we are unemployed.
> —Julia Carlisle, "Young, Privileged, and Unemployed"

The strong, straightforward tone and the stark juxtaposition of being "intelligent" with "unemployed" set the style for this letter to the editor.

Now consider the brutally sarcastic tone of Nathaniel Stein's hilarious parody of the Harvard grading policy, a piece he wrote following up on a professor's complaint of out-of-control grade inflation at the school. Stein borrows the formal language of a typical "grading standards" sheet to mock the decline in rigor that the professor has lamented:

> The A+ grade is used only in very rare instances for the recognition of truly exceptional achievement.
>
> For example: A term paper receiving the A+ is virtually indistinguishable from the work of a professional, both in its choice of paper

stock and its font. The student's command of the topic is expert, or at the very least intermediate, or beginner. Nearly every single word in the paper is spelled correctly; those that are not can be reasoned out phonetically within minutes. Content from Wikipedia is integrated with precision. The paper contains few, if any, death threats. . . .

An overall course grade of A+ is reserved for those students who have not only demonstrated outstanding achievement in coursework but have also asked very nicely.

Finally, the A+ grade is awarded to all collages, dioramas and other art projects.

—Nathaniel Stein, "Leaked! Harvard's Grading Rubric"

Both styles probably work, but they signal that the writers are about to make very different kinds of cases. Here, style alone tells readers what to expect.

Manipulating style also enables writers to shape readers' responses to their ideas. Devices as simple as repetition, parallelism, or even paragraph length can give sentences remarkable power. Consider this passage from an essay by Sherman Alexie in which he explores the complex reaction of straight men to the announcement of NBA star Jason Collins that he is gay:

Homophobic basketball fans will disparage his skills, somehow equating his NBA benchwarmer status with his sexuality. But let's not forget that Collins is still one of the best 1,000 basketball players in the world. He has always been better than his modest statistics would indicate, and his teams have been dramatically more efficient with him on the court. He is better at hoops than 99.9 percent of you are at anything you do. He might not be a demigod, but he's certainly a semi-demigod. Moreover, his basketball colleagues universally praise him as a physically and mentally tough player. In his prime, he ably battled that behemoth known as Shaquille O'Neal. Most of all, Collins is widely regarded as one of the finest gentlemen to ever play the game. Generous, wise, and supportive, he's a natural leader. And he has a degree from Stanford University.

In other words, he's a highly attractive dude.

—Sherman Alexie, "Jason Collins Is the Envy of
Straight Men Everywhere"

In this passage, Alexie uses a sequence of short, direct, and roughly parallel sentences ("He is . . . He might . . . He ably battled . . . He has") to present evidence justifying the playful point he makes in a pointedly

Jason Collins © Gary A. Vasquez/USA Today Sports Images

emphatic, one-sentence paragraph. The remainder of his short essay then amplifies that point.

In a rhetorical analysis, you can explore such stylistic choices. Why does a formal style work for discussing one type of subject matter but not another? How does a writer use humor or irony to underscore an important point or to manage a difficult concession? Do stylistic choices, even something as simple as the use of contractions or personal pronouns, bring readers close to a writer, or do technical words and an impersonal voice signal that an argument is for experts only?

To describe the stylistic effects of visual arguments, you may use a different vocabulary and talk about colors, camera angles, editing, balance, proportion, fonts, perspective, and so on. But the basic principle is this: the look of an item—whether a poster, an editorial cartoon, or a film documentary—can support the message that it carries, undermine it, or muddle it. In some cases, the look will be the message. In a rhetorical analysis, you can't ignore style.

This poster, promoting travel to the bicycle-friendly city of Münster, Germany, demonstrates visually the amount of space needed to transport the same number of people by car, bicycle, and bus. Foto Presseamt Münster, City of Münster, Press Office

RESPOND •

Find a recent example of a visual argument, either in print or on the Internet. Even though you may have a copy of the image, describe it carefully in your paper on the assumption that your description is all readers may have to go on. Then make a judgment about its effectiveness, supporting your claim with clear evidence from the "text."

Examining a Rhetorical Analysis

On the following pages, well-known political commentator and columnist for the *New York Times* David Brooks argues that today's college graduates have been poorly prepared for life after school because of what he sees as a radical excess of supervision. Responding to his argument with a detailed analysis is Rachel Kolb, a student at Stanford University.

It's Not about You

DAVID BROOKS

© David Levene/ eyevine/Redux Pictures

Over the past few weeks, America's colleges have sent another class of graduates off into the world. These graduates possess something of inestimable value. Nearly every sensible middle-aged person would give away all their money to be able to go back to age 22 and begin adulthood anew.

But, especially this year, one is conscious of the many ways in which this year's graduating class has been ill served by their elders. They enter a bad job market, the hangover from decades of excessive borrowing. They inherit a ruinous federal debt.

More important, their lives have been perversely structured. This year's graduates are members of the most supervised generation in American history. Through their childhoods and teenage years, they have been monitored, tutored, coached and honed to an unprecedented degree.

Yet upon graduation they will enter a world that is unprecedentedly wide open and unstructured. Most of them will not quickly get married, buy a home and have kids, as previous generations did. Instead, they will confront amazingly diverse job markets, social landscapes and lifestyle niches. Most will spend a decade wandering from job to job and clique to clique, searching for a role.

No one would design a system of extreme supervision to prepare people for a decade of extreme openness. But this is exactly what has emerged in modern America. College students are raised in an environment that demands one set of navigational skills, and they are then cast out into a different environment requiring a different set of skills, which they have to figure out on their own.

Worst of all, they are sent off into this world with the whole baby-boomer theology ringing in their ears. If you sample some of the commencement addresses being broadcast on C-Span these days, you see that many graduates are told to: Follow *your* passion, chart *your* own course, march to the beat of *your* own drummer, follow *your* dreams and find *your*self. This is the litany of expressive individualism, which is still the dominant note in American culture.

But, of course, this mantra misleads on nearly every front.

College grads are often sent out into the world amid rapturous talk of limitless possibilities. But this talk is of no help to the central business of adulthood, finding serious things to tie yourself down to. The successful young adult is beginning to make sacred commitments—to a spouse, a community and calling—yet mostly hears about freedom and autonomy.

Today's graduates are also told to find their passion and then pursue their dreams. The implication is that they should find themselves first and then go off and live their quest. But, of course, very few people at age 22 or 24 can take an inward journey and come out having discovered a developed self.

Most successful young people don't look inside and then plan a life. They look outside and find a problem, which summons their life. A relative suffers from Alzheimer's and a young woman feels called to help cure that disease. A young man works under a miserable boss and must develop management skills so his department can function. Another young woman finds herself confronted by an opportunity she never thought of in a job category she never imagined. This wasn't in her plans, but this is where she can make her contribution.

Most people don't form a self and then lead a life. They are called by a problem, and the self is constructed gradually by their calling.

The graduates are also told to pursue happiness and joy. But, of course, when you read a biography of someone you admire, it's rarely the things that made them happy that compel your admiration. It's the things they did to court unhappiness—the things they did that were arduous and miserable, which sometimes cost them friends and aroused hatred. It's excellence, not happiness, that we admire most.

Finally, graduates are told to be independent-minded and to express their inner spirit. But, of course, doing your job well often means suppressing yourself. As Atul Gawande mentioned during his countercultural address . . . at Harvard Medical School, being a good doctor often means being part of a team, following the rules of an institution, going down a regimented checklist.

Today's grads enter a cultural climate that preaches the self as the center of a life. But, of course, as they age, they'll discover that the tasks of a life are at the center. Fulfillment is a byproduct of how people engage their tasks, and can't be pursued directly. Most of us are egotistical and most are self-concerned most of the time, but it's nonetheless true that life comes to a point only in those moments when the self dissolves into some task. The purpose in life is not to find yourself. It's to lose yourself.

Understanding Brooks's Binaries

RACHEL KOLB

As a high school and college student, I was given an incredible range of educational and extracurricular options, from interdisciplinary studies to summer institutes to student-organized clubs. Although today's students have more opportunities to adapt their educations to their specific personal goals, as I did, David Brooks argues that the structure of the modern educational system nevertheless leaves young people ill-prepared to meet the challenges of the real world. In his *New York Times* editorial "It's Not about You," Brooks illustrates excessive supervision and uncontrolled individualistic rhetoric as opposing problems that complicate young people's entry into adult life, which then becomes less of a natural progression than an outright paradigm shift. Brooks's argument itself mimics the pattern of moving from "perversely structured" youth to "unprecedentedly wide open" adulthood: it operates on the basis of binary oppositions, raising familiar notions about how to live one's life and then dismantling them. Throughout, the piece relies less on factual evidence than on Brooks's own authoritative tone and skill in using rhetorical devices.

In his editorial, Brooks objects to mainstream cultural messages that sell students on individuality, but bases his conclusions more on general observations than on specific facts. His argument is, in itself, a loose form of rhetorical analysis. It opens by telling us to "sample some of the commencement addresses being broadcast on C-Span these days," where we will find messages such as: "Follow *your* passion, chart *your* own course, march to the beat of *your* own drummer, follow *your* dreams and find *yourself*." As though moving down a checklist, it then scrutinizes the problems with this rhetoric of "expressive individualism." Finally, it turns to Atul Gawande's "countercultural address" about working collectively, en route to confronting the

Courtesy of Rachel Kolb

Connects article to personal experience to create an ethical appeal.

Provides brief overview of Brooks's argument. States Brooks's central claim.

Transition sentence.

109

individualism of modern America. C-Span and Harvard Medical School aside, however, Brooks's argument is astonishingly short on external sources. He cites no basis for claims such as "this year's graduates are members of the most supervised generation in American history" or "most successful young people don't look inside and then plan a life," despite the fact that these claims are fundamental to his observations. Instead, his argument persuades through painting a picture—first of "limitless possibilities," then of young men and women called into action by problems that "summon their life"—and hoping that we will find the illustration familiar.

Instead of relying on the logos of his argument, Brooks assumes that his position as a baby boomer and *New York Times* columnist will provide a sufficient enough ethos to validate his claims. If this impression of age and social status did not enter our minds along with his bespectacled portrait, Brooks reminds us of it. Although he refers to the theology of the baby boomer generation as the "worst of all," from the beginning of his editorial he allots himself as another "sensible middle-aged person" and distances himself from college graduates by referring to them as "they" or as "today's grads," contrasting with his more inclusive reader-directed "you." Combined with his repeated use of passive sentence constructions that create a confusing sense of responsibility ("The graduates are sent off into the world"; "graduates are told"), this sense of distance could be alienating to the younger audiences for which this editorial seems intended. Granted, Brooks compensates for it by embracing themes of "excellence" and "fulfillment" and by opening up his message to "most of us" in his final paragraph, but nevertheless his self-defined persona has its limitations. Besides dividing his audience, Brooks risks reminding us that, just as his observations belong only to this persona, his arguments apply only to a subset of American society. More specifically, they apply only to the well-educated middle to upper class who might be more likely to fret after the implications of "supervision" and

Comments critically on author's use of evidence.

Analyzes author's intended audience.

"possibilities," or the readers who would be most likely to flip through the *New York Times*.

Brooks overcomes his limitations in logos and ethos through his piece's greatest strength: its style. He effectively frames cultural messages in binaries in order to reinforce the disconnect that exists between what students are told and what they will face as full members of society. Throughout his piece, he states one assumption after another, then prompts us to consider its opposite. "Serious things" immediately take the place of "rapturous talk"; "look[ing] inside" replaces "look[ing] outside"; "suppressing yourself" becomes an alternative to being "independent-minded." Brooks's argument is consumed with dichotomies, culminating with his statement "It's excellence, not happiness, that we admire most." He frames his ideas within a tight framework of repetition and parallel structure, creating muscular prose intended to engage his readers. His repeated use of the phrase "but, of course" serves as a metronomic reminder, at once echoing his earlier assertions and referring back to his air of authority.

Closely analyzes Brooks's style.

Brooks illustrates the power of words in swaying an audience, and in his final paragraph his argument shifts beyond commentary. Having tested our way of thinking, he now challenges us to change. His editorial closes with one final binary, the claim that "The purpose in life is not to find yourself" but "to lose yourself." And, although some of Brooks's previous binaries have clanged with oversimplification, this one rings truer. In accordance with his adoption of the general "you," his concluding message need not apply only to college graduates. By unfettering its restrictions at its climax, Brooks liberates his argument. After all, only we readers bear the responsibility of reflecting, of justifying, and ultimately of determining how to live our lives.

Analyzes author's conclusion.

WORK CITED

Brooks, David. "It's Not about You." *Everything's an Argument*, 7th ed., by Andrea A. Lunsford and John J. Ruszkiewicz, Bedford/St. Martin's, 2016, pp. 106-8. Reprint of "It's Not about You," *The New York Times*, 30 May 2011.

GUIDE | **to writing a rhetorical analysis**

● **Finding a Topic**

A rhetorical analysis is usually assigned: you're asked to show how an argument works and to assess its effectiveness. When you can choose your own subject for analysis, look for one or more of the following qualities:

- a complex verbal or visual argument that challenges you—or disturbs or pleases you
- a text that raises current or enduring issues of substance
- a text that you believe should be taken more seriously

Look for arguments to analyze in the editorial and op-ed pages of any newspaper, political magazines such as the *Nation* or *National Review*, Web sites of organizations and interest groups, political blogs such as *Huffington Post* or *Power Line*, corporate Web sites that post their TV ad spots, videos and statements posted to YouTube, and so on.

● **Researching Your Topic**

Once you've got a text to analyze, find out all you can about it. Use library or Web resources to explore:

- who the author is and what his or her credentials are
- if the author is an institution, what it does, what its sources of funding are, who its members are, and so on
- who is publishing or sponsoring the piece, and what the organization typically publishes
- what the leanings or biases of the author and publisher might be
- what the context of the argument is—what preceded or provoked it and how others have responded to it

● **Formulating a Claim**

Begin with a hypothesis. A full thesis might not become evident until you're well into your analysis, but your final thesis should reflect the complexity of the piece that you're studying. In developing a thesis, consider questions such as the following:

- How can I describe what this argument achieves?
- What is the purpose, and is it accomplished?
- What audiences does the argument address and what audiences does it ignore, and why?
- Which of its rhetorical features will likely influence readers most: ethos of the author? emotional appeals? logical progression? style?
- What aspects of the argument work better than others?
- How do the rhetorical elements interact?

Here's the hardest part for most writers of rhetorical analyses: whether you agree or disagree with an argument usually doesn't matter in a rhetorical analysis. You've got to stay out of the fray and pay attention only to how—and to how well—the argument works.

Examples of Possible Claims for a Rhetorical Analysis

- Some people admire the directness and confidence of Hillary Clinton; others are put off by her bland and sometimes tone-deaf rhetoric. A close look at several of her speeches and public appearances will illuminate both sides of this debate.

- Today's editorial in the *Daily Collegian* about campus crimes may scare first-year students, but its anecdotal reporting doesn't get down to hard numbers—and for a good reason. Those statistics don't back the position taken by the editors.

- The imageboard 4chan has been called an "Internet hate machine," yet others claim it as a great boon to creativity. A close analysis of its home-page can help to settle this debate.

- The original design of New York's Freedom Tower, with its torqued surfaces and evocative spire, made a stronger argument about American values than its replacement, a fortress-like skyscraper stripped of imagination and unable to make any statement except "I'm 1,776 feet tall."

Preparing a Proposal

If your instructor asks you to prepare a proposal for your rhetorical analysis, here's a format you might use:

- Provide a copy of the work you're analyzing, whether it's a print text, a photograph, a digital image, or a URL, for instance.

- Offer a working hypothesis or tentative thesis.

- Indicate which rhetorical components seem especially compelling and worthy of detailed study and any connections between elements. For example, does the piece seem to emphasize facts and logic so much that it becomes disconnected from potential audiences? If so, hint at that possibility in your proposal.

- Indicate background information you intend to research about the author, institution, and contexts (political, economic, social, and religious) of the argument.

- Define the audience you'd like to reach. If you're responding to an assignment, you may be writing primarily for a teacher and classmates. But they make up a complex audience in themselves. If you can do so within the spirit of the assignment, imagine that your analysis will be published in a local newspaper, Web site, or blog.

- Conclude by briefly discussing the key challenges you anticipate in preparing a rhetorical analysis.

● Considering Format and Media

Your instructor may specify that you use a particular format and/or medium. If not, ask yourself these questions to help you make a good choice:

- What format is most appropriate for your rhetorical analysis? Does it call for an academic essay, a report, an infographic, a brochure, or something else?

- What medium is most appropriate for your analysis? Would it be best delivered orally to a live audience? Presented as an audio essay or podcast? Presented in print only or in print with illustrations?

- Will you need visuals, such as moving or still images, maps, graphs, charts—and what function will they play in your analysis? Make sure they are not just "added on" but are necessary components of the analysis.

● Thinking about Organization

Your rhetorical analysis is likely to include the following:

- Facts about the text you're analyzing: Provide the author's name; the title or name of the work; its place of publication or its location; the date it was published or viewed.

- Contexts for the argument: Readers need to know where the text is coming from, to what it may be responding, in what controversies it might be embroiled, and so on. Don't assume that they can infer the important contextual elements.

- A synopsis of the text that you're analyzing: If you can't attach the original argument, you must summarize it in enough detail so that a reader can imagine it. Even if you attach a copy of the piece, the analysis should include a summary.

- Some claim about the work's rhetorical effectiveness: It might be a simple evaluative claim or something more complex. The claim can come early in the paper, or you might build up to it, providing the evidence that leads toward the conclusion you've reached.

- A detailed analysis of how the argument works: Although you'll probably analyze rhetorical components separately, don't let your analysis become a dull roster of emotional, ethical, and logical appeals. Your rhetorical analysis should be an argument itself that supports a claim; a simple list of rhetorical appeals won't make much of a point.

- Evidence for every part of the analysis.

- An assessment of alternative views and counterarguments to your own analysis.

● Getting and Giving Response: Questions for Peer Response

If you have access to a writing center, discuss the text that you intend to analyze with a writing consultant before you write the paper. Try to find people who agree with the argument and others who disagree, and take notes on their observations. Your instructor may assign you to a peer group for the purpose of reading and responding to one another's drafts; if not, share your draft with someone on your own. You can use the following questions to evaluate a draft. If you're evaluating someone else's draft, be sure to illustrate your points with examples. Specific comments are always more helpful than general observations.

The Claim

- Does the claim address the rhetorical effectiveness of the argument itself rather than the opinion or position that it takes?

- Is the claim significant enough to interest readers?

- Does the claim indicate important relationships between various rhetorical components?
- Would the claim be one that the creator of the piece would regard as serious criticism?

Evidence for the Claim

- Is enough evidence given to support all your claims? What evidence do you still need?
- Is the evidence in support of the claim simply announced, or are its significance and appropriateness analyzed? Is a more detailed discussion needed?
- Do you use appropriate evidence, drawn from the argument itself or from other materials?
- Do you address objections readers might have to the claim, criteria, or evidence?
- What kinds of sources might you use to explain the context of the argument? Do you need to use sources to check factual claims made in the argument?
- Are all quotations introduced with appropriate signal phrases (for instance, "As Áida Álvarez points out"), and do they merge smoothly into your sentences?

Organization and Style

- How are the parts of the argument organized? How effective is this organization? Would some other structure work better?
- Will readers understand the relationships among the original text, your claims, your supporting reasons, and the evidence you've gathered (from the original text and any other sources you've used)? If not, what could be done to make those connections clearer? Are more transitional words and phrases needed? Would headings or graphic devices help?
- Are the transitions or links from point to point, sentence to sentence, and paragraph to paragraph clear and effective? If not, how could they be improved?
- Is the style suited to the subject and appropriate to your audience? Is it too formal? Too casual? Too technical? Too bland or boring?
- Which sentences seem particularly effective? Which ones seem weakest, and how could they be improved? Should some short sentences be combined, or should any long ones be separated into two or more sentences?

- How effective are the paragraphs? Do any seem too skimpy or too long? Do they break the analysis at strategic points?

- Which words or phrases seem particularly effective, accurate, and powerful? Do any seem dull, vague, unclear, or inappropriate for the audience or your purpose? Are definitions provided for technical or other terms that readers might not know?

Spelling, Punctuation, Mechanics, Documentation, and Format

- Check the spelling of the author's name, and make sure that the name of any institution involved with the work is correct. Note that the names of many corporations and institutions use distinctive spelling and punctuation.

- Get the title of the text you're analyzing right.

- Are there any errors in spelling, punctuation, capitalization, and the like?

- Does the assignment require a specific format? Check the original assignment sheet to be sure.

RESPOND•

Find an argument on the editorial page or op-ed page in a recent newspaper. Then analyze it rhetorically, using principles discussed in this chapter. Show how it succeeds, fails, or does something else entirely. Perhaps you can show that the author is unusually successful in connecting with readers but then has nothing to say. Or perhaps you discover that the strong logical appeal is undercut by a contradictory emotional argument. Be sure that the analysis includes a summary of the original essay and basic publication information about it (its author, place of publication, and publisher).

PART 2

WRITING arguments

7

Structuring Arguments

I get hives after eating ice cream.
My mouth swells up when I eat cheese.
Yogurt triggers my asthma.

↓

Dairy products make me sick.

Dairy products make me sick.
Ice cream is a dairy product.

↓

Ice cream makes me sick.

These two sets of statements illustrate the most basic ways in which Western culture structures logical arguments. The first piles up specific examples and draws a conclusion from them: that's **inductive reasoning** and structure. The second sets out a general principle (the major premise of a syllogism) and applies it to a specific case (the minor premise) in order to reach a conclusion: that's **deductive reasoning** and structure. In everyday reasoning, we often omit the middle statement, resulting in what Aristotle called an *enthymeme*: "Since dairy products make me sick, I better leave that ice cream alone." (See p. 65 for more on enthymemes.)

But the arguments you will write in college call for more than just the careful critical thinking offered within inductive and deductive reasoning. You will also need to define claims, explain the contexts in which you are offering them, consider counterarguments fairly and carefully, defend your assumptions, offer convincing evidence, appeal to particular audiences, and more. And you will have to do so using a clear structure that moves your argument forward. This chapter introduces you to three helpful ways to structure arguments. Feel free to borrow from all of them!

The Classical Oration

The authors of this book once examined a series of engineering reports and found that—to their great surprise—these reports were generally structured in ways similar to those used by Greek and Roman rhetors two thousand years ago. Thus, this ancient structuring system is alive and well in twenty-first-century culture. The classical oration has six parts, most of which will be familiar to you, despite their Latin names:

Exordium: You try to win the attention and goodwill of an audience while introducing a topic or problem.

Narratio: You present the facts of the case, explaining what happened when, who is involved, and so on. The *narratio* puts an argument in context.

Partitio: You divide up the topic, explaining what the claim is, what the key issues are, and in what order they will be treated.

Confirmatio: You offer detailed support for the claim, using both logical reasoning and factual evidence.

Refutatio: You carefully consider and respond to opposing claims or evidence.

Peroratio: You summarize the case and move the audience to action.

This structure is powerful because it covers all the bases: readers or listeners want to know what your topic is, how you intend to cover it, and what evidence you have to offer. And you probably need a reminder to present a pleasing *ethos* when beginning a presentation and to conclude with enough *pathos* to win an audience over completely. Here, in outline form, is a five-part updated version of the classical pattern, which you may find useful on many occasions:

Introduction

- gains readers' interest and willingness to listen
- establishes your qualifications to write about your topic
- establishes some common ground with your audience
- demonstrates that you're fair and even-handed
- states your claim

Background

- presents information, including personal stories or anecdotes that are important to your argument

Lines of Argument

- presents good reasons, including logical and emotional appeals, in support of your claim

Alternative Arguments

- carefully considers alternative points of view and opposing arguments
- notes the advantages and disadvantages of these views
- explains why your view is preferable to others

Conclusion

- summarizes the argument
- elaborates on the implications of your claim
- makes clear what you want the audience to think or do
- reinforces your credibility and perhaps offers an emotional appeal

Not every piece of rhetoric, past or present, follows the structure of the oration or includes all its components. But you can identify some of its elements in successful arguments if you pay attention to their design. Here are the words of the 1776 Declaration of Independence:

When in the Course of human events, it becomes necessary for one people to dissolve the political bands which have connected them with another, and to assume among the powers of the earth, the separate and equal station to which the Laws of Nature and of Nature's God entitle them, a decent respect to the opinions of mankind requires that they should declare the causes which impel them to the separation.

— Opens with a brief *exordium* explaining why the document is necessary, invoking a broad audience in acknowledging a need to show "a decent respect to the opinions of mankind." Important in this case, the lines that follow explain the assumptions on which the document rests.

We hold these truths to be self-evident, that all men are created equal, that they are endowed by their Creator with certain unalienable Rights, that among these are Life, Liberty, and the pursuit of Happiness—that to secure these rights, Governments are instituted among Men, deriving their just powers from the consent of the governed—That whenever any Form of Government becomes destructive to these ends, it is the Right of the People to alter or to abolish it and to institute new Government, laying its Foundation on such principles and organizing its powers in such form, as to them shall seem most likely to effect their Safety and Happiness. Prudence, indeed, will dictate that Governments long established should not be changed for light and transient causes; and accordingly all experience hath shewn that mankind are more disposed to suffer, while evils are sufferable, than to right themselves by abolishing the forms to which they are accustomed. But when a long train of abuses and usurpations, pursuing invariably the same Object evinces a design to reduce them under absolute Despotism, it is their right, it is their duty, to throw off such Government and to

A *narratio* follows, offering background on the situation: because the government of George III has become destructive, the framers of the Declaration are obligated to abolish their allegiance to him.

provide new Guards for their future security.— Such has been the patient sufferance of these Colonies; and such is now the necessity which constrains them to alter their former Systems of Government. The history of the present King of Great Britain is a history of repeated injuries and usurpations, all having in direct object the establishment of an absolute Tyranny over these States. To prove this, let Facts be submitted to a candid world.

Arguably, the *partitio* begins here, followed by the longest part of the document (not reprinted here), a *confirmatio* that lists the "long train of abuses and usurpations" by George III.

— Declaration of Independence, July 4, 1776

The authors might have structured this argument by beginning with the last two sentences of the excerpt and then listing the facts intended to prove the king's abuse and tyranny. But by choosing first to explain the purpose and "self-evident" assumptions behind their argument and only then moving on to demonstrate how these "truths" have been denied by the British, the authors forge an immediate connection with readers and build up to the memorable conclusion. The structure is both familiar and inventive— as your own use of key elements of the oration should be in the arguments you compose.

The Declaration of Independence National Archives

Rogerian and Invitational Arguments

In trying to find an alternative to confrontational and angry arguments like those that so often erupt in legislative bodies around the world, scholars and teachers of rhetoric have adapted the nonconfrontational principles employed by psychologist Carl Rogers in personal therapy sessions. In simple terms, Rogers argued that people involved in disputes should not respond to each other until they could fully, fairly, and even sympathetically state the other person's position. Scholars of rhetoric Richard E. Young, Alton L. Becker, and Kenneth L. Pike developed a four-part structure that is now known as Rogerian argument:

1. **Introduction:** You describe an issue, a problem, or a conflict in terms rich enough to show that you fully understand and respect any alternative position or positions.

2. **Contexts:** You describe the contexts in which alternative positions may be valid.

3. **Writer's position:** You state your position on the issue and present the circumstances in which that opinion would be valid.

4. **Benefits to opponent:** You explain to opponents how they would benefit from adopting your position.

The key to Rogerian argumentation is a willingness to think about opposing positions and to describe them fairly. In a Rogerian structure, you have to acknowledge that alternatives to your claims exist and that they might be reasonable under certain circumstances. In tone, Rogerian arguments steer clear of heated and stereotypical language, emphasizing instead how all parties in a dispute might gain from working together.

In the same vein, feminist scholars Sonja Foss and Cindy Griffin have outlined a form of argument they label "invitational," one that begins with careful attention to and respect for the person or the audience you are in conversation with. Foss and Griffin show that such listening—in effect, walking in the other person's shoes—helps you see that person's points of view more clearly and thoroughly and thus offers a basis for moving together toward new understandings. The kind of argument they describe is what another rhetorician, Krista Ratcliffe, calls "rhetorical listening," which helps to establish productive connections between people and thus helps enable effective cross-cultural communications.

Invitational rhetoric has as its goal not winning over opponents but getting people and groups to work together and identify with each other;

it strives for connection, collaboration, and the mutually informed creation of knowledge. As feminist scholar Sally Miller Gearhart puts it, invitational argument offers a way to disagree without hurting one another, to disagree with respect. This kind of argument is especially important in a society that increasingly depends on successful collaboration to get things done. In college, you may have opportunities to practice invitational rhetoric in peer-review sessions, when each member of a group listens carefully in order to work through problems and issues. You may also practice invitational rhetoric looking at any contested issue from other people's points of view, taking them into account, and engaging them fairly and respectfully in your own argument. Students we know who are working in high-tech industries also tell us how much such arguments are valued, since they fuel innovation and "out of the box" thinking.

Invitational arguments, then, call up structures that more resemble good two-way conversations or free-ranging dialogues than straight-line marches from thesis to conclusion. Even conventional arguments benefit from invitational strategies by giving space early on to a full range of perspectives, making sure to present them thoroughly and clearly. Remember that in such arguments your goal is enhanced understanding so that you can open up a space for new perceptions and fresh ideas.

Consider how Frederick Douglass tried to broaden the outlook of his audiences when he delivered a Fourth of July oration in 1852. Most nineteenth-century Fourth of July speeches followed a pattern of praising the Revolutionary War heroes and emphasizing freedom, democracy, and justice. Douglass, a former slave, had that tradition in mind as he delivered his address, acknowledging the "great principles" that the "glorious anniversary" celebrates. But he also asked his (white) listeners to see the occasion from another point of view:

> Fellow-citizens, pardon me, allow me to ask, why am I called upon to speak here today? What have I, or those I represent, to do with your national independence? Are the great principles of political freedom and natural justice, embodied in the Declaration of Independence, extended to us? And am I, therefore, called upon to bring our humble offering to the national altar, and to confess the benefits and express devout gratitude for the blessings resulting from your independence to us? . . . I say it with a sad sense of the disparity between us. I am not included within the pale of this glorious anniversary! Your high independence only reveals the immeasurable distance between us. The blessings in which you, this day, rejoice, are not enjoyed in common.

Frederick Douglass © World History
Archive/Alamy

> The rich inheritance of justice, liberty, prosperity and independence, bequeathed by your fathers, is shared by you, not by me. The sunlight that brought life and healing to you, has brought stripes and death to me. This Fourth of July is yours, not mine. You may rejoice, I must mourn.
>
> —Frederick Douglass, "What to the Slave Is the Fourth of July?"

Although his speech is in some ways confrontational, Douglass is also inviting his audience to see a version of reality that they could have discovered on their own had they dared to imagine the lives of African Americans living in the shadows of American liberty. Issuing that invitation, and highlighting its consequences, points a way forward in the conflict between slavery and freedom, black and white, oppression and justice, although response to Douglass's invitation was a long time in coming.

In May 2014, First Lady Michelle Obama used elements of invitational argument in delivering a speech to high school graduates from several high schools in Topeka, Kansas. Since the speech occurred on the sixtieth anniversary of the Supreme Court's decision to disallow "separate but equal" schools in the landmark *Brown v. Board of Education* case, which was initiated in Topeka, Mrs. Obama invited the audience to experience the ups and downs of students before and after the decision, putting themselves in the places of the young African Americans who, in 1954, desperately wanted the freedom to attend well-funded schools open to white students. So she tells the stories of some of these young people, inviting those there to walk a while in their shoes. And she concludes her speech with a call for understanding and cooperation:

> Every day, you have the same power to choose our better history—by opening your hearts and minds, by speaking up for what you know is right, by sharing the lessons of *Brown v. Board of Education*, the lessons you learned right here in Topeka, wherever you go for the rest of our lives. I know you all can do it. I am so proud of all of you, and I cannot wait to see everything you achieve in the years ahead.

Michelle Obama speaking in Topeka, Kansas AP Photo/Orlin Wagner

In this speech, Mrs. Obama did not castigate audience members for failing to live up to the ideals of *Brown v. Board of Education* (though she could have done so), nor does she dwell on current ills in Topeka. Rather, she invokes "our better history" and focuses on the ways those in Topeka have helped to write that history. She identifies with her audience and asks them to identify with her—and she aims to inspire the young graduates to follow her example.

The use of invitational argument and careful listening in contemporary political life are rare, but in spite of much evidence to the contrary (think of the repeatedly demonstrated effectiveness of political attack ads), the public claims to prefer nonpartisan and invitational rhetoric to one-on-one, winner-take-all battles, suggesting that such an approach strikes a chord in many people, especially in a world that is increasingly open to issues of diversity. The lesson to take from Rogerian or invitational argument is that it makes good sense in structuring your own arguments to learn opposing positions well enough to state them accurately and honestly, to strive to understand the points of view of your opponents, to acknowledge those views fairly in your own work, and to look for solutions that benefit as many people as possible.

RESPOND ●

Choose a controversial topic that is frequently in the news, and decide how you might structure an argument on the subject, using the general principles of the classical oration. Then look at the same subject from a Rogerian or invitational perspective. How might your argument differ? Which approach would work better for your topic? For the audiences you might want to address?

Toulmin Argument

In *The Uses of Argument* (1958), British philosopher Stephen Toulmin presented structures to describe the way that ordinary people make reasonable arguments. Because Toulmin's system acknowledges the complications of life—situations when we qualify our thoughts with words such as *sometimes, often, presumably, unless,* and *almost*—his method isn't as airtight as formal logic that uses syllogisms (see p. 121 in this chapter and p. 63 in Chapter 4). But for that reason, Toulmin logic has become a powerful and, for the most part, practical tool for understanding and shaping arguments in the real world.

Toulmin argument will help you come up with and test ideas and also figure out what goes where in many kinds of arguments. Let's take a look at the basic elements of Toulmin's structure:

Claim	the argument you wish to prove
Qualifiers	any limits you place on your claim
Reason(s)/ Evidence	support for your claim
Warrants	underlying assumptions that support your claim
Backing	evidence for warrant

If you wanted to state the relationship between them in a sentence, you might say:

> My claim is true, to a qualified degree, because of the following reasons, which make sense if you consider the warrant, backed by these additional reasons.

These terms—claim, evidence, warrants, backing, and qualifiers—are the building blocks of the Toulmin argument structure. Let's take them one at a time.

Making Claims

Toulmin arguments begin with **claims**, debatable and controversial statements or assertions you hope to prove.

A claim answers the question *So what's your point?* or *Where do you stand on that?* Some writers might like to ignore these questions and avoid stating a position. But when you make a claim worth writing about, then it's worth standing up and owning it.

Is there a danger that you might oversimplify an issue by making too bold a claim? Of course. But making that sweeping claim is a logical first step toward eventually saying something more reasonable and subtle. Here are some fairly simple, undeveloped claims:

Congress should enact legislation that establishes a path to citizenship for illegal immigrants.

It's time for the World Health Organization (WHO) to exert leadership in coordinating efforts to stem the Ebola epidemic in West Africa.

NASA should launch a human expedition to Mars.

Veganism is the most responsible choice of diet.

Military insurance should not cover the cost of sex change surgery for service men and women.

Good claims often spring from personal experiences. You may have relevant work or military or athletic experience—or you may know a lot about music, film, sustainable agriculture, social networking, inequities in government services—all fertile ground for authoritative, debatable, and personally relevant claims.

RESPOND●

Claims aren't always easy to find. Sometimes they're buried deep within an argument, and sometimes they're not present at all. An important skill in reading and writing arguments is the ability to identify claims, even when they aren't obvious.

Collect a sample of six to eight letters to the editor of a daily newspaper (or a similar number of argumentative postings from a political blog). Read each item, and then identify every claim that the writer makes. When you've compiled your list of claims, look carefully at the words that the writer or writers use when stating their positions. Is there a common vocabulary? Can you find words or phrases that signal an impending claim? Which of these seem most effective? Which ones seem least effective? Why?

Offering Evidence and Good Reasons

You can begin developing a claim by drawing up a list of reasons to support it or finding **evidence** that backs up the point.

Evidence and Reason(s) ⟶ So Claim

One student writer wanted to gather good reasons in support of an assertion that his college campus needed more official spaces for parking bicycles. He did some research, gathering statistics about parking-space allocation, numbers of people using particular designated slots, and numbers of bicycles registered on campus. Before he went any further, however, he listed his primary reasons for wanting to increase bicycle parking:

- **Personal experience:** At least twice a week for two terms, he was unable to find a designated parking space for his bike.

- **Anecdotes:** Several of his friends told similar stories. One even sold her bike as a result.

- **Facts:** He found out that the ratio of car to bike parking spaces was 100 to 1, whereas the ratio of cars to bikes registered on campus was 25 to 1.

- **Authorities:** The campus police chief told the college newspaper that she believed a problem existed for students who tried to park bicycles legally.

On the basis of his preliminary listing of possible reasons in support of the claim, this student decided that his subject was worth more research. He was on the way to amassing a set of good reasons and evidence that were sufficient to support his claim.

In shaping your own arguments, try putting claims and reasons together early in the writing process to create enthymemes. Think of these enthymemes as test cases or even as topic sentences:

> Bicycle parking spaces should be expanded because the number of bikes on campus far exceeds the available spots.

> It's time to lower the driving age because I've been driving since I was fourteen and it hasn't hurt me.

> National legalization of marijuana is long overdue since it is already legal in over twenty states, has shown to be less harmful than alcohol, and provides effective relief from pain associated with cancer.

> Violent video games should be carefully evaluated and their use monitored by the industry, the government, and parents because these games cause addiction and psychological harm to players.

As you can see, attaching a reason to a claim often spells out the major terms of an argument.

"I know your type, you're the type who'll make me prove every claim I make."

Anticipate challenges to your claims. © 2009 Charles Barsotti/The New Yorker Collection/The Cartoon Bank

But your work is just beginning when you've put a claim together with its supporting reasons and evidence—because readers are certain to begin questioning your statement. They might ask whether the reasons and evidence that you're offering really do support the claim: should the driving age really be changed just because you've managed to drive since you were fourteen? They might ask pointed questions about your evidence: exactly how do you know that the number of bikes on campus far exceeds the number of spaces available? Eventually, you've got to address potential questions about the quality of your assumptions and the quality of your evidence. The connection between claim and reason(s) is a concern at the next level in Toulmin argument.

Determining Warrants

Crucial to Toulmin argument is appreciating that there must be a logical and persuasive connection between a claim and the reasons and data supporting it. Toulmin calls this connection the **warrant**. It answers the question *How exactly do I get from the data to the claim?* Like the warrant in legal situations (a search warrant, for example), a sound warrant in an argument gives you authority to proceed with your case.

The warrant tells readers what your (often unstated) assumptions are—for example, that any practice that causes serious disease should be banned by the government. If readers accept your warrant, you can then present specific evidence to develop your claim. But if readers dispute your warrant, you'll have to defend it before you can move on to the claim itself.

Stating warrants can be tricky because they can be phrased in various ways. What you're looking for is the general principle that enables you to justify the move from a reason to a specific claim—the bridge connecting them. The warrant is the assumption that makes the claim seem believable. It's often a value or principle that you share with your readers. Here's an easy example:

> Don't eat that mushroom: it's poisonous.

The warrant supporting this enthymeme can be stated in several ways, always moving from the reason (it's poisonous) to the claim (Don't eat that mushroom):

> Anything that is poisonous shouldn't be eaten.

> If something is poisonous, it's dangerous to eat.

Here's the relationship, diagrammed:

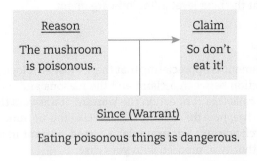

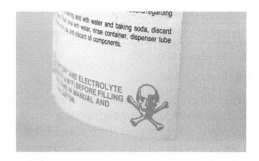

A simple icon—a skull and crossbones—can make a visual argument that implies a claim, a reason, and a warrant. PhotoLink/Getty Images

Perfectly obvious, you say? Exactly—and that's why the statement is so convincing. If the mushroom in question is a death cap or destroying angel (and you might still need expert testimony to prove that it is), the warrant does the rest of the work, making the claim that it supports seem logical and persuasive.

Let's look at a similar example, beginning with the argument in its basic form:

> We'd better stop for gas because the gauge has been reading empty for more than thirty miles.

In this case, you have evidence that is so clear (a gas gauge reading empty) that the reason for getting gas doesn't even have to be stated: the tank is almost empty. The warrant connecting the evidence to the claim is also pretty obvious:

> If the fuel gauge of a car has been reading empty for more than thirty miles, then that car is about to run out of gas.

Since most readers would accept this warrant as reasonable, they would also likely accept the statement the warrant supports.

Naturally, factual information might undermine the whole argument: the fuel gauge might be broken, or the driver might know that the car will go another fifty miles even though the fuel gauge reads empty. But in most cases, readers would accept the warrant.

Now let's consider how stating and then examining a warrant can help you determine the grounds on which you want to make a case. Here's a political enthymeme of a familiar sort:

> Flat taxes are fairer than progressive taxes because they treat all tax-payers in the same way.

Warrants that follow from this enthymeme have power because they appeal to a core American value—equal treatment under the law:

Treating people equitably is the American way.

All people should be treated in the same way.

You certainly could make an argument on these grounds. But stating the warrant should also raise a flag if you know anything about tax policy. If the principle is obvious and universal, then why do federal and many progressive state income taxes require people at higher levels of income to pay at higher tax rates than people at lower income levels? Could the warrant not be as universally popular as it seems at first glance? To explore the argument further, try stating the contrary claim and warrants:

Progressive taxes are fairer than flat taxes because people with more income can afford to pay more, benefit more from government, and shelter more of their income from taxes.

People should be taxed according to their ability to pay.

People who benefit more from government and can shelter more of their income from taxes should be taxed at higher rates.

Now you see how different the assumptions behind opposing positions really are. If you decided to argue in favor of flat taxes, you'd be smart to recognize that some members of your audience might have fundamental reservations about your position. Or you might even decide to shift your entire argument to an alternative rationale for flat taxes:

Flat taxes are preferable to progressive taxes because they simplify the tax code and reduce the likelihood of fraud.

Here, you have two stated reasons that are supported by two new warrants:

Taxes that simplify the tax code are desirable.

Taxes that reduce the likelihood of fraud are preferable.

Whenever possible, you'll choose your warrant knowing your audience, the context of your argument, and your own feelings.

Be careful, though, not to suggest that you'll appeal to any old warrant that works to your advantage. If readers suspect that your argument for progressive taxes really amounts to *I want to stick it to people who work harder than I*, your credibility may suffer a fatal blow.

Examples of Claims, Reasons, and Warrants

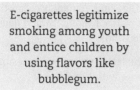 E-cigarettes legitimize smoking among youth and entice children by using flavors like bubblegum.

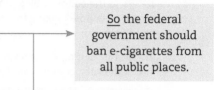 So the federal government should ban e-cigarettes from all public places.

Since

The Constitution was established to "promote the general welfare," and citizens are thus entitled to protection from harmful actions by others.

The Electoral College gives small states undue influence.

So it should be abolished.

Since

No states should have undue influence on presidential elections.

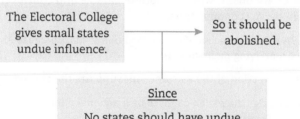 I've been drinking since age fourteen without problems.

So the legal age for drinking should be lowered.

Since

What works for me should work for everyone else.

RESPOND ●

At their simplest, warrants can be stated as "X is good" or "X is bad." Return to the letters to the editor or blog postings that you analyzed in the exercise on p. 131, this time looking for the warrant that is behind each claim. As a way to start, ask yourself these questions:

> If I find myself agreeing with the letter writer, what assumptions about the subject matter do I share with him/her?
>
> If I disagree, what assumptions are at the heart of that disagreement?

The list of warrants you generate will likely come from these assumptions.

Offering Evidence: Backing

The richest, most interesting part of a writer's work—backing—remains to be done after the argument has been outlined. Clearly stated claims and warrants show you how much evidence you will need. Take a look at this brief argument, which is both debatable and controversial, especially in tough economic times:

> NASA should launch a human expedition to Mars because Americans need a unifying national goal.

Here's one version of the warrant that supports the enthymeme:

> What unifies the nation ought to be a national priority.

Sticker honoring the retirement of the Space Shuttle program
© Steven Barrymore

To run with this claim and warrant, you'd first need to place both in context. Human space exploration has been debated with varying intensity following the 1957 launch of the Soviet Union's *Sputnik* satellite, after the losses of the U.S. space shuttles *Challenger* (1986) and *Columbia* (2003), and after the retirement of the Space Shuttle program in 2011. Acquiring such background knowledge through reading, conversation, and inquiry of all kinds will be necessary for making your case. (See Chapter 3 for more on gaining authority.)

There's no point in defending any claim until you've satisfied readers that questionable warrants on which the claim is based are defensible. In Toulmin argument, evidence you offer to support a warrant is called **backing**.

Warrant

What unifies the nation ought to be a national priority.

Backing

Americans want to be part of something bigger than themselves. (Emotional appeal as evidence)

In a country as diverse as the United States, common purposes and values help make the nation stronger. (Ethical appeal as evidence)

In the past, government investments such as the Hoover Dam and the *Apollo* moon program enabled many—though not all—Americans to work toward common goals. (Logical appeal as evidence)

In addition to evidence to support your warrant (backing), you'll need evidence to support your claim:

Argument in Brief (Enthymeme/Claim)

NASA should launch a human expedition to Mars because Americans now need a unifying national goal.

Evidence

The American people are politically divided along lines of race, ethnicity, religion, gender, and class. (Fact as evidence)

A common challenge or problem often unites people to accomplish great things. (Emotional appeal as evidence)

A successful Mars mission would require the cooperation of the entire nation—and generate tens of thousands of jobs. (Logical appeal as evidence)

A human expedition to Mars would be a valuable scientific project for the nation to pursue. (Appeal to values as evidence)

As these examples show, appeals to values and emotions can be just as appropriate as appeals to logic and facts, and all such claims will be stronger if a writer presents a convincing ethos. In most arguments, appeals work together rather than separately, reinforcing each other. (See Chapter 3 for more on ethos.)

Using Qualifiers

Experienced writers know that qualifying expressions make writing more precise and honest. Toulmin logic encourages you to acknowledge limitations to your argument through the effective use of **qualifiers**. You can save time if you qualify a claim early in the writing process. But you might not figure out how to limit a claim effectively until after you've explored your subject or discussed it with others.

Qualifiers

few	more or less	often
it is possible	in some cases	perhaps
rarely	many	under these conditions
it seems	typically	possibly
some	routinely	for the most part
it may be	most	if it were so
sometimes	one might argue	in general

Never assume that readers understand the limits you have in mind. Rather, spell them out as precisely as possible, as in the following examples:

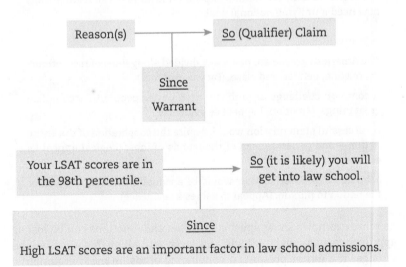

Unqualified Claim	People who don't go to college earn less than those who do.
Qualified Claim	*In most cases*, people who don't go to college earn less than those who do.

Understanding Conditions of Rebuttal

In the Toulmin system, potential objections to an argument are called **conditions of rebuttal**. Understanding and reacting to these conditions are essential to support your own claims where they're weak and also to recognize and understand the reasonable objections of people who see the world differently. For example, you may be a big fan of the Public Broadcasting Service (PBS) and the National Endowment for the Arts (NEA) and prefer that federal tax dollars be spent on these programs. So you offer the following claim:

Claim	The federal government should support the arts.

You need reasons to support this thesis, so you decide to present the issue as a matter of values:

Argument in Brief	The federal government should support the arts because it also supports the military.

Now you've got an enthymeme and can test the warrant, or the premises of your claim:

Warrant	If the federal government can support the military, then it can also support other programs.

But the warrant seems frail: you can hear a voice over your shoulder saying, "In essence, you're saying that *Because we pay for a military, we should pay for everything!*" So you decide to revise your claim:

Revised Argument	If the federal government can spend huge amounts of money on the military, then it can afford to spend moderate amounts on arts programs.

Now you've got a new warrant, too:

Revised Warrant	A country that can fund expensive programs can also afford less expensive programs.

This is a premise that you can defend, since you believe strongly that the arts are just as essential as a strong military is to the well-being of the

ART WORKS. | **National Endowment for the Arts**
arts.gov

The new NEA logo

country. Although the warrant now seems solid, you still have to offer strong grounds to support your specific and controversial claim. So you cite statistics from reputable sources, this time comparing the federal budgets for the military and the arts. You break them down in ways that readers can visualize, demonstrating that much less than a penny of every tax dollar goes to support the arts.

But then you hear those voices again, saying that the "common defense" is a federal mandate; the government is constitutionally obligated to support a military, and support for the arts is hardly in the same league! Looks like you need to add a paragraph explaining all the benefits the arts provide for very few dollars spent, and maybe you should suggest that such funding falls under the constitutional mandate to "promote the general welfare." Though not all readers will accept these grounds, they'll appreciate that you haven't ignored their point of view: you've gained credibility by anticipating a reasonable objection.

Dealing with conditions of rebuttal is an essential part of argument. But it's important to understand rebuttal as more than mere opposition. Anticipating objections broadens your horizons, makes you more open to alternative viewpoints, and helps you understand what you need to do to support your claim.

Within Toulmin argument, conditions of rebuttal remind us that we're part of global conversations: Internet newsgroups and blogs provide potent responses to positions offered by participants in discussions; instant messaging and social networking let you respond to and challenge others; links on Web sites form networks that are infinitely variable and open. In cyberspace, conditions of rebuttal are as close as your screen.

RESPOND●

Using an essay or a project you are composing, do a Toulmin analysis of the argument. When you're done, see which elements of the Toulmin scheme are represented. Are you short of evidence to support the warrant? Have you considered the conditions of rebuttal? Have you qualified your claim adequately? Next, write a brief revision plan: How will you buttress the argument in the places where it is weakest? What additional evidence will you offer for the warrant? How can you qualify your claim to meet the conditions of rebuttal? Then show your paper to a classmate and have him/her do a Toulmin analysis: a new reader will probably see your argument in different ways and suggest revisions that may not have occurred to you.

Outline of a Toulmin Argument

Consider the claim that was mentioned on p. 137:

Claim	The federal government should ban e-cigarettes.
Qualifier	The ban would be limited to public spaces.
Good Reasons	E-cigarettes have not been proven to be harmless.
	E-cigarettes legitimize smoking and also are aimed at recruiting teens and children with flavors like bubblegum and cotton candy.
Warrants	The Constitution promises to "promote the general welfare."
	Citizens are entitled to protection from harmful actions by others.
Backing	The United States is based on a political system that is supposed to serve the basic needs of its people, including their health.
Evidence	Analysis of advertising campaigns that reveal direct appeals to children
	Lawsuits recently won against e-cigarette companies, citing the link between e-cigarettes and a return to regular smoking
	Examples of bans on e-cigarettes already imposed in many public places
Authority	Cite the FDA and medical groups on effect of e-cigarette smoking.
Conditions of Rebuttal	E-cigarette smokers have rights, too.
	Smoking laws should be left to the states.
	Such a ban could not be enforced.
Responses	The ban applies to public places; smokers can smoke in private.

A Toulmin Analysis

You might wonder how Toulmin's method holds up when applied to an argument that is longer than a few sentences. Do such arguments really work the way that Toulmin predicts? In the following short argument, well-known linguist and author Deborah Tannen explores the consequences of a shift in the meaning of one crucial word: *compromise*. Tannen's essay, which originally appeared as a posting on Politico.com on June 15, 2011, offers a series of interrelated claims based on reasons, evidence, and warrants that culminate in the last sentence of the essay. She begins by showing that the word *compromise* is now rejected by both the political right and the political left and offers good reasons and evidence to support that claim. She then moves back to a time when "a compromise really was considered great," and offers three powerful pieces of evidence in support of that claim. The argument then comes back to the present, with a claim that the compromise and politeness of the nineteenth century have been replaced by "growing enmity." That claim is supported with reasoning and evidence that rest on an underlying warrant that "vituperation and seeing opponents as enemies is corrosive to the human spirit." The claims in the argument—that *compromise* has become a dirty word and that enmity and an adversarial spirit are on the rise—lead to Tannen's conclusion: rejecting compromise breaks the trust necessary for a democracy and thus undermines the very foundation of our society. While she does not use traditional qualifying words, she does say that the situation she describes is a "threat" to our nation, which qualifies the claim to some extent: the situation is not the "death" of our nation but rather a "threat." Tannen's annotated essay follows.

Photo: Stephen
Voss, courtesy of
Deborah Tannen

Why Is "Compromise" Now a Dirty Word?

DEBORAH TANNEN

Contextual
information
leading up to
initial claim

When did the word "compromise" get compromised?

When did the negative connotations of "He was caught in a compromising position" or "She compromised her ethics" replace the positive connotations of "They reached a compromise"?

House Speaker John Boehner said it outright on *60 Minutes* last year. When talking about "compromise," Boehner said, "I reject the word."

"When you say the word 'compromise,'" he explained, ". . . a lot of Americans look up and go, 'Uh-oh, they're gonna sell me out.'" His position is common right now.

In the same spirit, Tony Perkins wrote in a recent CNN.com op-ed piece, "When it comes to conservative principles, compromise is the companion of losers."

The political right is particularly vehement when it comes to compromise. Conservatives are now strongly swayed by the tea party movement, whose clarion call is a refusal to compromise, regardless of the practical consequences.

But the rejection of compromise is more widespread than that. The left regularly savages President Barack Obama for compromising too soon, too much or on the wrong issues. Many who fervently sought universal health coverage, for example, could not celebrate its near accomplishment because the president gave up the public option.

Initial claim

Reason

The death of compromise has become a threat to our nation as we confront crucial issues such as the debt ceiling and that most basic of legislative responsibilities: a federal budget. At stake is the very meaning of what had once seemed unshakable: "the full faith and credit" of the U.S. government.

Evidence

Back when the powerful nineteenth-century senator Henry Clay was called "the great compromiser," achieving a compromise really was considered great. On three occasions, the Kentucky statesman helped the Senate preserve the Union by crafting compromises between the deadlocked slave-holding South and the Northern free states. In 1820, his Missouri Compromise stemmed the spread of slavery. In 1833, when the South was poised to defy federal tariff laws favored by the North and the federal government was about to authorize military action, Clay found a last-minute compromise. And his Compromise of 1850 averted civil war for at least a decade.

It was during an 1850 Senate debate that Clay stated his conviction: "I go for honorable compromise whenever it can be made." Something else he said then holds a key to how the dwindling respect for compromise is related to larger and more dangerous developments in our nation today.

Warrant

"All legislation, all government, all society," Clay said, "is formed upon the principle of mutual concession, politeness, comity, courtesy; upon these, everything is based."

Claim

Concession, politeness, comity, courtesy—none of these words could be uttered now with the assurance of

Reason

listeners' approval. The word "comity" is rarely heard; "concession" sounds weak; "politeness" and "courtesy" sound quaint—much like the contemporary equivalent, "civility."

That Clay lauded both compromise and civil discourse in the same speech reveals the link between, on the one hand, the word "compromise" falling into disre-

Evidence

pute, and, on the other, the glorification of aggression that I wrote about in my book, *The Argument Culture: Stopping America's War of Words.*

Claim

Today we have an increasing tendency to approach every task—and each other—in an ever more adversarial spirit. Nowhere is this more evident, or more destructive, than in the Senate.

Though the two-party system is oppositional by nature, there is plenty of evidence that a certain (yes) comity has been replaced by growing enmity. We don't have to look as far back as Clay for evidence. In 1996, for example, an unprecedented fourteen incumbent senators announced that they would not seek reelection. And many, in farewell essays, described an increase in vituperation and partisanship that made it impossible to do the work of the Senate.

Rebuttal

Evidence

"The bipartisanship that is so crucial to the operation of Congress," Howell Heflin of Alabama wrote, "especially the Senate, has been abandoned." J. James Exon of Nebraska described an "ever-increasing vicious polarization of the electorate" that had "all but swept aside the former preponderance of reasonable discussion."

Evidence

But this is not happening only in the Senate. There is a rising adversarial spirit among the people and the press. It isn't only the obvious invective on TV and radio. A newspaper story that criticizes its subject is praised as "tough"; one that refrains from criticism is scorned as a "puff piece."

Claim

The notion of "balance" today often leads to a search for the most extreme opposing views — so they can be presented as "both sides," leaving no forum for subtlety, multiple perspectives or the middle ground, where most people stand. Framing issues in this polarizing way reinforces the impression that Boehner voiced: that compromising is selling out.

Reason

Evidence

Being surrounded by vituperation and seeing opponents as enemies is corrosive to the human spirit. It's also dangerous to our democracy. The great anthropologist Margaret Mead explained this in a 1962 speech.

Warrant

Claim

"We are essentially a society which must be more committed to a two-party system than to either party," Mead said. "The only way you can have a two-party system is to belong to a party formally and to fight to the death . . ." not for your party to win but "for the right of the other party to be there too."

Reason

Today, this sounds almost as quaint as "comity" in political discourse.

Reason

Mead traced our two-party system to our unique revolution: "We didn't kill a king and we didn't execute a large number of our people, and we came into our own without the stained hands that have been associated with most revolutions."

With this noble heritage, Mead said, comes "the obligation to keep the kind of government we set up"—where members of each party may "disagree mightily" but still "trust in each other and trust in our political opponents."

Conclusion

Losing that trust, Mead concluded, undermines the foundation of our democracy. That trust is exactly what is threatened when the very notion of compromise is rejected.

What Toulmin Teaches

As Tannen's essay demonstrates, few arguments you read have perfectly sequenced claims or clear warrants, so you might not think of Toulmin's terms in building your own arguments. Once you're into your subject, it's easy to forget about qualifying a claim or finessing a warrant. But remembering what Toulmin teaches will always help you strengthen your arguments:

- Claims should be clear, reasonable, and carefully qualified.

- Claims should be supported with good reasons and evidence. Remember that a Toulmin structure provides the framework of an argument, which you fill out with all kinds of data, including facts, statistics, precedents, photographs, and even stories.

- Claims and reasons should be based on assumptions your audience will likely accept. Toulmin's focus on warrants can be confusing because it asks us to look at the assumptions that underlie our arguments—something many would rather not do. Toulmin pushes us to probe the values that support any argument and to think of how those values relate to particular audiences.

- Effective arguments respectfully anticipate objections readers might offer. Toulmin argument acknowledges that any claim can crumble under certain conditions, so it encourages a complex view that doesn't demand absolute or unqualified positions.

It takes considerable experience to write arguments that meet all these conditions. Using Toulmin's framework brings them into play automatically. If you learn it well enough, constructing good arguments can become a habit.

Organization

As you think about organizing your argument, remember that cultural factors are at work: patterns that you find persuasive are probably ones that are deeply embedded in your culture. In the United States, many people expect a writer to "get to the point" as directly as possible and to articulate that point efficiently and unambiguously. The organizational patterns favored by many in business hold similarities to the classical oration—a highly explicit pattern that leaves little or nothing unexplained—introduction and thesis, background, overview of the parts that follow, evidence, other viewpoints, and conclusion. If a piece of writing follows this pattern, American readers ordinarily find it "well organized."

So it's no surprise that student writers in the United States are expected to make their structures direct and their claims explicit, leaving little unspoken. Their claims usually appear early in an argument, often in the first paragraph.

But not all cultures take such an approach. Some expect any claim or thesis to be introduced subtly, indirectly, and perhaps at the end of a work, assuming that audiences will "read between the lines" to understand what's being said. Consequently, the preferred structure of arguments (and face-to-face negotiations, as well) may be elaborate, repetitive, and full of digressions. Those accustomed to such writing may find more direct Western styles overly simple, childish, or even rude.

When arguing across cultures, look for cues to determine how to structure your presentations effectively. Here are several points to consider:

- Do members of your audience tend to be very direct, saying explicitly what they mean? Or are they restrained, less likely to call a spade a spade? Consider adjusting your work to the expectations of the audience.

- Do members of your audience tend to respect authority and the opinions of groups? They may find blunt approaches disrespectful or contrary to their expectations.

- Consider when to state your thesis: At the beginning? At the end? Somewhere else? Not at all?

- Consider whether digressions are a good idea, a requirement, or an element to avoid.

8
Arguments of Fact

Left to right: Zoonar/N.Sorokin/age fototstock; Alfred Eisenstaedt/Getty Images; © David R. Frazier, Photolibrary, Inc./Alamy

Many people believe that extensive use of the Internet, and especially social media, is harmful to memory and to learning, but recent research by scholars of literacy provides evidence suggesting that they are probably wrong.

In the past, female screen stars like Marilyn Monroe could be buxom and curvy, less concerned about their weight than actresses today. Or so the legend goes. But measuring the costumes worn by Monroe and other actresses reveals a different story.

When an instructor announces a tough new attendance policy for her course, a student objects that there is no evidence that students who regularly attend classes perform any better than those who do not. The instructor begs to differ.

Understanding Arguments of Fact

Factual arguments come in many varieties, but they all try to establish whether something is or is not so, answering questions such as *Is a historical legend true? Has a crime occurred?* or *Are the claims of a scientist accurate?* At first glance, you might object that these aren't arguments at all but just a matter of looking things up and then writing reports. And you'd be correct to an extent: people don't usually argue factual matters that are settled or undisputed (*The earth revolves around the sun*), that might be decided with simple research (*The Mendenhall Glacier has receded 1.75 miles since 1958*), or that are the equivalent of a rule (*One mile measures 5,280 feet*). Reporting facts, you might think, should be free of the friction of argument.

Yet facts become arguments whenever they're controversial on their own or challenge people's beliefs and lifestyles. Disagreements about childhood obesity, endangered species, or energy production ought to have a kind of clean, scientific logic to them. But that's rarely the case because the facts surrounding them must be interpreted. Those interpretations then determine what we feed children, where we can build a dam, or how we heat our homes. In other words, serious factual arguments almost always have consequences. *Can we rely on wind and solar power to solve our energy needs? Will the Social Security trust fund really go broke? Is it healthy to eat fatty foods?* People need well-reasoned factual arguments on subjects of this kind to make informed decisions. Such arguments educate the public.

For the same reason, we need arguments to challenge beliefs that are common in a society but held on the basis of inadequate or faulty information. Corrective arguments appear daily in the media, often based on studies written by scientists or researchers that the public would not encounter on their own. Many people, for example, believe that talking on a cell phone while driving is just like listening to the radio. But their intuition is not based on hard data: scientific studies show that using a cell phone in a car is comparable to driving under the influence of alcohol. That's a fact. As a result, fourteen states (and counting) have banned the use of handheld phones in cars.

Factual arguments also routinely address broad questions about how we understand the past. For example, are the accounts that we have of the American founding—or the Civil War, Reconstruction, or the heroics of the "Greatest Generation" in World War II—accurate? Or

© Bagley/Cagle Cartoons, Inc.

do the "facts" that we teach today sometimes reflect the perspectives and prejudices of earlier times or ideologies? The telling of history is almost always controversial and rarely settled: the British and Americans will always tell different versions of what happened in North America in 1776.

The Internet puts mountains of information at our fingertips, but we need to be sure to confirm whether or not that information is fact, using what Howard Rheingold calls "crap detection," the ability to distinguish between accurate information and inaccurate information, misinformation, or disinformation. (For more on "crap detection," see Chapter 19, "Evaluating Sources.")

As you can see, arguments of fact do much of the heavy lifting in our world. They report on what has been recently discovered or explore the implications of that new information. They also add interest and complexity to our lives, taking what might seem simple and adding new dimensions to it. In many situations, they're the precursors to other forms of analysis, especially causal and proposal arguments. Before we can explore why things happen as they do or solve problems, we need to do our best to determine the facts.

RESPOND•

For each topic in the following list, decide whether the claim is worth arguing to a college audience, and explain why or why not.

Earthquakes are increasing in number and intensity.

Many people die annually of heart disease.

Fewer people would be obese if they followed the Paleo Diet.

Japan might have come to terms more readily in 1945 if the Allies in World War II hadn't demanded unconditional surrender.

Boys would do better in school if there were more men teaching in elementary and secondary classrooms.

The sharp drop in oil prices could lead drivers to go back to buying gas-guzzling trucks and SUVs.

There aren't enough high-paying jobs for college graduates these days.

Hydrogen may never be a viable alternative to fossil fuels because it takes too much energy to change hydrogen into a usable form.

Proponents of the Keystone Pipe Line have exaggerated the benefits it will bring to the American economy.

Characterizing Factual Arguments

Factual arguments are often motivated by simple human curiosity or suspicion: *Are people who earn college degrees happier than those who don't? If being fat is so unhealthy, why aren't mortality rates rising?* Researchers may notice a pattern that leads them to look more closely at some phenomenon or behavior, exploring questions such as *What if?* or *How come?* Or maybe a writer first notes something new or different or unexpected and wants to draw attention to that fact: *Contrary to expectations, suicide rates are much higher in rural areas than in urban ones.*

Such observations can lead quickly to **hypotheses**—that is, toward tentative and plausible statements of fact whose merits need to be examined more closely. *Maybe being a little overweight isn't as bad for people as we've been told? Maybe people in rural areas have less access to mental health services?* To support such hypotheses, writers then have to uncover evidence that reaches well beyond the casual observations that triggered an initial interest—like a news reporter motivated to see whether there's a verifiable story behind a source's tip.

For instance, the authors of *Freakonomics*, Stephen J. Dubner and Steven D. Levitt, were intrigued by the National Highway Traffic Safety Administration's claim that car seats for children were 54 percent effective in preventing deaths in auto crashes for children below the age of four. In a *New York Times* op-ed column entitled "The Seat-Belt Solution," they posed an important question about that factual claim:

> But 54 percent effective compared with what? The answer, it turns out, is this: Compared with a child's riding completely unrestrained.

Their initial question about that claim led them to a more focused inquiry, then to a database on auto crashes, and then to a surprising conclusion: for kids above age twenty-four months, those in car seats were statistically safer than those without any protection but weren't safer than those confined by seat belts (which are much simpler, cheaper, and more readily available devices). Looking at the statistics every which way, the authors wonder if children older than two years would be just as well off physically — and their parents less stressed and better off financially — if the government mandated seat belts rather than car seats for them.

What kinds of evidence typically appear in sound factual arguments? The simple answer might be "all sorts," but a case can be made that factual arguments try to rely more on "hard evidence" than do "constructed" arguments based on logic and reason (see Chapter 4). Even so, some pieces of evidence are harder than others!

Developing a Factual Argument

Entire Web sites are dedicated to finding and posting errors from news and political sources. Some, like Media Matters for America and Accuracy in Media, take overtly partisan stands. Here's a one-day sampling of headlines from Media Matters:

> **Hillary Clinton Overcompensates on Foreign Policy Because She's a Woman**
>
> **Fox Host Defends Calling Michelle Obama Fat**
>
> **Fox News Decries Granting Undocumented Children Their Right to Public Education**

And here's a listing from Accuracy in Media:

An Inside Look at How Democrats Rig the Election Game

Why Obamacare Is Unfixable

The American Left: Friends to Our Country's Enemies

It would be hard to miss the blatant political agendas at work on these sites.

Other fact-checking organizations have better reputations when it comes to assessing the truths behind political claims and media presentations. Though both are also routinely charged with bias, Pulitzer Prize–winning PolitiFact.com and FactCheck.org at least make an effort to be fair-minded across a broader political spectrum. FactCheck, for example, provides a detailed analysis of the claims it investigates in relatively neutral and denotative language, and lists the sources its researchers used—just as if its writers were doing a research paper. At its best, FactCheck.org demonstrates what one valuable kind of factual argument can accomplish.

Any factual argument that you might compose—from how you state your claim to how you present evidence and the language you

PolitiFact uses a meter to rate political claims from "True" to "Pants on Fire."

use—should be similarly shaped by the occasion for the argument and a desire to serve the audiences that you hope to reach. We can offer some general advice to help you get started.

RESPOND•

The Annenberg Public Policy Center at the University of Pennsylvania hosts FactCheck.org, a Web site dedicated to separating facts from opinion or falsehood in the area of politics. It claims to be politically neutral. Find a case that interests you, either a recent controversial item listed on its homepage or another from its archives. Carefully study the item. Pay attention to the devices that FactCheck uses to suggest or ensure objectivity and the way that it handles facts and statistics. Then offer your own brief *factual* argument about the site's objectivity.

Identifying an Issue

To offer a factual argument of your own, you need to identify an issue or problem that will interest you and potential readers. Look for situations or phenomena—local or national—that seem out of the ordinary in the expected order of things. For instance, you might notice that many people you know are deciding not to attend college. How widespread is this change, and who are the people making this choice?

Or follow up claims that strike you as at odds with the facts as you know them or believe them. Maybe you doubt explanations being offered for your favorite sport team's current slump or for the declining number of minority men in your college courses. Or you might give a local spin to factual questions that other people have already formulated on a national level. Do people in your town seem to be flocking to high-MPG vehicles or resisting bans on texting while driving or smoking in public places outdoors? You will likely write a better paper if you take on a factual question that genuinely interests you.

In fact, whole books are written when authors decide to pursue factual questions that intrigue them. But you want to be careful not to argue matters that pose no challenge for you or your audiences. You're not offering anything new if you just try to persuade readers that smoking is harmful to their well-being. So how about something fresh in the area of health?

Quick preliminary research and reading might allow you to move from an intuition to a hypothesis, that is, a tentative statement of your claim: *Having a dog is good for your health.* As noted earlier, factual arguments often provoke other types of analysis. In developing this claim, you'd need to explain what "good for your health" means, potentially an argument of definition. You'd also likely find yourself researching causes of the phenomenon if you can demonstrate that it is factual. As it turns out, your canine hypothesis would have merit if you defined "good for health" as "encouraging exercise." Here's the lead to a *New York Times* story reporting recent research:

> If you're looking for the latest in home exercise equipment, you may want to consider something with four legs and a wagging tail.
>
> Several studies now show that dogs can be powerful motivators to get people moving. Not only are dog owners more likely to take regular walks, but new research shows that dog walkers are more active overall than people who don't have dogs.
>
> One study even found that older people are more likely to take regular walks if the walking companion is canine rather than human.
>
> —Tara Parker-Pope, "Forget the Treadmill. Get a Dog," March 14, 2011

As always, there's another side to the story: what if people likely to get dogs are the very sort already inclined to be more physically active? You could explore that possibility as well (and researchers have) and then either modify your initial hypothesis or offer a new one. That's what hypotheses are for. They are works in progress.

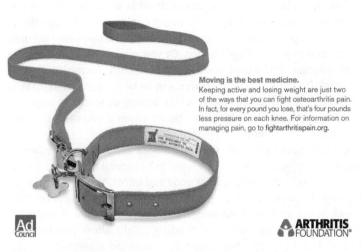

Moving is the best medicine.
Keeping active and losing weight are just two of the ways that you can fight osteoarthritis pain. In fact, for every pound you lose, that's four pounds less pressure on each knee. For information on managing pain, go to fightarthritispain.org.

Here's an actual ad based on the claim that exercise (and dog ownership) is good for health.

RESPOND •

Working with a group of colleagues, generate a list of twenty favorite "mysteries" explored on TV shows, in blogs, or in tabloid newspapers. Here are three to get you started—the alien crash landing at Roswell, the existence of Atlantis, and the uses of Area 51. Then decide which—if any—of these puzzlers might be resolved or explained in a reasonable factual argument and which ones remain eternally mysterious and improbable. Why are people attracted to such topics? Would any of these items provide material for a noteworthy factual argument?

Researching Your Hypothesis

How and where you research your subject will depend, naturally, on your subject. You'll certainly want to review Chapter 18, "Finding Evidence," Chapter 19, "Evaluating Sources," and Chapter 20, "Using Sources," before constructing an argument of fact. Libraries and the Web will provide you with deep resources on almost every subject. Your task will typically be to separate the best sources from all the rest. The word *best* here has many connotations: some reputable sources may be too technical for your audiences; some accessible sources may be pitched too low or be too far removed from the actual facts.

You'll be making judgment calls like this routinely. But do use primary sources whenever you can. For example, when gathering a comment from a source on the Web, trace it whenever possible to its original site, and read the comment in its full context. When statistics are quoted, follow them back to the source that offered them first to be sure that they're recent and reputable. Instructors and librarians can help you appreciate the differences. Understand that even sources with pronounced biases can furnish useful information, provided that you know how to use them, take their limitations into account, and then share what you know about the sources with your readers.

Sometimes, you'll be able to do primary research on your own, especially when your subject is local and you have the resources to do it. Consider conducting a competent survey of campus opinions and attitudes, for example, or study budget documents (often public) to determine trends in faculty salaries, tuition, student fees, and so on. Primary research of this sort can be challenging because even the simplest surveys or polls have to be intelligently designed and executed in a way that samples a representative population (see Chapter 4). But the work could pay off in an argument that brings new information to readers.

Refining Your Claim

As you learn more about your subject, you might revise your hypothesis to reflect what you've discovered. In most cases, these revised hypotheses will grow increasingly complex and specific. Following are three versions of essentially the same claim, with each version offering more information to help readers judge its merit:

- Americans really did land on the moon, despite what some people think!

- Since 1969, when the *Eagle* supposedly landed on the moon, some people have been unjustifiably skeptical about the success of the United States' *Apollo* program.

- Despite plentiful hard evidence to the contrary—from *Saturn V* launches witnessed by thousands to actual moon rocks tested by independent labs worldwide—some people persist in believing falsely that NASA's moon landings were actually filmed on deserts in the American Southwest as part of a massive propaganda fraud.

'...And, of course, there are the conspiracy theorists who say that it was all a big hoax and I didn't jump over it at all.'

© KES/CartoonStock.com

The additional details about the subject might also suggest new ways to develop and support it. For example, conspiracy theorists claim that the absence of visible stars in photographs of the moon landing is evidence that it was staged, but photographers know that the camera exposure needed to capture the foreground—astronauts in their bright space suits—would have made the stars in the background too dim to see. That's a key bit of evidence for this argument.

As you advance in your research, your thesis will likely pick up even more qualifying words and expressions, which help you to make reasonable claims. Qualifiers—words and phrases such as *some, most, few, for most people, for a few users, under specific conditions, usually, occasionally, seldom,* and so on—will be among your most valuable tools in a factual argument. (See p. 140 in Chapter 7 for more on qualifiers.)

Sometimes it is important to set your factual claim into a context that helps explain it to others who may find it hard to accept. You might have to concede some ground initially in order to see the broader picture. For instance, professor of English Vincent Carretta anticipated strong objections after he uncovered evidence that Olaudah Equiano—the author of *The Interesting Narrative* (1789), a much-cited autobiographical account of his Middle Passage voyage and subsequent life as a slave—may actually have been born in South Carolina and not in western Africa. Speaking to the *Chronicle of Higher Education* about why Equiano may have fabricated his African origins to serve a larger cause, Carretta explains:

> "Whether [Equiano] invented his African birth or not, he knew that what that movement needed was a first-person account. And because they were going after the slave trade, it had to be an account of someone who had been born in Africa and was brought across the Middle Passage. An African American voice wouldn't have done it."
>
> —Jennifer Howard, "Unraveling the Narrative"

Carretta asks readers to appreciate that the new facts that he has discovered about *The Interesting Narrative* do not undermine the work's historical significance. If anything, his research has added new dimensions to its meaning and interpretation.

Deciding Which Evidence to Use

In this chapter, we've blurred the distinction between factual arguments for scientific and technical audiences and those for the general public (in magazines, blogs, social media sites, television documentaries, and so on). In the former kind of arguments, readers will expect specific types of evidence arranged in a formulaic way. Such reports may include a hypothesis, a review of existing research on the subject, a description of methods, a presentation of results, and finally a formal discussion of the findings. If you are thinking "lab report," you are already familiar with an academic form of a factual argument with precise standards for evidence.

Less scientific factual arguments—claims about our society, institutions, behaviors, habits, and so on—are seldom so systematic, and they may draw on evidence from a great many different media. For instance, you might need to review old newspapers, scan videos, study statistics on government Web sites, read transcripts of congressional hearings, record the words of eyewitnesses to an event, glean information by following experts on Twitter, and so on. Very often, you will assemble your arguments from material found in credible, though not always concurring, authorities and resources—drawing upon the factual findings of scientists and scholars, but perhaps using their original insights in novel ways.

For example, you might be intrigued by a comprehensive report from the Kaiser Family Foundation (2010) providing the results of a study of more than 2,000 eight- to eighteen-year-old American children:

> The study found that the average time spent reading books for pleasure in a typical day rose from 21 minutes in 1999 to 23 minutes in 2004, and finally to 25 minutes in 2010. The rise of screen-based media has not melted children's brains, despite ardent warnings otherwise: "It does not appear that time spent using screen media (TV, video games and computers) displaces time spent with print media," the report stated. Teens are not only reading more books, they're involved in communities of like-minded book lovers.
> —Hannah Withers and Lauren Ross,
> "Young People Are Reading More Than You"

Reading about these results, however, may raise some new questions for you: Is twenty-five minutes of reading a day really something to be happy about? What is the quality of what these young people are reading? Such questions might lead you to do a new study that could challenge the conclusion of the earlier research by bringing fresh facts to the table.

Often, you may have only a limited number of words or pages in which to make a factual argument. What do you do then? You present your best evidence as powerfully as possible. But that's not difficult. You can make a persuasive factual case with just a few examples: three or four often suffice to make a point. Indeed, going on too long or presenting even good data in ways that make it seem uninteresting or pointless can undermine a claim.

Presenting Your Evidence

In *Hard Times* (1854), British author Charles Dickens poked fun at a pedagogue he named Thomas Gradgrind, who preferred hard facts before all things human or humane. When poor Sissy Jupe (called "girl number twenty" in his awful classroom) is unable at his command to define *horse*, Gradgrind turns to his star pupil:

> "Bitzer," said Thomas Gradgrind. "Your definition of a horse."
>
> "Quadruped. Graminivorous. Forty teeth, namely twenty-four grinders, four eyeteeth, and twelve incisive. Sheds coat in the spring; in marshy countries, sheds hoofs, too. Hoofs hard, but requiring to be shod with iron. Age known by marks in mouth." Thus (and much more) Bitzer.
>
> "Now girl number twenty," said Mr. Gradgrind. "You know what a horse is."
>
> —Charles Dickens, *Hard Times*

But does Bitzer? Rattling off facts about a subject isn't quite the same thing as knowing it, especially when your goal is, as it is in an argument of fact, to educate and persuade audiences. So you must take care how you present your evidence.

Factual arguments, like any others, take many forms. They can be as simple and pithy as a letter to the editor (or Bitzer's definition of a horse) or as comprehensive and formal as a senior thesis or even a dissertation. Such a thesis might have just two or three readers mainly interested in the facts you are presenting and the competence of your work. So your presentation can be lean and relatively simple.

But to earn the attention of readers in some more public forum, you may need to work harder to be persuasive. For instance, Pew Research Center's May 2014 formal report, *Young Adults, Student Debt, and Economic Well-Being*, which spends time introducing its authors and establishing their expertise, is twenty-three pages long, cites a dozen sources, and contains sixteen figures and tables. Like many such studies, it also includes a foreword, an overview, and a detailed table of contents. All these elements help readers find the facts they need while also establishing the ethos of the work, making it seem serious, credible, well conceived, and worth reading.

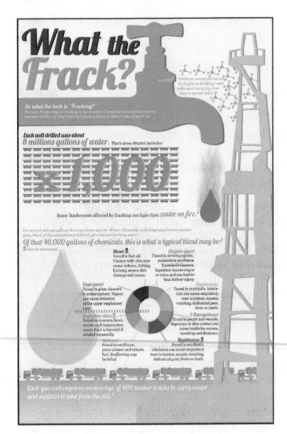

"What the Frack?" uses images to present its case against fracking.
© Jess Nelson Design

Considering Design and Visuals

When you prepare a factual argument, consider how you can present your evidence most effectively. Precisely because factual arguments often rely on evidence that can be measured, computed, or illustrated, they benefit from thoughtful, even artful presentation of data. If you have lots of examples, you might arrange them in a list (bulleted or otherwise) and keep the language in each item roughly parallel. If you have an argument that can be translated into a table, chart, or graph (see Chapter 14), try it. And if there's a more dramatic medium for your factual argument—a Prezi slide show, a multimedia mashup, a documentary video posted via a social network—experiment with it, checking to be sure it would satisfy the assignment.

Infographics like this one turn facts and data into arguments. USAID

Images and photos—from technical illustrations to imaginative re-creations—have the power to document what readers might otherwise have to imagine, whether actual conditions of drought, poverty, or a disaster like devastating typhoon Haiyan that displaced over 4 million people in the Philippines in 2013, or the dimensions of the Roman forum as it existed in the time of Julius Caesar. Readers today expect the arguments they read to include visual elements, and there's little reason not to offer this assistance if you have the technical skills to create them.

Consider the rapid development of the genre known as infographics—basically data presented in bold visual form. These items can be humorous and creative, but many, such as "Learning Out of Poverty" on the preceding page, make powerful factual arguments even when they leave it to viewers to draw their own conclusions. Just search "infographics" on the Web to find many examples.

<hr>

GUIDE | **to writing an argument of fact**

<hr>

● Finding a Topic

You're entering an argument of fact when you:

- make a claim about fact or existence that's controversial or surprising: *Climate change is threatening species in all regions by extending the range of non-native plants and animals.*

- correct an error of fact: *The overall abortion rate is not increasing in the United States, though rates are increasing in some states.*

- challenge societal myths: *Many Mexicans fought alongside Anglos in battles that won Texas its independence from Mexico.*

- wish to discover the state of knowledge about a subject or examine a range of perspectives and points of view: *The rationales of parents who homeschool their children reveal some surprising differences.*

● Researching Your Topic

Use both a library and the Web to locate the information you need. A research librarian is often a valuable resource, as are experts or eyewitnesses. Begin research by consulting the following types of sources:

- scholarly books on your subject
- newspapers, magazines, reviews, and journals (online and print)
- online databases
- government documents and reports
- Web sites, blogs, social networking sites, and listservs or newsgroups
- experts in the field, some of whom might be right on your campus

Do field research if appropriate—a survey, a poll, or systematic observation. Or invite people with a stake in the subject to present their interpretations of the facts. Evaluate all sources carefully, making sure that each is authoritative and credible.

● Formulating a Hypothesis

Don't rush into a thesis. Instead, begin with a hypothesis that expresses your beliefs at the beginning of the project but that may change as you learn more. It's OK to start with a question to which you don't have an answer or with a broad, general interest in a subject:

- **Question:** Have higher admissions standards at BSU reduced the numbers of entering first-year students from small, rural high schools?

- **Hypothesis:** Higher admissions standards at BSU are reducing the number of students admitted from rural high schools, which tend to be smaller and less well-funded than those in suburban and urban areas.

- **Question:** Have music sites like Pandora and Spotify reduced the amount of illegal downloading of music?

- **Hypothesis:** Services like Pandora and Spotify may have done more than lawsuits by record companies to discourage illegal downloads of music.

- **Question:** How dangerous is nuclear energy, really?

- **Hypothesis:** The danger posed by nuclear power plants is far less than that attributable to other viable energy sources.

- **Question:** Why can't politicians and citizens agree about the threat posed by the huge federal deficit?

- **Hypothesis:** People with different points of view read different threats into the budget numbers and so react differently.

● Examples of Arguable Factual Claims

- A campus survey that shows that far more students have read *Harry Potter and the Prisoner of Azkaban* than *Hamlet* indicates that our current core curriculum lacks depth.

- Evidence suggests that the European conquest of the Americas may have had more to do with infectious diseases than any superiority in technology or weaponry.

- In the long run, dieting may be more harmful than moderate overeating.

● Preparing a Proposal

If your instructor asks you to prepare a proposal for your project, here's a format that may help:

State your thesis or hypothesis completely. If you are having trouble doing so, try outlining it in Toulmin terms:

Claim:

Reason(s):

Warrant(s):

Alternatively, you might describe the complications of a factual issue you hope to explore in your project, with the thesis perhaps coming later.

- Explain why the issue you're examining is important, and provide the context for raising the issue. Are you introducing new information, making available information better known, correcting what has been reported incorrectly, or complicating what has been understood more simply?

- Identify and describe those readers you most hope to reach with your argument. Why is this group of readers most appropriate for your project? What are their interests in the subject? How might you involve them in the paper?

- Discuss the kinds of evidence you expect to use in the project and the research the paper will require.

- Briefly discuss the key challenges you anticipate in preparing your argument.

● Considering Format and Media

Your instructor may specify that you use a particular format and/or medium. If not, ask yourself these questions to help you make a good choice:

- What format is most appropriate for your argument of fact? Does it call for an academic essay, a report, an infographic, a brochure, or something else?

- What medium is most appropriate for your argument? Would it be best delivered orally to a live audience? Presented as an audio essay or podcast? Presented in print only or in print with illustrations?

- Will you need visuals, such as moving or still images, maps, graphs, charts—and what function will they play in your argument? Make sure they are not just "added on" but are necessary components of the argument.

Thinking about Organization

The simplest structure for a factual argument is to make a claim and then prove it. But even a basic approach needs an introductory section that provides a context for the claim and a concluding section that assesses the implications of the argument. A factual argument that corrects an error or provides an alternative view of some familiar concept or historical event will also need a section early on explaining what the error or the common belief is. Be sure your opening section answers the *who, what, where, when, how,* and (maybe) *why* questions that readers will bring to the case.

Factual arguments offered in some academic fields follow formulas and templates. A format favored in the hard sciences and also in the social and behavioral sciences is known by its acronym, IMRAD, which stands for Introduction, Methods, Research, and Discussion. Another typical format calls for an abstract, a review of literature, a discussion of method, an analysis, and a references list. When you have flexibility in the structure of your argument, it makes sense to lead with a striking example to interest readers in your subject and then to conclude with your strongest evidence. Pay particular attention to transitions between key points.

If you are defending a specific claim, anticipate the ways people with different points of view might respond to your argument. Consider how to address such differences respectfully in the body of your argument. But don't let a factual argument with a persuasive thesis end with concessions or refutations, especially in pieces for the general public. Such a strategy leaves readers thinking about problems with your claim at precisely the point when they should be impressed by its strengths. On the other hand, if your factual argument becomes exploratory, you may find yourself simply presenting a range of positions.

Getting and Giving Response: Questions for Peer Response

Your instructor may assign you to a group for the purpose of reading and responding to each other's drafts. If not, ask for responses from serious readers or consultants at a writing center. Use the following questions to evaluate a colleague's draft. Since specific comments help more than general observations, be sure to illustrate your comments with examples. Some of the questions below assume a conventional, thesis-driven project, but more exploratory or invitational arguments of fact also need to be clearly phrased, organized, and supported with evidence.

The Claim

- Does the claim clearly raise a serious and arguable factual issue?
- Is the claim as clear and specific as possible?
- Is the claim qualified? If so, how?

Evidence for the Claim

- Is the evidence provided enough to persuade readers to believe your claim? If not, what additional evidence would help? Does any of the evidence seem inappropriate or ineffective? Why?

- Is the evidence in support of the claim simply announced, or do you explain its significance and appropriateness? Is more discussion needed?

- Are readers' potential objections to the claim or evidence addressed adequately? Are alternative positions understood thoroughly and presented fairly?

- What kinds of sources are cited? How credible and persuasive will they be to readers? What other kinds of sources might work better?

- Are all quotations introduced with appropriate signal phrases (such as "As Tyson argues, . . .") and blended smoothly into the writer's sentences?

- Are all visuals titled and labeled appropriately? Have you introduced them and commented on their significance?

Organization and Style

- How are the parts of the argument organized? Is this organization effective?

- Will readers understand the relationships among the claims, supporting reasons, warrants, and evidence? If not, how might those connections be clearer? Is the function of every visual clear? Are more transitions needed? Would headings or graphic devices help?

- Are the transitions or links from point to point, sentence to sentence, and paragraph to paragraph clear and effective? If not, how could they be improved?

- Are all visuals carefully integrated into the text? Is each visual introduced and commented on to point out its significance? Is each visual labeled as a figure or a table and given a caption as well as a citation?
- Is the style suited to the subject? Is it too formal, casual, or technical? Can it be improved?
- Which sentences seem effective? Which ones seem weaker, and how could they be improved? Should short sentences be combined, and any longer ones be broken up?
- How effective are the paragraphs? Too short or too long? How can they be improved?
- Which words or phrases seem effective? Do any seem vague or inappropriate for the audience or the writer's purpose? Are technical or unfamiliar terms defined?

Spelling, Punctuation, Mechanics, Documentation, and Format

- Are there any errors in spelling, punctuation, capitalization, and the like?
- Is an appropriate and consistent style of documentation used for parenthetical citations and the list of works cited or references? (See Chapter 22.)
- Does the paper or project follow an appropriate format? Is it appropriately designed and attractively presented? How could it be improved?

PROJECTS •

1. Turn a database of information you find in the library or online into a traditional argument or, alternatively, into an infographic that offers a variety of potential claims. FedStats, a government Web site, provides endless data, but so can the sports or financial sections of a newspaper. Once you find a rich field of study, examine the data and draw your ideas from it, perhaps amplifying these ideas with material from other related sources of information. If you decide to create an infographic, you'll find good examples at VizWorld or Cool Infographics online. Software tools you can use to create infographics include Piktochart and Google Public Data. Have fun.

2. Write an argument about one factual matter you are confident—based on personal experience or your state of knowledge—that most people get wrong, time and again. Use your expertise to correct this false impression.

3. Tough economic and political times sometimes reinforce and sometimes undermine cultural myths. With your classmates, generate a list of common beliefs about education, employment, family life, marriage, social progress, technology, and so on that seem to be under unusual scrutiny today. *Does it still pay to invest in higher education? Do two-parent households matter as much as they used to? Can children today expect to do better than their parents? Is a home still a good investment?* Pick one area to explore in depth, narrow the topic as much as you can, and then gather facts that inform it by doing research, perhaps working collaboratively to expand your findings. Turn your investigation into a factual argument.

4. Since critic and writer Nicholas Carr first asked "Is Google Making Us Stupid?" many have answered with a resounding "yes," arguing that extensive time online is reducing attention spans and leaving readers less critical than ever. Others have disagreed, saying that new technologies are doing just the opposite—expanding our brain power. Do some research on this controversy, on the Web or in the library, and consult with a wide range of people interested in the subject, perhaps gathering them together for a discussion or panel discussion. Then offer a factual argument based on what you uncover, reflecting the range of perspectives and opinions you have encountered.

Readers will
certainly notice
the title.

Why You Should Fear Your Toaster More Than Nuclear Power

TAYLOR PEARSON

A recent nuclear
disaster in Japan
provides a chal-
lenging context
for Pearson's
claim: we need
nuclear energy.

For the past month or so, headlines everywhere have been warning us of the horrible crises caused by the damaged Japanese nuclear reactors. Titles like "Japan Nuclear Disaster Tops Scale" have fueled a new wave of protests against anything nuclear—namely, the construction of new nuclear plants or even the continued operation of existing plants. However, all this reignited fear of nuclear energy is nothing more than media sensationalism. We need nuclear energy. It's clean, it's efficient, it's economic, and it's probably the only thing that will enable us to quickly phase out fossil fuels.

The first-person
plural point
of view (*we*)
helps Pearson to
connect with his
audience.

DEATH TOLL

First, let's address what is probably everyone's main concern about nuclear energy: the threat it poses to us and the likelihood of a nuclear power plant killing large numbers of people. The actual number of deaths caused by nuclear power plant accidents, even in worst-case scenarios, have been few. Take the Chernobyl accident—the worst and most lethal nuclear incident to date. As tragic

---

Taylor Pearson wrote "Why You Should Fear Your Toaster More Than Nuclear Power" while he was a sophomore at the University of Texas at Austin. The assignment asked for a public argument—one good enough to attract readers who could put it down if they lost interest. In other words, a purely academic argument wouldn't work. So Pearson allows himself to exercise his sense of humor. Nor did the paper have to be formally documented. However, Pearson was expected to identify crucial sources the way writers do in magazines and newspapers. The paper provides an example of a factual argument with a clear thesis: "We need nuclear energy."

as it was, the incident has killed only eighty-two people. More specifically, according to a 2005 release by the World Health Organization, thirty-two were killed in the effort to put out the fires caused by the meltdown and thirty-eight died within months of the accident as a result of acute radiation poisoning. Since the accident occurred in 1986, an additional twelve people have died from the radiation they were exposed to during the accident. Almost all deaths were highly exposed rescue workers. Other nuclear power accidents have been few and never resulted in more than ten deaths per incident. Still think that's too dangerous? To provide some perspective, let's consider an innocuous household appliance, the toaster: over three thousand people died from toaster accidents the first year the appliances were produced and sold in the 1920s, and they still cause around fifty accident-related deaths every year in the United States. So your toaster is far more likely to kill you than any nuclear power plant and subsequently give you a painfully embarrassing epitaph.

In fact, in comparison to the other major means of energy production in the United States, nuclear power is remarkably safe. According to the U.S. Department of Labor, coal mining currently causes about sixty-five deaths and eleven thousand injuries per year, while oil drilling is responsible for approximately 125 deaths per year in the United States. Annual death tolls fluctuate depending upon the demand for these resources and the subsequent drilling or mining required, but the human cost is still exponentially more than that of nuclear energy. However, in the decades that nuclear power has been used in the United States, there have been zero deaths caused by nuclear power accidents—none at all. That's much better than the thousands of lives coal, oil, and toasters have cost us. If you care about saving human lives, then you should like nuclear energy.

Pearson deflates fears by putting deaths caused by nuclear plants in perspective.

RADIATION

Despite nuclear energy causing remarkably few deaths, people are also terrified of another aspect of nuclear power—radiation. Everyone's scared of developing a boulder-size tumor or our apples growing to similar size as a result of the awful radiation given off by nuclear power plants or their potential meltdowns. However, it should comfort you to know (or perhaps not) that you receive more radiation from a brick wall than from a nuclear power plant.

The argument uses technical terms but makes sure they are accessible to readers.

We live in a radioactive world—nearly everything gives off at least a trace amount of radiation; that includes brick walls. Yes, while such a wall emits about 3.5 millirems of radiation per year, a nuclear power plant gives off about .3 millirems per year. (Millirem is just a unit of radiation dosage.) Of course, this low level of emission is a result of the numerous safeguards set up around the reactors to suppress radiation. So what happens if those safeguards fail? Will everyone surrounding the plant turn into a mutant?

To answer that question, let's examine the reactor failures in the recent Japanese nuclear crisis following several devastating earthquakes. The damage from the quakes took out the power to several nuclear plants, which caused their core cooling systems to go offline. To prevent reactor meltdowns, workers had to douse the failing reactors in thousands of gallons of seawater to cool the fuel rods, which contain all the radioactive materials. Worries about the resulting radioactive seawater contaminating the ocean and sea life flared as a result. But just how radioactive is the water? Officials from Tokyo Electric Power Company said the water "would have to be drunk for a whole year in order to accumulate one millisievert." People are generally exposed to about 1 to 10 millisieverts each year from background radiation caused by substances in the air and soil. "You would have to eat or drink an awful lot to

The argument is full of data and statistics from what seem to be reputable authorities and sources.

get any level of radiation that would be harmful," said British nuclear expert Laurence Williams. You get exposed to 5 millisieverts during a coast-to-coast flight across the United States. According to the U.S. Food and Drug Administration, you receive between 5 and 60 millisieverts in a CAT scan, depending on the type. So drinking water for a year that was in direct contact with containers of radioactive material used in those Japanese nuclear plants will expose you to a fifth of the radiation you would get from the weakest CAT scan. How dangerous!

WASTE

But even if we have little to fear from nuclear power plants themselves, what about the supposedly deadly by-products of these plants? Opponents of nuclear energy cite the fact that while nuclear power plants don't emit greenhouse gases, they do leave behind waste that remains radioactive for thousands of years. However, this nuclear waste problem is exaggerated. According to Professor Emeritus of Computer Science at Stanford University, John McCarthy, a 1,000-megawatt reactor produces only 1.5 cubic meters of waste after a year of operation. The current solution is to put the waste in protective containers and store them in caverns cut in granite. At the very least, with such a small amount of waste per reactor, the caverns don't have to be dug very fast.

Nuclear power plants do produce waste that needs to be kept away from living things, but the actual amount of waste produced is small and therefore manageable. If the United States got all its power from nuclear plants, the amount of waste produced would be equivalent to one pill of aspirin per person, per year—tiny compared to the amount of waste produced by plants that use fossil fuels; the U.S. Energy Information Administration notes that coal alone produces about 1.8 billion metric tons of CO_2 emissions per year.

As the argument explores various aspects of nuclear energy, headings keep the reader on track.

Pearson strategically concedes a downside of nuclear energy.

Quantity is not the only factor that has been exaggerated—the amount of time the waste remains dangerously radioactive has also been inflated. After about five hundred years, the fission products' radiation levels drop to below the level at which we typically find them in nature; the thousands of years opponents of nuclear energy refer to are the years the waste will be radioactive, not excessively so. You don't want to stand right next to this material even after those first five hundred years, but if it can exist in nature without doing any noticeable damage, then it doesn't pose any serious threat. Essentially, everything is radioactive; to criticize something for being radioactive without specifying the level of radioactivity means nothing.

MEETING OUR ENERGY DEMANDS

Although I've done a lot here in an attempt to defend nuclear energy, I still acknowledge it's not perfect. While the nuclear waste problem isn't something to be too worried about, it would still be better if we could satisfy our demand for energy without producing waste, radioactive or otherwise. However, I believe nuclear energy is the only realistic option we have to one day achieve an entirely clean energy reality.

We live in an age dominated by energy—to power our cars, our homes, and our computers. Let's face it: we're not going to give up the lifestyle that energy gives us. But under the current means of energy production—primarily coal in the United States—we're pumping out billions of tons of greenhouse gases that will eventually destroy our planet. So we have a dilemma. While we want to do something about global warming, we don't want to change our high-energy-consumption way of life. What are our options?

The concluding paragraphs compare nuclear power to potential alternatives.

Currently, completely clean sources of energy haven't been developed enough to make them a realistic option to supply all our energy needs. For solar energy to match the energy production of nuclear power plants presently in use, we would have to cover an area the size of New Jersey with solar panels. That's not a realistic option; we're not going to build that many panels just to get ourselves off of our addiction to fossil fuels. The same is true of the other renewable energy sources: wind, geothermal, hydroelectric, etc. The technologies simply aren't mature enough.

However, nuclear power is realistic. We have the means and the technology to make enough nuclear power plants to satisfy our electricity demands. Nuclear plants produce a lot of power with relatively little waste. Moving from coal to nuclear plants could provide us with adequate power until we develop more efficient renewable sources of electricity.

So what's stopping us? Of course, those heavily invested in coal and other fossil fuels lobby the government to keep their industries profitable, but a large source of opposition is also the American public. Because of the atom bombs of World War II, the Cold War, and Chernobyl, we're scared of all things nuclear. Anytime we hear the word "radiation," images of mushroom clouds and fallout enter our minds. But nuclear power plants aren't bombs. No matter what happens to them, they will never explode. Strong as it might be, our fear of nuclear power is overblown and keeping us from using a source of energy that could literally save our planet. We need to stop the fearmongering before we burn our planet to a crisp.

Of course, that's if our toasters don't kill us first.

Pearson ends his argument by asking readers to acknowledge that their fears of nuclear power aren't based in fact.

What the Numbers Show about N.F.L. Player Arrests

NEIL IRWIN

Off-the-field violence by professional football players is coming under new focus this week after the release of a video involving the star Baltimore Ravens running back Ray Rice, followed by a bungled response by the National Football League.

But what do the numbers show about N.F.L. players' tangles with the law more broadly? Are some teams' players more likely to get into legal trouble? Are arrests rising or falling? What are the most common offenses?

USA Today maintains a database of arrests, charges, and citations of N.F.L. players for anything more serious than a traffic citation. Maintained by Brent Schrotenboer, it goes back to 2000 and covers, to date, 713 instances in which pro football players have had a run-in with the law that was reported by the news media.

The data set is imperfect; after all, it depends on news media outlets finding out about every time a third-string offensive lineman is pulled

Ray Rice was arraigned on domestic violence charges in May 2014. He was fired by the Baltimore Ravens in September 2014. AP Photo/The Philadelphia Inquirer, Tom Gralish, Pool

over for driving drunk, and so some arrests may well fall through the cracks. Moreover, arrests are included even if charges are dropped or the player is found not guilty, so it presumably includes legal run-ins in which the player did nothing wrong.

Finally, for purposes of these tabulations, a simple drug possession charge in which no one was hurt counts the same as a case like that of Mr. Rice, who is on tape punching his fiancée out cold (she is now his wife), or even that of the former New England Patriot Aaron Hernandez, who is in jail awaiting trial on murder charges.

But with those caveats aside, here's what the data show about how pro football players are interacting with the law. The numbers show a league in which drunk-driving arrests are a continuing problem and domestic violence charges are surprisingly common; in which the teams that have the most players getting in legal trouble don't always fit the impressions fans might have; and in which teams with high arrest rates tend to stay that way over time.

One N.F.L. player in 40 is arrested in a given year. There are 32 teams, each with 53 players on its roster plus another eight on its practice squad (plus more players who show up for training camp but do not make the team, but we didn't attempt to account for them). Thus over the nearly 15 years that the USA *Today* data goes back, the 713 arrests mean that 2.53 percent of players have had a serious run-in with the law in an average year. That may sound bad, but the arrest rate is lower than the national average for men in that age range.

Arrests peaked in the mid-2000s, and are way down this year. The peak year for arrests of N.F.L. players was 2006, followed closely by 2007 and 2008. (These are calendar years, not N.F.L. seasons.) One important caveat: The apparent increase could be a result of increased coverage of professional athletes' legal troubles by Internet media. In other words, we don't know for sure whether more N.F.L. players were being arrested in those years, or whether TMZ and other outlets were better positioned to find out about it.

Despite the Ray Rice episode, 2014 is on track to be the year with the fewest arrests of N.F.L. players on record. Through Sept. 10, there had only been 21. If the final four months of the year proceed at the same pace of arrests as the first eight, that will come to 28, well below the previous low of 36 in 2004.

The most common accusation is driving while drunk, but domestic violence is a big problem. Some 28 percent of the arrests in the database were for driving under the influence, with 202 incidents. Other frequent categories of charges include assault and battery (88 cases) and drug-related offenses (82). This data is also a reminder that domestic violence has been a problem among N.F.L. players since long before Ray and Janay Rice got on that Atlantic City elevator: There have been 85 charges for domestic violence and related offenses since 2000.

The Minnesota Vikings have had the most players arrested since 2000. The number of arrests by team range from a low of 11 (tie between the Arizona Cardinals and St. Louis Rams) versus a high of 44 (the Vikings), with the Cincinnati Bengals and Denver Broncos close behind. (The Houston Texans also have 11 but started playing in 2002.)

To look at it a different way, across the league from 2000 through 2013, 2.53 percent of players were arrested per year, but for the Vikings, that number is 5 percent. For the teams tied for fewest arrests, it is 1.3 percent.

The Ravens have received negative publicity over Rice, whom they fired, and over other players' legal troubles this year, but their 22 player

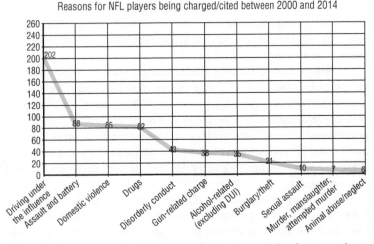

Reasons for NFL players being charged/cited between 2000 and 2014

Although driving under the influence is the top reason NFL players ran into trouble with the law, the next three biggest reasons are very concerning.

Data from *USA Today*

arrests since 2000 make them right at the leaguewide average. The Oakland Raiders have cultivated an image of being a franchise for tough, rowdy bad boys. The team's players, however, have had 19 scrapes with the law since 2000, below average.

The frequency of arrests in a franchise tends to be consistent over time. One might imagine that the number of players from a given franchise who are arrested is a random phenomenon. Maybe, in the rankings above, for example, the Vikings and the Bengals were just unlucky and the Cardinals and Rams were just lucky.

But there's a simple way to test that. If the results were random, you would expect there to be no correlation between the number of player arrests in one time period with a subsequent time period. You could even imagine a negative correlation, if teams that had a run of players getting in trouble took extra care not to sign players reputed to have character issues.

But that is not what happened over the last 14 years. If you chart the number of arrests of players from each franchise in the first seven years of the data, 2000 to 2006, versus the number of arrests that franchise experienced from 2007 to 2013, the correlation is a pretty solid 53 percent. [This] shows a clear pattern in which those franchises with high numbers of arrests in the early years also tended to have high numbers of arrests in later years and vice versa.

The data don't tell us anything about why these patterns are so persistent, but there are two possibilities that seem to stand out. First, there could be club culture. The top management of a franchise may send a message to personnel scouts and coaches that they are either more or less tolerant of signing players who have had legal problems in the past. (One might imagine that the personal style of the coach could play a role as well, but coaches tend not to have long tenures in the modern N.F.L.; no coach has led his team continuously for the entirety of the time covered by this arrest data, though the Patriots' Bill Belichick misses that honor by only a few weeks, having been hired in late January 2000.)

Second, there is geography. Different cities have different patterns of living and different approaches to law enforcement. Perhaps players for the Jets and the Giants (both with persistently low arrest rates) are at less risk of arrest for D.U.I. because people are less likely to need to drive themselves to nightclubs in Manhattan. Or perhaps in some cities, young African-American men driving expensive cars attract more police attention than in others.

Regardless of the reasons, a handful of franchises have persistently higher numbers of players who end up being arrested, and may want to learn from their rivals in other cities as to why.

9

Arguments of Definition

Left to right: AP Photo/Seth Wenig; Bill Wight/Getty Images; Frederick M. Brown/Getty Images

A student writes a cookbook for her master's thesis, hoping to make it easier for people to eat good, healthy food for less money. Her work helps redefine current definitions of *thesis*.

A panel of judges must decide whether computer-enhanced images will be eligible in a contest for landscape photography. At what point is an electronically manipulated image no longer a *photograph*?

A conservative student group accuses the student government on campus of sponsoring a lecture series featuring a disproportionate number of "left-wing" writers and celebrities. A spokesperson for the student government defends its program by questioning the definition of *left-wing* used to classify some of the speakers.

Understanding Arguments of Definition

Definitions matter. Just ask a scientist, a mathematician, an engineer, a judge—or just an everyday person who wants to marry someone of the same sex. In 1996, the Congress passed, and President Clinton signed, the Defense of Marriage Act (DOMA), which defined marriage in federal law this way:

> In determining the meaning of any Act of Congress, or of any ruling, regulation, or interpretation of the various administrative bureaus and agencies of the United States, the word "marriage" means only a legal union between one man and one woman as husband and wife, and the word "spouse" refers only to a person of the opposite sex who is a husband or a wife. 1 U.S.C. 7.

This decision and its definitions of *marriage* and *spouse* have been challenged over and over again in the ensuing decades, leading eventually to another Supreme Court decision, in the summer of 2013, that declared DOMA unconstitutional. The majority opinion, written by Justice Kennedy, found that the earlier law was discriminatory and that it labeled same-sex unions as "less worthy than the marriage of others." In so ruling, the court affirmed that the federal government cannot differentiate between a "marriage" of heterosexuals and one of homosexuals. Laws regarding marriage—and thus attempting to define or redefine the term—are still ongoing, and you might want to check the status of such controversies in your own state.

In any case, such decisions demonstrate that arguments of definition aren't abstract academic exercises: they are contentious and very often have important consequences for ordinary people. That's because they wield the power to say what someone or something is or can be. Such arguments can both include or exclude: A wolf in Montana either is an endangered species or it isn't. An unsolicited kiss is or is not sexual harassment. A person merits official political refugee status in the United States or doesn't. Another way of approaching definitional arguments, however, is to think of what falls between *is* and *is not* in a definitional claim. In fact, many definitional disputes occur in that murky realm.

Consider the controversy over how to define *human intelligence*. Some argue that human intelligence is a capacity that is measured by tests of verbal and mathematical reasoning. In other words, it's defined by IQ and SAT scores. Others define *intelligence* as the ability to perform specific practical tasks. Still others interpret *intelligence* in emotional terms as a competence in relating to other people. Any of these positions could be defended reasonably, but perhaps the wisest approach would be to construct a definition of *intelligence* that is rich enough to incorporate all these perspectives—and maybe more.

The fact is that crucial political, social, and scientific terms—such as *intelligence, social justice, war,* or *marriage*—are reargued, reshaped, and updated for the times.

The use of drones in air strikes—and the loss of civilian lives involved—has led to a heated national controversy. Commenting in *The Daily Kos*, MinistryOfTruth wrote:

> We all cringe when we hear of the innocent lives lost at war and civilians caught in the crossfire. These civilian deaths are always sad and tragic reminders of the cost of war. The Military/Industrial Complex doesn't like that. Reports of civilian deaths make the wars unpopular, and that's not the right way to continue to justify an ever growing military budget full of expensive drone missiles and the longest war in American history, is it? Nope. So what do they do? Re-define the dead civilians.
>
> —MinistryOfTruth, in *The Daily Kos*

Blogger MinistryOfTruth goes on to quote from a lengthy article in the *New York Times* concluding that the administration "embraced a disputed method for counting civilian casualties that . . . in effect counts all military-age males in a strike zone as combatants, . . . unless there is explicit intelligence posthumously proving them innocent." As this example illustrates, during war times it is especially important to watch how definitions get shifted and changed to shape or change reality.

Red DaxLuma Gallery/
Shutterstock

The argument over how to define *militants* and *combatants* will not be settled simply by consulting a dictionary, no matter how up to date it is. In fact, dictionaries inevitably reflect the way that particular groups of people use words at a specified time and place. And like any form of writing, these reference books mirror the prejudices of their makers—as shown, perhaps most famously, in the entries of lexicographer Samuel Johnson (1709–1784), who gave the English language its first great dictionary. Johnson, no friend of the Scots, defined *oats* as "a grain which in England is generally given to horses, but in Scotland supports the people." (To be fair, he also defined *lexicographer* as "a writer of dictionaries, a harmless drudge.") Thus, it's possible to disagree with dictionary definitions or to regard them merely as starting points for arguments.

The *Dictionary for Landlubbers* defines words according to their point of view! Excerpted from *SAILING: A Dictionary for Landlubbers, Old Salts, & Armchair Drifters.* Copyright © 1981 by Henry Beard and Roy McKie. Used by permission of Workman Publishing Co., Inc., New York. All rights reserved.

sail·ing (sā'lĩng), 1.n. the fine art of getting wet and becoming ill while slowly going nowhere at great expense.

A DICTIONARY FOR LANDLUBBERS, OLD SALTS, & ARMCHAIR DRIFTERS • BY HENRY BEARD & ROY McKIE •

RESPOND●

Briefly discuss how you might define the italicized terms in the following controversial claims of definition. Compare your definitions of the terms with those of your classmates.

Graphic novels are *serious literature.*

Burning a nation's flag is a *hate crime.*

Matt Drudge and Arianna Huffington aren't *journalists.*

College sports programs have become *big businesses.*

Plagiarism can be an act of *civil disobedience.*

Satanism is a *religion* properly protected by the First Amendment.

Campaign contributions are acts of *free speech* that should never be regulated.

The District of Columbia should not have all the privileges of an American *state.*

Polygamous couples should have the legal privileges of *marriage.*

Kinds of Definition

Because there are different kinds of definitions, there are also different ways to make a definition argument. Fortunately, identifying a particular type of definition is less important than appreciating when an issue of definition is at stake. Let's explore some common definitional issues.

Formal Definitions

Formal definitions are what you find in dictionaries. Such definitions place a term in its proper **genus** and **species**—first determining its class and then identifying the features or criteria that distinguish it from other members of that class. That sounds complicated, but a definition will help you see the principle. To define *hybrid car*, you might first place it in a general class—*passenger vehicles*. Then the formal definition would distinguish hybrid cars from other passenger vehicles: *they can move using two or more sources of power, either separately or in combination.* So the full definition might look like this: *a hybrid car is a passenger vehicle* (genus) *that can operate using two or more sources of power, separately or in combination* (species).

Many arguments involve deciding whether an object meets the criteria set by a formal definition. For instance, suppose that you are

2014 Honda Insight: fully hybrid or something else?
PHOTOEDIT/PhotoEdit, Inc.

considering whether a Toyota Prius and a Honda Insight are comparable hybrid vehicles. Both are clearly passenger cars, so the genus raises no questions. But not all vehicles that claim to be hybrids are powered by two sources: some of them are just electrically *assisted* versions of a regular gasoline car. That's the species question. Looking closely, you discover that a Prius can run on either gas or electric power alone. But does the Insight have that flexibility? Not quite. It has an electric motor that assists its small gas engine, but the vehicle never runs on electricity alone. So technically the Insight is labeled a *mild hybrid* whereas the Prius is called a *full hybrid*. This definitional distinction obviously has consequences for consumers concerned about CO_2 emissions.

Operational Definitions

Operational definitions identify an object or idea by what it does or by what conditions create it. For example, someone's offensive sexual imposition on another person may not meet the technical definition of *harassment* unless it is considered *unwanted, unsolicited*, and *repeated*. These three conditions then define what makes an act that might be acceptable in some situations turn into harassment. But they might also then become part of a highly contentious debate: were the conditions actually present in a given case? For example, could an offensive act really be harassment if the accused believed sexual interest was mutual and therefore solicited?

As you might imagine, arguments arise from operational definitions whenever people disagree about what the conditions define or whether these conditions have been fulfilled. Here are some examples of those types of questions:

Questions Related to Conditions

- Can institutional racism occur in the absence of specific and individual acts of racism?
- Can someone who is paid for their community service still be called a volunteer?
- Can an offensive act be termed harassment if the accused believed sexual interest was mutual and therefore solicited?

Questions Related to Fulfillment of Conditions

- Has an institution supported traditions or policies that have led to widespread racial inequities?

- Was the compensation given to a volunteer really "pay" or simply "reimbursement" for expenses?

- Should a person be punished for harassment if he or she believed the offensive action to be solicited?

Prince Charming considers whether an action would fulfill the conditions for an operational definition. Cartoonstock Ltd./www.CartoonStock.com

RESPOND •

This chapter opens with several rhetorical situations that center on definitional issues. Select one of these situations, and then, using the strategy of formal definition, set down some criteria of definition. For example, identify the features of a photograph that make it part of a larger class (*art, communication method, journalistic technique*). Next, identify the features that make it distinct from other members of that larger class. Then use the strategy of operational definition to establish criteria for the same object: what does it do? Remember to ask questions related to conditions (*Is a computer-scanned photograph still a photograph?*) and questions related to fulfillment of conditions (*Does a good photocopy of a photograph achieve the same effect as the photograph itself?*).

Definitions by Example

Resembling operational definitions are **definitions by example**, which define a class by listing its individual members. Such definitions can be helpful when it is easier to illustrate or show what related people or

An app like Discovr Music defines musical styles by example when it connects specific artists or groups to others who make similar sounds.
Discovr Music 2012

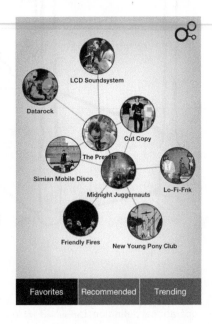

things have in common than to explain each one in precise detail. For example, one might define the broad category of *tablets* by listing the major examples of these products or define *heirloom tomatoes* by recalling all those available at the local farmers' market.

Arguments of this sort may focus on who or what may be included in a list that defines a category — *classic movies, worst natural disasters, groundbreaking painters*. Such arguments often involve comparisons and contrasts with the items that most readers would agree belong in this list. One could ask why Washington, D.C., is denied the status of a state: how does it differ from the fifty recognized American states? Or one might wonder why the status of planet is denied to asteroids, when both planets and asteroids are bodies that orbit the sun. A comparison between planets and asteroids might suggest that size is one essential feature of the eight recognized planets that asteroids don't meet. (In 2006, in a famous exercise in definitional argument, astronomers decided to deny poor Pluto its planetary classification.)

Developing a Definitional Argument

Definitional arguments don't just appear out of the blue; they often evolve out of daily life. You might get into an argument over the definition of *ordinary wear and tear* when you return a rental car with some soiled upholstery. Or you might be asked to write a job description for a new position to be created in your office: you have to define the job position in a way that doesn't step on anyone else's turf. Or maybe employees on your campus object to being defined as *temporary workers* when they've held their same jobs for years. Or someone derides one of your best friends as *just a nerd*. In a dozen ways every day, you encounter situations that are questions of definition. They're so frequent and indispensable that you barely notice them for what they are.

Formulating Claims

In addressing a question of definition, you'll likely formulate a *tentative claim* — a declarative statement that represents your first response to such situations. Note that such initial claims usually don't follow a single definitional formula.

Claims of Definition

A person paid to do public service is not a *volunteer*.

Institutional racism can exist—maybe even thrive—in the absence of overt civil rights violations.

Political bias has been consistently practiced by the mainstream media.

Theatergoers shouldn't confuse *musicals* with *operas*.

White lies are hard to define but easy to recognize.

None of the statements listed here could stand on its own because it likely reflects a first impression and gut reaction. But that's fine because making a claim of definition is typically a starting point, a cocky moment that doesn't last much beyond the first serious rebuttal or challenge. Statements like these aren't arguments until they're attached to reasons, data, warrants, and evidence (see Chapter 7).

Finding good reasons to support a claim of definition usually requires formulating a general definition by which to explore the subject. To be persuasive, the definition must be broad and not tailored to the specific controversy:

A volunteer is . . .

Institutional racism is . . .

Political bias is . . .

A musical is . . . but an opera is . . .

A white lie is . . .

Now consider how the following claims might be expanded with a general definition to become full-fledged definitional arguments:

Arguments of Definition

Someone paid to do public service is not a volunteer because volunteers are people who . . .

Institutional racism can exist even in the absence of overt violations of civil rights because, by definition, institutional racism is . . .

Political bias in the media is evident when . . .

Musicals focus on words first while operas . . .

The most important element of a white lie is its destructive nature; the act of telling one hurts both the receiver and the sender.

Notice, too, that some of the issues can involve comparisons between things—such as operas and musicals.

Crafting Definitions

Imagine that you decide to tackle the concept of *paid volunteer* in the following way:

> Participants in the federal AmeriCorps program are not really volunteers because they receive "education awards" for their public service. Volunteers are people who work for a cause without receiving compensation.

In Toulmin terms, as explained in Chapter 7, the argument looks like this:

Claim	Participants in AmeriCorps aren't volunteers . . .
Reason	. . . because they are paid for their service.
Warrant	People who are compensated for their services are, ordinarily, employees.

As you can see, the definition of *volunteers* will be crucial to the shape of the argument. In fact, you might think you've settled the matter with this tight little formulation. But now it's time to listen to the readers over your shoulder (again, see Chapter 7), who are pushing you further. Do the terms of your definition account for all pertinent cases of volunteerism—in particular, any related to the types of public service AmeriCorps members might be involved in? What do you do with unpaid interns: how do they affect your definition of *volunteers*? Consider, too, the word *cause* in your original claim of the definition:

> Volunteers are people who work for a cause without receiving compensation.

Cause has political connotations that you may or may not intend. You'd better clarify what you mean by *cause* when you discuss its definition in your paper. Might a phrase such as *the public good* be a more comprehensive or appropriate substitute for *a cause*? And then there's the matter of *compensation* in the second half of your definition:

> Volunteers are people who work for a cause without receiving compensation.

Aren't people who volunteer to serve on boards, committees, and commissions sometimes paid, especially for their expenses? What about members of the so-called all-volunteer military? They're financially compensated during their years of service, and they enjoy benefits after they complete their tours of duty.

As you can see, you can't just offer up a definition as part of an argument and expect that readers will accept it. Every part of a definition has to be interrogated, critiqued, and defended. So investigate your subject in the library, on the Internet, and in conversation with others, including experts if you can. You might then be able to present your definition in a single paragraph, or you may have to spend several pages coming to terms with the complexity of the core issue.

After conducting research of this kind, you'll be in a better position to write an extended definition that explains to your readers what you believe makes a volunteer a volunteer, how to identify institutional racism, or how to distinguish between a musical and an opera.

Matching Claims to Definitions

Once you've formulated a definition that readers will accept — a demanding task in itself — you might need to look at your particular subject to see if it fits your general definition. It should provide evidence of one of the following:

- It is a clear example of the class defined.
- It clearly falls outside the defined class.
- It falls between two closely related classes or fulfills some conditions of the defined class but not others.
- It defies existing classes and categories and requires an entirely new definition.

How do you make this key move in an argument? Here's an example from an article by Anthony Tommasini entitled "Opera? Musical? Please Respect the Difference." Early in the piece, Tommasini argues that a key element separates the two musical forms:

> Both genres seek to combine words and music in dynamic, felicitous and, to invoke that all-purpose term, artistic ways. But in opera, music is the driving force; in musical theater, words come first.

His claim of definition (or of difference) makes sense because it clarifies aspects of the two genres.

> This explains why for centuries opera-goers have revered works written in languages they do not speak. . . . As long as you basically know

what is going on and what is more or less being said, you can be swept away by a great opera, not just by music, but by visceral drama.

In contrast, imagine if the exhilarating production of Cole Porter's *Anything Goes* now on Broadway . . . were to play in Japan without any kind of titling technology. The wit of the musical is embedded in its lyrics. . . .

But even after having found a distinction so perceptive, Tommasini (like most writers making arguments of definition) still has to acknowledge exceptions.

Theatergoing audiences may not care much whether a show is a musical or an opera. But the best achievements in each genre . . . have been from composers and writers who grounded themselves in a tradition, *even while reaching across the divide.* [emphasis added]

If evidence you've gathered while developing an argument of definition suggests that similar limitations may be necessary, don't hesitate to modify your claim. It's amazing how often seemingly cut-and-dried matters of definition become blurry—and open to compromise and accommodation—as you learn more about them. That has proved to be the case as various campuses across the country have tried to define *hate speech* or *internship*—tricky matters. And even the Supreme Court has never said exactly what *pornography* is. Just when matters seem to be settled, new legal twists develop. Should virtual child pornography created with software be illegal, as is the real thing? Or is a virtual image—even a lewd one—an artistic expression that is protected (as other works of art are) by the First Amendment?

Considering Design and Visuals

In thinking about how to present your argument of definition, you may find a simple visual helpful, such as the Venn diagram on page 198 from Wikimedia Commons that defines *sustainability* as the place where our society and its economy intersect with the environment. Such a visual might even suggest a structure for an oral presentation.

Remember too that visuals like photographs, charts, and graphs can also help you make your case. Such items might demonstrate that the conditions for a definition have been met—as the widely circulated and horrific photographs from Abu Ghraib prison in Iraq helped to define *torture*. Or you might create a graphic yourself to illustrate a concept you are defining, perhaps through comparison and contrast.

Finally, don't forget that basic design elements—such as boldface and italics, headings, or links in online text—can contribute to (or detract from) the credibility and persuasiveness of your argument of definition. (See Chapter 14 for more on "Visual Rhetoric.")

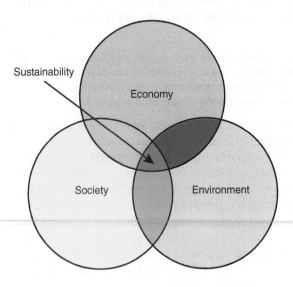

GUIDE to writing an argument of definition

● Finding a Topic

You're entering an argument of definition when you:

- formulate a controversial or provocative definition: *The American Dream, which once meant a McMansion in a gated community, now has taken on a new definition.*

- challenge a definition: *For most Americans today, the American Dream involves not luxury but the secure pensions, cheap energy costs, and health insurance that workers in the 1950s and 1960s supposedly enjoyed.*

- try to determine whether something fits an existing definition: *Expanding opportunity is (or is not) central to the American Dream.*

- seek to broaden an existing definition or create a new definition to accommodate wider or differing perspectives: *In a world where information is easily and freely shared, it may be time to explore alternative understandings of the American Dream.*

Look for issues of definition in your everyday affairs—for instance, in the way that jobs are classified at work, that key terms are used in your academic major, that politicians characterize social issues that concern you, and so on. Be especially alert to definitional arguments that may arise when you or others deploy adjectives such as *true, real, actual,* or *genuine: a true patriot, real reform, authentic Mexican food.*

● Researching Your Topic

You can research issues of definition by using the following sources:

- college dictionaries and encyclopedias
- unabridged dictionaries
- specialized reference works and handbooks, such as legal and medical dictionaries
- your textbooks (check their glossaries)
- newsgroups and blogs that focus on particular topics, especially political ones
- community or advocacy groups that are engaged in legal or social issues
- social media postings by experts you respect

Browse in your library reference room and use the electronic indexes and databases to determine how often disputed or contentious terms or phrases occur in influential online newspapers, journals, and Web sites.

When dealing with definitions, ask librarians about the most appropriate and reliable sources. For instance, to find the definition of a legal term, *Black's Law Dictionary* or a database such as FindLaw may help. Check USA.gov for how the government defines terms.

● Formulating a Claim

After exploring your subject, try to formulate a thesis that lets readers know where you stand or what issues are at stake. Begin with the following types of questions:

- questions related to genus: *Is assisting in suicide a crime?*

- questions related to species: *Is marijuana a harmful addictive drug or a useful medical treatment?*

- questions related to conditions: *Must the imposition of sexual attention be both unwanted and unsolicited to be considered sexual harassment?*

- questions related to fulfillment of conditions: *Has our college kept in place traditions or policies that might constitute racial discrimination?*

- questions related to membership in a named class: *Can a story put together out of thirty-one retweets be called a novel, or even a short story?*

If you start with a thesis, it should be a complete statement that makes a claim of definition and states the reasons supporting it. You may later decide to separate the claim from its supporting reasons. But a working thesis should be a fully articulated thought that spells out all the details and qualifications: *Who? What? Where? When? How many? How regularly? How completely?*

However, since arguments of definition are often exploratory and tentative, an initial thesis (if you have one) may simply describe problems in formulating a particular definition: *What we mean by X is likely to remain unsettled until we can agree more fully about Y and Z; The key to understanding what constitutes X may lie in appreciating how different groups approach Y and Z.*

● Examples of Definitional Claims

- Assisting a gravely ill person in committing suicide should not be considered *murder* when the motive for the act is to ease a person's suffering and not to benefit from the death.

- Although somewhat addictive, marijuana should not be classified as a *dangerous drug* because it damages individuals and society less than heroin or cocaine and because it helps people with life-threatening diseases live more comfortably.

- Giving college admission preference to all racial minorities can be an example of *class discrimination* because such policies may favor middle- and upper-class students who are already advantaged.

- Attempts to define the concept of *freedom* need to take into account the way the term is historically understood in cultures worldwide, not just in the countries of Western Europe and North America.

● Preparing a Proposal

If your instructor asks you to prepare a proposal for your project, here's a format that may help:

State your thesis or hypothesis completely. If you're having trouble doing so, try outlining it in Toulmin terms:

Claim:

Reason(s):

Warrant(s):

Alternatively, you might describe the complications of a definitional issue you hope to explore in your project, with the thesis perhaps coming later.

- Explain why this argument of definition deserves attention. What's at stake? Why is it important for your readers to consider?

- Identify whom you hope to reach through your argument and why these readers would be interested in it. How might you involve them in the paper?

- Briefly discuss the key challenges that you anticipate in preparing your argument.

- Determine what sources you expect to consult: Web? Databases? Dictionaries? Encyclopedias? Periodicals?

- Determine what visuals to include in your definitional argument.

● Considering Format and Media

Your instructor may specify that you use a particular format and/or medium. If not, ask yourself these questions to help you make a good choice:

- What format is most appropriate for your argument of definition? Does it call for an academic essay, a report, an infographic, a brochure, or something else?

- What medium is most appropriate for your argument? Would it be best delivered orally to a live audience? Presented as an audio essay or podcast? Presented in print only or in print with illustrations?

- Will you need visuals, such as moving or still images, maps, graphs, charts—and what function will they play in your argument? Make sure they are not just "added on" but are necessary components of the argument.

● Thinking about Organization

Your argument of definition is likely to include some of the following parts:

- a claim involving a question of definition
- a general definition of some key concept
- a careful look at your subject in terms of that general definition
- evidence for every part of the argument, including visual evidence if appropriate
- a careful consideration of alternative views and counterarguments
- a conclusion drawing out the implications of the argument

It's impossible, however, to predict what emphasis each of those parts might receive or what the ultimate shape of an argument of definition will be. Try to account for the ways people with different points of view will likely respond to your argument. Then, consider how to address such differences civilly in the body of your argument.

● Getting and Giving Response: Questions for Peer Response

Your instructor may assign you to a group for the purpose of reading and responding to each other's drafts. If not, ask for responses from serious readers or consultants at a writing center. Use the following questions to evaluate a colleague's draft. Be sure to illustrate your comments with examples; specific comments help more than general observations.

The Claim

- Is the claim clearly an issue of definition?
- Is the claim significant enough to interest readers?
- Are clear and specific criteria established for the concept being defined? Do the criteria define the term adequately? Using this definition, could most readers identify what's being defined and distinguish it from other related concepts?

Evidence for the Claim

- Is enough evidence furnished to explain or support the definition? If not, what kind of additional evidence is needed?
- Is the evidence in support of the claim simply announced, or are its significance and appropriateness analyzed? Is a more detailed discussion needed?
- Are all the conditions of the definition met in the concept being examined?
- Are any objections readers might have to the claim, criteria, evidence, or way the definition is formulated adequately addressed? Have you represented other points of view completely and fairly?
- What kinds of sources are cited? How credible and persuasive will they be to readers? What other kinds of sources might work better?
- Are all quotations introduced with appropriate signal phrases (such as "As Tyson argues, . . .") and blended smoothly into the writer's sentences?
- Are all visual sources labeled, introduced, and commented upon?

Organization and Style

- How are the parts of the argument organized? Is this organization effective?

- Will readers understand the relationships among the claims, supporting reasons, warrants, and evidence? If not, how might those connections be clearer? Is the function of every visual clear? Are more transitions needed? Would headings or graphic devices help?

- Are the transitions or links from point to point, sentence to sentence, and paragraph to paragraph clear and effective? If not, how could they be improved?

- Are all visuals (or other elements such as audio or video clips) carefully integrated into the text? Is each visual introduced and commented on to point out its significance? Is each visual labeled as a figure or a table and given a caption as well as a citation?

- Is the style suited to the subject? Is it too formal, casual, or technical? Can it be improved?

- Which sentences seem effective? Which ones seem weaker, and how could they be improved? Should short sentences be combined, and any longer ones be broken up?

- How effective are the paragraphs? Too short or too long? How can they be improved?

- Which words or phrases seem effective? Do any seem vague or inappropriate for the audience or the writer's purpose? Are technical or unfamiliar terms defined?

Spelling, Punctuation, Mechanics, Documentation, and Format

- Are there any errors in spelling, punctuation, capitalization, and the like?

- Is the documentation appropriate and consistent? (See Chapter 22.)

- Does the paper or project follow an appropriate format? Is it appropriately designed and attractively presented?

PROJECTS •

1. Write an argument of definition about a term such as *military combatants* or *illegal alien* that has suddenly become culturally significant or recently changed in some important way. Either defend the way the term has come to be defined or raise questions about its appropriateness, offensiveness, inaccuracy, and so on. Consider words or expressions such as *terrorism, marriage equality, racist, assisted suicide, enhanced interrogation, tea partier, collateral damage, forcible rape, net neutrality,* etc.

2. Write an essay in which you compare or contrast the meaning of two related terms, explaining the differences between them by using one or more methods of definition: formal definition, operational definition, definition by example. Be clever in your choice of the initial terms: look for a pairing in which the differences might not be immediately apparent to people unfamiliar with how the terms are used in specific communities. Consider terms such as *liberal/progressive, classy/cool, lead soprano/prima donna, student athlete/jock, highbrow /intellectual,* and so on.

3. In an essay at the end of this chapter, Natasha Rodriguez explores the adjective *underprivileged,* trying to understand why this label bothers her so much. She concludes that needing financial aid should not be conflated with being disadvantaged. After reading this selection carefully, respond to Rodriguez's argument in an argument of definition of your own. Or, alternatively, explore a concept similar to "underprivileged" with the same intensity that Rodriguez brings to her project. Look for a term to define and analyze either from your major or from an area of interest to you.

4. Because arguments of definition can have such important consequences, it helps to develop one by first getting input from lots of "stakeholders," that is, from people or groups likely to be affected by any change in the way a term is defined. Working with a small group, identify a term in your school or wider community that might need a fresh formulation or a close review. It could be a familiar campus word or phrase such as *nontraditional student, diversity, scholastic dishonesty,* or *social justice;* or it may be a term that has newly entered the local environment, perhaps reflecting an issue of law enforcement, safety, transportation, health, or even entertainment. Once you have settled on a significant term, identify a full range of stakeholders. Then, through some systematic field research (interviews, questionnaires) or by examining existing documents and materials (such as library sources, Web sites, pamphlets, publications), try to understand how the term currently functions in your community. Your definitional argument will, in effect, be what you can learn about the meanings that word or phrase has today for a wide variety of people.

Who Are You Calling Underprivileged?

NATASHA RODRIGUEZ

Courtesy of
Natasha Rodriguez

I have come to loathe the word "underprivileged." When I filled out my college applications, I checked off the Latino/Hispanic box whenever I was asked to give my ethnicity. My parents in turn indicated their income, hoping that we would qualify for financial aid. But while I waited for acceptances and rejections, several colleges I was considering sent me material that made me feel worthless rather than excited about attending those institutions.

The first mailing I received was a brochure that featured a photograph of African-American, Asian, and Latino teens standing around in a cluster, their faces full of laughter and joy. The title of the brochure was "Help for Underprivileged Students." At first I was confused: "Underprivileged" was not a word that I associated with myself. But there was the handout, with my name printed boldly on the surface.

The author questions the connotations of underprivileged.

The text went on to inform me that, since I was a student who had experienced an underprivileged life, I could qualify for several kinds of financial aid and scholarships. While I appreciated the intent, I was turned off by that one word—"underprivileged."

I had never been called that before. The word made me question how I saw myself in the world. Yes, I needed financial aid, and I had received generous scholarships to help me attend a private high school on the Upper East Side of New York. Surely that didn't mean that I had

Natasha Rodriguez is a student at Sarah Lawrence College, where she edits the features section of her school newspaper, the *Phoenix*.

lived a less-privileged life than others. My upbringing had been very happy.

What does "underprivileged" actually mean? According to most dictionaries, the word refers to a person who does not enjoy the same standard of living or rights as a majority of people in a society. I don't fit that definition. Even though my family does not have a lot of money, we have always had enough to get by, and I have received an excellent education.

The author then gives a standard definition for *underprivileged* and explains why she refuses the label.

What angered me most about the label was why colleges would ever use such a term. Who wants to be called underprivileged? I'm sure that even those who have had no opportunities would not want their social status rubbed in their faces so blatantly. People should be referred to as underprivileged only if they're the ones who are calling themselves that.

Misfortune, like beauty, is in the eye of the beholder. It's not appropriate to slap labels on people that they might not like or even agree with. Social research has found that those who are negatively labeled usually have lower self-esteem than others who are not labeled in that way. So why does the label of "underprivileged" persist?

Most colleges brag about the diversity of their students. But I don't want to be bragged about if my ethnicity is automatically associated with "underprivileged." Several colleges that had not even received information on my parents' finances just assumed that I was underprivileged because I had checked "Latino/Hispanic" on their applications.

The author examines the assumptions colleges make based on ethnicity and income.

That kind of labeling has to stop. Brochures and handouts could be titled "Help for Students in Need" rather than "Help for Underprivileged Students." I am sure that many people, myself included, are more than willing to admit that they require financial aid, and would feel fine about a college that referred to them as a student in need.

The essay concludes with the author's own self-definition.

That's a definition I can agree with. I am a student in need; I'm just not an underprivileged one.

Friending: The Changing Definition of Friendship in the Social Media Era

JOYCE XINRAN LIU

March 6, 2014

In just two months, I boosted my LinkedIn connections from 300 to almost 500. I was proud of winning the numbers game. However, recently when I was trying to request an informational interview via LinkedIn, I was depressed that less than 5% actually responded to me. I think I know most of them, but I actually don't. Or they don't think so. Maybe this is social media's fault. It creates the illusion of intimacy and closeness that doesn't actually exist. Maybe I should blame myself. I rushed to think of my social media connections as true friends that I could rely on.

I forgot the rules of friendship. Social media is a new platform for communication that expands and accelerates the way we connect and engage people, but the old rules of thumb for building relationships are still there. To understand what makes a friend a "friend" in social media, we'd better step back and think about the chemistry needed in true friendship (sans social media).

To make a true friend, we first need to get to know the person well, such that we understand what she likes and dislikes, what experiences have made her who she is today, and what her values are in life. Yet knowing someone does not guarantee a lasting friendship. For example, some people know their boss pretty well, yet they may not define their boss as a friend. In addition to knowing each other well, building friendships takes time; it's necessary for both sides to have some investment in the relationship.

Now let's get back to the world of social media and reconsider the process of making friends. Facebook, Twitter, LinkedIn, and many other social

Joyce Xinran Liu is a graduate in Integrated Marketing Communications at Northwestern University's Medill School. She posted this piece on a blog called *Vitamin IMC*, a site developed by the graduate students in the program to "educate marketers, potential students and companies about integrated marketing communications—what it is, how it's applied and how it builds profit within organizations."

media platforms have provided tons of personal information—both ongoing and historical—about people we want to know. For example, we can gain insights into someone's social life and interests through Facebook, get up-to-the-minute status updates from Twitter, and read someone's full professional experience on LinkedIn. A five-minute search on a social media platform can make us feel that we are old friends of the person we want to make friends with. But this is only one side of the story since the person we are searching into may not feel the same way as we do. This is often the case. A one-way connection without reciprocal engagement can never be thought of as a friendship, even on social media.

When acquaintances share their joys, complaints or even private information on social media, does it mean that they deem all of these online connections as real friends? Probably not. But why share their private information then? My argument is that they sacrifice their privacy in exchange for intimacy. Some people may want to make more friends, attract more attention, or even enhance self-esteem with the inflated intimacy they receive from friends, acquaintances and mere strangers on social media. These shared social media updates make people feel close, but it doesn't always mean they are close.

It's not social media's fault that it helps us develop a wide net of connections, yet still leaves us wanting more. We've created the myth of building strong relationships via social media. It's possible to build friendship online, but more often we need to integrate online engagement with offline interaction. Overall, social media has changed ways people interact with each other, but it has not affected the rooted norms and socialization process of making friends either online or offline. And it's time to adjust our expectations for building relationships in this new media space.

10
Evaluations

Left to right: Mario Tama/Getty Images; Jonah Willihnganz, The Stanford Storytelling Project; Hulton Archive/Getty Images

"We don't want to go there for coffee. Their beans aren't fair trade, the drinks are high in calories, and the stuff is *way* overpriced."

The campus storytelling project has just won a competition sponsored by NPR, and everyone involved is thrilled. Then they realize that this year all but one of the leaders of this project will graduate and that they have very few new recruits. So they put their heads together to figure out what qualities they need in new recruits that will help maintain the excellence of their project.

Orson Welles's masterpiece *Citizen Kane* is playing at the Student Union for only one more night, but the new *Captain America* is featured across the street in 3-D. Guess which movie your roomie wants to see? You intend to set her straight.

Understanding Evaluations

Evaluations are everyday arguments. By the time you leave home in the morning, you've likely made a dozen informal evaluations: You've selected dressy clothes because you have a job interview with a law firm. You've chosen low-fat yogurt and fruit over the pancakes you really love. You've queued up the perfect playlist on your iPhone for your hike to campus. In each case, you've applied criteria to a particular problem and then made a decision. That's evaluating on the fly.

Some professional evaluations require more elaborate standards, evidence, and paperwork (imagine an aircraft manufacturer certifying a new jet for passenger service), but they don't differ structurally from the simpler choices that people make all the time. People love to voice their opinions, and they always have. In fact, a mode of ancient rhetoric—called the *ceremonial* or *epideictic* (see Chapter 1)—was devoted entirely to speeches of praise and blame.

Today, rituals of praise and blame are a significant part of American life. Adults who would choke at the notion of debating causal or definitional claims will happily spend hours appraising the Oakland Raiders, Boston Red Sox, or Tampa Bay Rays. Other evaluative spectacles in our culture include awards shows, beauty pageants, most-valuable-player presentations, lists of best-dressed or worst-dressed celebrities, "sexiest people" magazine covers, literary prizes, political opinion polls, consumer product magazines, and—the ultimate formal public gesture of evaluation—elections. Indeed, making evaluations is a form of entertainment in America and generates big audiences (think of *The Voice*) and revenues.

Arguments about sports are usually evaluations of some kind. Cal Sport Media via AP Images

RESPOND •

The last ten years have seen a proliferation of "reality" talent shows—
Dancing with the Stars, So You Think You Can Dance, American (or *Canadian* or
Australian or many other) *Idol, America's Got Talent, The Voice,* and so on.
Write a short opinion piece assessing the merits of a particular "talent"
show. What should a proper event of this kind accomplish? Does the event
you're reviewing do so?

Criteria of Evaluation

Arguments of evaluation can produce simple rankings and winners or
can lead to profound decisions about our lives, but they always involve
standards. The particular standards we establish for judging
anything—whether an idea, a work of art, a person, or a product—are
called **criteria of evaluation.** Sometimes criteria are self-evident: a car
that gets fifteen miles per gallon is a gas hog, and a piece of fish that
smells even a little off shouldn't be eaten. But criteria get complicated
when a subject is abstract: *What features make a song a classic? What constitutes a fair wage? How do we measure a successful foreign policy or college
career?* Struggling to identify such difficult criteria of evaluation can lead
to important insights into your values, motives, and preferences.

Why make such a big deal about criteria when many acts of evaluation seem effortless? We should be suspicious of our judgments especially when we make them casually. It's irresponsible simply to think
that spontaneous and uninformed quips should carry the same weight
as well-informed and well-reasoned opinions. Serious evaluations
always require reflection, and when we look deeply into our judgments,
we sometimes discover important questions that typically go unasked,
many prefaced by *why*:

- You challenge the grade you received in a course, but you don't question the practice of grading.

- You argue passionately that a Republican Congress is better for America than a Democratic alternative, but you fail to ask why voters get
  only two choices.

- You argue that buying a hybrid car makes more sense than keeping
  an SUV, but you don't ask whether taking alternative forms of transportation (like the bus or a bike) makes the most sense of all.

Push an argument of evaluation hard enough and even simple judgments become challenging and intriguing.

In fact, for many writers, grappling with criteria is the toughest step in producing an evaluation. When you offer an opinion about a topic you know reasonably well, you want readers to learn something from your judgment. So you need time to think about and then justify the criteria for your opinion, whatever the subject.

Do you think, for instance, that you could explain what (if anything) makes a veggie burger good? Though many people have eaten veggie burgers, they probably haven't spent much time thinking about them. But it wouldn't be enough to claim merely that a proper one should be juicy or tasty—such trite claims are not even interesting. The following criteria offered on the *Cook's Illustrated* Web site show what happens when experts give the issue a closer look:

> We wanted to create veggie burgers that even meat eaters would love. We didn't want them to taste like hamburgers, but we did want them to act like hamburgers, *having a modicum of chew, a harmonious blend of savory ingredients, and the ability to go from grill to bun without falling apart.* [emphasis added]
>
> —*Cook's Illustrated*

After a lot of experimenting, *Cook's Illustrated* came up with a recipe that met these criteria.

What criteria of evaluation are embedded in this visual argument? © Ildi Papp/age fotostock

Criteria of evaluation aren't static, either. They differ according to time and audience. Much market research, for example, is designed to find out what particular consumers want now and may want in the future—what their criteria are for buying a product. In good times, people may demand homes with soaring entryways, lots of space, and premium appliances. In tougher times, they may care more about efficient use of space, quality insulation, and energy-efficient stoves and dishwashers. Shifts in values, attitudes, and criteria happen all the time.

RESPOND•

Choose one item from the following list that you understand well enough to evaluate. Develop several criteria of evaluation that you could defend to distinguish excellence from mediocrity in the area. Then choose an item that you don't know much about and explain the research you might do to discover reasonable criteria of evaluation for it.

smartwatches	U.S. vice presidents
NFL quarterbacks	organic vegetables
social networking sites	all-electric cars
TV journalists	spoken word poetry
video games	athletic shoes
graphic narratives	country music bands
Navajo rugs	sci-fi films

Characterizing Evaluation

One way of understanding evaluative arguments is to consider the types of evidence they use. A distinction explored in Chapter 4 between hard evidence and constructed arguments based on reason is helpful here: we defined **hard evidence** as facts, statistics, testimony, and other kinds of arguments that can be measured, recorded, or even found—the so-called smoking gun in a criminal investigation. We defined constructed arguments based on reason as those that are shaped by language and various kinds of logic.

We can talk about arguments of evaluation the same way, looking at some as quantitative and others as qualitative. **Quantitative arguments** of evaluation rely on criteria that can be measured, counted, or demonstrated in some mechanical fashion (something is taller, faster, smoother, quieter, or more powerful than something else). In contrast, **qualitative arguments** rely on criteria that must be explained through language and media, relying on such matters as values, traditions, and emotions (something is more ethical, more beneficial, more handsome, or more noble than something else). A claim of evaluation might be supported by arguments of both sorts.

Quantitative Evaluations

At first glance, quantitative evaluations seem to hold all the cards, especially in a society as enamored of science and technology as our own is. Making judgments should be easy if all it involves is measuring and counting—and in some cases, that's the way things work out. *Who's the tallest or heaviest or loudest person in your class?* If your classmates allow themselves to be measured, you could find out easily enough, using the right equipment and internationally sanctioned standards of measurement—the meter, the kilo, or the decibel.

But what if you were to ask, *Who's the smartest person in class?* You could answer this more complex question quantitatively, using IQ tests or college entrance examinations that report results numerically. In fact, almost all college-bound students in the United States submit to this kind of evaluation, taking either the SAT or the ACT to demonstrate their verbal and mathematical prowess. Such measures are widely accepted by educators and institutions, but they are also vigorously challenged. What do they actually measure? They predict likely academic success only in college, which is one kind of intelligence.

Quantitative measures of evaluation can be enormously useful, but even the most objective measures have limits. They've been devised by fallible people who look at the world from their own inevitably limited perspectives.

Qualitative Evaluations

Many issues of evaluation that are closest to people's hearts aren't subject to quantification. *What makes a movie great?* If you suggested a quantitative measure like length, your friends would probably hoot, "Get serious!" But what about box-office receipts, adjusted for inflation? Would films that made the most money—an easily quantifiable measure—be the "best pictures"? That select group would include movies such as *Star Wars*, *The Sound of Music*, *Gone with the Wind*, *Titanic*, *Avatar*, and *E.T.* An interesting group of films—but the best?

To define the criteria for "great movie," you'd more likely look for the standards and evidence that serious critics explore in their arguments, abstract or complicated issues such as their societal impact, cinematic technique, dramatic structures, intelligent casting, and so on. Most of these markers of quality could be defined and identified with some precision but not measured or counted. You'd also have to make your case rhetorically, convincing the audience to accept the markers of quality you are offering and yet appreciating that they might not. A movie reviewer making qualitative judgments might spend as much time defending criteria of evaluation as providing evidence that these standards are present in a particular film. But putting those standards into action can be what makes a review something worth reading. Consider how Roger Ebert, in writing about *Toy Story*, the first all-computer-made feature film, teaches his readers how to find evidence of quality in a great movie:

> **Toy Story** creates a universe out of a couple of kids' bedrooms, a gas station, and a stretch of suburban highway. Its heroes are toys, which come to life when nobody is watching. Its conflict is between an

Web sites such as Netflix and Rotten Tomatoes offer recommendations for films based on users' past selections and the ratings of other users and critics. Sometimes those judgments are at odds. Then whom do you trust? © Denis ALLARD/REA/Redux

old-fashioned cowboy who has always been a little boy's favorite toy, and the new space ranger who may replace him. The villain is the mean kid next door who takes toys apart and puts them back together again in macabre combinations. And the result is a visionary roller-coaster ride of a movie.

For the kids in the audience, a movie like this will work because it tells a fun story, contains a lot of humor, and is exciting to watch. Older viewers may be even more absorbed, because *Toy Story*, the first feature made entirely by computer, achieves a three-dimensional reality and freedom of movement that is liberating and new. The more you know about how the movie was made, the more you respect it.

RESPOND●

For examples of powerful evaluation arguments, search the Web or your library for eulogies or obituaries of famous, recently deceased individuals. Try to locate at least one such item, and then analyze the types of claims it makes about the accomplishments of the deceased. What types of criteria of evaluation hold the obituary or eulogy together? Why should we respect or admire the person?

Developing an Evaluative Argument

Developing an argument of evaluation can seem like a simple process, especially if you already know what your claim is likely to be. To continue the movie theme for one more example:

Citizen Kane is the finest film ever made by an American director.

Having established a claim, you would then explore the implications of your belief, drawing out the reasons, warrants, and evidence that might support it:

Claim	*Citizen Kane* is the finest film ever made by an American director . . .
Reason	. . . because it revolutionizes the way we see the world.
Warrant	Great films change viewers in fundamental ways.
Evidence	Shot after shot, *Citizen Kane* presents the life of its protagonist through cinematic images that viewers can never forget.

The warrant here is, in effect, an implied statement of criteria—in this case, the quality that defines "great film" for the writer. It may be important for the writer to share that assumption with readers and perhaps to identify other great films that similarly make viewers appreciate new perspectives.

As you can see, in developing an evaluative argument, you'll want to pay special attention to criteria, claims, and evidence.

Formulating Criteria

Although even casual evaluations (*The band sucks!*) might be traced to reasonable criteria, most people don't defend their positions until they are challenged (*Oh yeah?*). Similarly, writers who address readers with whom they share core values rarely discuss their criteria in great detail. A film critic like the late Roger Ebert (see p. 216) isn't expected to restate all his principles every time he writes a movie review. Ebert assumes that his readers will—over time—come to appreciate his standards. Still, criteria can make or break a piece.

So spend time developing your criteria of evaluation. What exactly makes a shortstop an all-star? Why is a standardized test an unreliable measure of intelligence? Fundamentally, what distinguishes an inspired rapper from a run-of-the-mill one? List the possibilities and then pare them down to the essentials. If you offer vague, dull, or unsupportable principles, expect to be challenged.

You're most likely to be vague about your beliefs when you haven't thought (or read) enough about your subject. Push yourself at least as far as you imagine readers will. Anticipate readers looking over your shoulder, asking difficult questions. Say, for example, that you intend to argue that anyone who wants to stay on the cutting edge of personal technology will obviously want Apple's latest iPad because it does so many amazing things. But what does that mean exactly? What makes the device "amazing"? Is it that it gives access to email and the Web, has a high-resolution screen, offers an astonishing number of apps, and makes a good e-reader? These are particular features of the device. But can you identify a more fundamental quality to explain the product's appeal, such as an iPad user's experience, enjoyment, or feeling of productivity? You'll often want to raise your evaluation to a higher level of generality like this so that your appraisal of a product, book, performance, or political figure works as a coherent argument, and not just as a list of random observations.

Be certain, too, that your criteria of evaluation apply to more than just your topic of the moment. Your standards should make sense on their own merits and apply across the board. If you tailor your criteria to get the outcome you want, you are doing what is called "special pleading." You might be pleased when you prove that the home team is awesome, but it won't take skeptics long to figure out how you've cooked the books.

RESPOND ●

Local news and entertainment magazines often publish "best of" issues or articles that catalog their readers' and editors' favorites in such categories as "best place to go on a first date," "best ice cream sundae," and "best dentist." Sometimes the categories are specific: "best places to say 'I was retro before retro was cool'" or "best movie theater seats." Imagine that you're the editor of your own local magazine and that you want to put out a "best of" issue tailored to your hometown. Develop ten categories for evaluation. For each category, list the evaluative criteria that you would use to make your judgment. Next, consider that because your criteria are warrants, they're especially tied to audience. (The criteria for "best dentist," for example, might be tailored to people whose major concern is avoiding pain, to those whose children will be regular patients, or to those who want the cheapest possible dental care.) For several of the evaluative categories, imagine that you have to justify your judgments to a completely different audience. Write a new set of criteria for that audience.

Making Claims

In evaluations, claims can be stated directly or, more rarely, strongly implied. For most writers, strong statements followed by reasonable qualifications work best. Consider the differences between the following three claims and how much greater the burden of proof is for the first claim:

Jessica Williams is the funniest "correspondent" ever on *The Daily Show.*

Jessica Williams has emerged as one of the funniest of *The Daily Show*'s "correspondents."

Jessica Williams may come to be regarded as one of the funniest and most successful of the "correspondents" on *The Daily Show.*

The funniest of all? Jessica Williams reporting on *The Daily Show.*

Here's a second set of examples demonstrating the same principle, that qualifications generally make a claim of evaluation easier to deal with and smarter:

> The Common Core Standards movement sure is a dumb idea.

> The Common Core Standards movement in educational reform is likely to do more harm than good.

> While laudable in their intentions to raise standards and improve student learning, the Common Core Standards adopted throughout the United States continue to put so high a premium on testing that they may well undermine the goals they seek to achieve.

The point of qualifying a statement isn't to make evaluative claims bland but to make them responsible and reasonable. Consider how Reagan Tankersley uses the criticisms of a musical genre he enjoys to frame a claim he makes in its defense:

> Structurally, dubstep is a simple musical form, with formulaic progressions and beats, something that gives a musically tuned ear little to grasp or analyze. For this reason, a majority of traditionally trained musicians find the genre to be a waste of time. These people have a legitimate position. . . . However, I hold that it is the simplicity of dubstep that makes it special: the primal nature of the song is what digs so deeply into fans. It accesses the most primitive area in our brains that connects to the uniquely human love of music.
> —Reagan Tankersley, "Dubstep: Why People Dance"

Tankersley doesn't pretend that dubstep is something it's not, nor does he expect his argument to win over traditionally minded critics. Yet he still makes a claim worth considering.

Dubstep DJs Benga, Artwork, and Skream of
Magnetic Man perform. Chiaki Nozu/Wire Image/
Getty Images

One tip: Nothing adds more depth to an opinion than letting others
challenge it. When you can, use the resources of the Internet or local
discussion boards to get responses to your opinions or topic proposals. It
can be eye-opening to realize how strongly people react to ideas or
points of view that you regard as perfectly normal. Share your claim and
then, when you're ready, your first draft with friends and classmates,
asking them to identify places where your ideas need additional support, either in the discussion of criteria or in the presentation of
evidence.

Presenting Evidence

Generally, the more evidence in an evaluation the better, provided that
the evidence is relevant. For example, in evaluating the performance of
two laptops, the speed of their processors would be essential; the quality
of their keyboards or the availability of service might be less crucial yet
still worth mentioning. But you have to decide how much detail your
readers want in your argument. For technical subjects, you might make
your basic case briefly and then attach additional supporting documents
at the end—tables, graphs, charts—for those who want more data.

Just as important as relevance in selecting evidence is presentation.
Not all pieces of evidence are equally convincing, nor should they
be treated as such. Select evidence that is most likely to influence
your readers, and then arrange the argument to build toward your

best material. In most cases, that best material will be evidence that's specific, detailed, memorable, and derived from credible sources. The details in these paragraphs from Sean Wilsey's review of *Fun Home: A Family Tragicomic*, a graphic novel by Alison Bechdel, tell you precisely what makes the work "lush," "absorbing," and well worth reading:

> It is a pioneering work, pushing two genres (comics and memoir) in multiple new directions, with panels that combine the detail and technical proficiency of R. Crumb with a seriousness, emotional complexity, and innovation completely its own. Then there are the actual words. Generally this is where graphic narratives stumble. Very few cartoonists can also write—or, if they can, they manage only to hit a few familiar notes. But *Fun Home* quietly succeeds in telling a story, not only through well-crafted images but through words that are equally revealing and well chosen. Big words, too! In 232 pages this memoir sent me to the dictionary five separate times (to look up "bargeboard," "buss," "scutwork," "humectant," and "perseverated").
>
> A comic book for lovers of words! Bechdel's rich language and precise images combine to create a lush piece of work—a memoir where concision and detail are melded for maximum, obsessive density. She has obviously spent years getting this memoir right, and it shows. You can read *Fun Home* in a sitting, or get lost in the pictures within the pictures on its pages. The artist's work is so absorbing you feel you are living in her world.
>
> —Sean Wilsey, "The Things They Buried"

The details in this passage make the case that Alison Bechdel's novel is one that pushes both comics and memoirs in new directions.

In evaluation arguments, don't be afraid to concede a point when evidence goes contrary to the overall claim you wish to make. If you're really skillful, you can even turn a problem into an argumentative asset, as Bob Costas does in acknowledging the flaws of baseball great Mickey Mantle in the process of praising him:

> None of us, Mickey included, would want to be held to account for every moment of our lives. But how many of us could say that our best moments were as magnificent as his?
>
> —Bob Costas, "Eulogy for Mickey Mantle"

RESPOND.

Take a close look at the cover of Alison Bechdel's graphic novel *Fun Home: A Family Tragicomic*. In what various ways does it make an argument of evaluation designed to make you want to read the work? Examine other books, magazines, or media packages (such as video game or software boxes) and describe any strategies they use to argue for their merit.

Fun Home: A Family Tragicomic by Alison Bechdel. Cover illustration © 2007 by Alison Bechdel. Reprinted by permission of Houghton Mifflin Harcourt Publishing Company. All rights reserved.

Considering Design and Visuals

Visual components play a significant role in many arguments of evaluation, especially those based on quantitative information. As soon as numbers are involved in supporting a claim, think about ways to arrange them in tables, charts, graphs, or infographics to make the information more accessible to readers. Visual elements are especially helpful when comparing items. Indeed, a visual spread like the one in the federal government's comparison of electric and hybrid cars (see p. 224) becomes an argument in itself about the vehicles the government has analyzed for fuel economy. The facts seem to speak for themselves because they are presented with care and deliberation. In the same way, you will want to make sure that you use similar care when using visuals to inform and persuade readers.

But don't ignore other basic design features of a text—such as headings for the different criteria you're using or, in online evaluations, links to material related to your subject.

Compare Side-by-Side

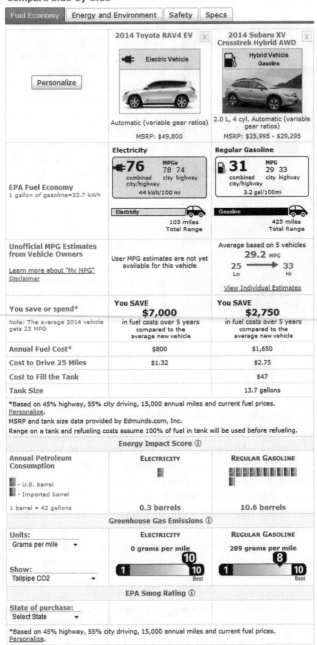

	2014 Toyota RAV4 EV ⊠	2014 Subaru XV Crosstrek Hybrid AWD ⊠
Personalize	Electric Vehicle	Hybrid Vehicle Gasoline
	Automatic (variable gear ratios) MSRP: $49,800	2.0 L, 4 cyl, Automatic (variable gear ratios) MSRP: $25,995 - $29,295
EPA Fuel Economy 1 gallon of gasoline=33.7 kWh	**Electricity** **76** MPGe 78 74 combined city highway city/highway 44 kWh/100 mi	**Regular Gasoline** **31** MPG 29 33 combined city highway city/highway 3.2 gal/100mi
	Electricity 103 miles Total Range	Gasoline 425 miles Total Range
Unofficial MPG Estimates from Vehicle Owners Learn more about "My MPG" Disclaimer	User MPG estimates are not yet available for this vehicle	Average based on 5 vehicles **29.2** MPG 25 → 33 Lo Hi View Individual Estimates
You save or spend* Note: The average 2014 vehicle gets 23 MPG	**You SAVE** **$7,000** in fuel costs over 5 years compared to the average new vehicle	**You SAVE** **$2,750** in fuel costs over 5 years compared to the average new vehicle
Annual Fuel Cost*	$800	$1,650
Cost to Drive 25 Miles	$1.32	$2.75
Cost to Fill the Tank		$47
Tank Size		13.7 gallons

*Based on 45% highway, 55% city driving, 15,000 annual miles and current fuel prices. Personalize.
MSRP and tank size data provided by Edmunds.com, Inc.
Range on a tank and refueling costs assume 100% of fuel in tank will be used before refueling.

Energy Impact Score ⓘ		
Annual Petroleum Consumption ▮ - U.S. barrel ▮ - Imported barrel 1 barrel = 42 gallons	ELECTRICITY 0.3 barrels	REGULAR GASOLINE 10.6 barrels
Greenhouse Gas Emissions ⓘ		
Units: Grams per mile ▾ **Show:** Tailpipe CO2 ▾	ELECTRICITY 0 grams per mile **10** 1 — 10 Best	REGULAR GASOLINE 289 grams per mile **8** 1 — 10 Best
EPA Smog Rating ⓘ		
State of purchase: Select State ▾		

*Based on 45% highway, 55% city driving, 15,000 annual miles and current fuel prices. Personalize.

U.S. Department of Energy

GUIDE to writing an evaluation

● Finding a Topic

You're entering an argument of evaluation when you:

- make a judgment about quality: Citizen Kane *is probably the finest film ever made by an American director.*

- challenge such a judgment: Citizen Kane *is vastly overrated by most film critics.*

- construct a ranking or comparison: Citizen Kane *is a more intellectually challenging movie than* Casablanca.

- explore criteria that might be used in making evaluative judgments: *Criteria for judging films are evolving as the production and audiences of films become ever more international.*

Issues of evaluation crop up everywhere—in the judgments you make about public figures or policies; in the choices you make about instructors and courses; in the recommendations you offer about books, films, or television programs; in the preferences you exercise in choosing products, activities, or charities. Evaluations typically use terms that indicate value or rank—*good/ bad, effective/ineffective, best/worst, competent/incompetent, successful/unsuccessful.* When you can choose a topic for an evaluation, consider writing about something on which others regularly ask your opinion or advice.

● Researching Your Topic

You can research issues of evaluation by using the following sources:

- journals, reviews, and magazines (for current political and social issues)
- books (for assessing judgments about history, policy, etc.)
- biographies (for assessing people)
- research reports and scientific studies
- books, magazines, and Web sites for consumers
- periodicals and Web sites that cover entertainment and sports
- blogs and social media sites that explore current topics

Surveys and polls can be useful in uncovering public attitudes: *What kinds of movies are young people seeing today? Who are the most admired people in the country? What activities or businesses are thriving or waning?* You'll discover that Web sites, newsgroups, and blogs thrive on evaluation. (Ever receive an invitation to "like" something on social media?) Browse these public forums for ideas, and, when possible, explore your own topic ideas there. But remember that all sources need to be evaluated themselves; examine each source carefully, making sure that it is legitimate and credible.

● Formulating a Claim

After exploring your subject, try to draw up a full and specific claim that lets readers know where you stand and on what criteria you'll base your judgments. Come up with a thesis that's challenging enough to attract readers' attention. In developing a thesis, you might begin with questions like these:

- What exactly is my opinion? Where do I stand?
- Can I make my judgment more clear-cut?
- Do I need to narrow or qualify my claim?
- By what standards will I make my judgment?
- Will readers accept my criteria, or will I have to defend them, too? What criteria might others offer?
- What evidence or major reasons can I offer in support of my evaluation?

For a conventional evaluation, your thesis should be a complete statement. In one sentence, make a claim of evaluation and state the reasons that support it. Be sure your claim is specific. Anticipate the questions readers might have: *Who? What? Where? Under what conditions? With what exceptions? In all cases?* Don't expect readers to guess where you stand.

For a more exploratory argument, you might begin (and even end) with questions about the process of evaluation itself. *What are the qualities we seek—or ought to—in our political leaders? What does it say about our cultural values when we find so many viewers entertained by so-called reality shows on television? What might be the criteria for collegiate athletic programs consistent with the values of higher education?* Projects that explore topics like these might not begin with straightforward theses or have the intention to persuade readers.

Examples of Evaluative Claims

- Though they may never receive Oscars for their work, Tom Cruise and Keanu Reeves deserve credit as actors who have succeeded in a wider range of film roles than most of their contemporaries.

- People are returning to cities because they find life there more civilized than in the suburbs.

- Lena Dunham's writing and acting on *Girls* is the most honest presentation of the lives of twentysomething women today.

- Jimmy Carter has been highly praised for his work as a former president of the United States, but history may show that even his much-derided term in office laid the groundwork for the foreign policy and economic successes now attributed to later administrations.

- Young adults today are shying away from diving into the housing market because they no longer believe that homeownership is a key element in economic success.

Preparing a Proposal

If your instructor asks you to prepare a proposal for your project, here's a format that may help:

State your thesis completely. If you're having trouble doing so, try outlining it in Toulmin terms:

Claim:

Reason(s):

Warrant(s):

Alternatively, you might describe your intention to explore a particular question of evaluation in your project, with the thesis perhaps coming later.

- Explain why this issue deserves attention. What's at stake?

- Identify whom you hope to reach through your argument and why these readers would be interested in it.

- Briefly discuss the key challenges you anticipate in preparing your argument.

- Determine what research strategies you'll use. What sources do you expect to consult?

● Considering Format and Media

Your instructor may specify that you use a particular format and/or medium. If not, ask yourself these questions to help you make a good choice:

- What format is most appropriate for your argument of evaluation? Does it call for an academic essay, a report, an infographic, a brochure, or something else?

- What medium is most appropriate for your argument? Would it be best delivered orally to a live audience? Presented as an audio essay or podcast? Presented in print only or in print with illustrations?

- Will you need visuals, such as moving or still images, maps, graphs, charts—and what function will they play in your argument? Make sure they are not just "added on" but are necessary components of the argument.

● Thinking about Organization

Your evaluation will likely include elements such as the following:

- an evaluative claim that makes a judgment about a person, idea, or object
- the criterion or criteria by which you'll measure your subject
- an explanation or justification of the criteria (if necessary)
- evidence that the particular subject meets or falls short of the stated criteria
- consideration of alternative views and counterarguments

All these elements may be present in arguments of evaluation, but they won't follow a specific order. In addition, you'll often need an opening paragraph to explain what you're evaluating and why. Tell readers why they should care about your subject and take your opinion seriously.

● Getting and Giving Response: Questions for Peer Response

Your instructor may assign you to a group for the purpose of reading and responding to each other's drafts. If not, ask for responses from serious readers or consultants at a writing center. Use the following questions to evaluate a colleague's draft. Be sure to illustrate your comments with examples; specific comments help more than general observations.

The Claim

- Is the claim an argument of evaluation? Does it make a judgment about something?

- Does the claim establish clearly what's being evaluated?

- Is the claim too sweeping? Does it need to be qualified?

- Will the criteria used in the evaluation be clear to readers? Do the criteria need to be defined more precisely?

- Are the criteria appropriate ones to use for this evaluation? Are they controversial? Should they be defended?

Evidence for the Claim

- Is enough evidence provided to show that what's being evaluated meets the established criteria? If not, what additional evidence is needed?

- Is the evidence in support of the claim simply announced, or are its significance and appropriateness analyzed? Is more detailed discussion needed?

- Are any objections readers might have to the claim, criteria, or evidence adequately addressed?

- What kinds of sources are cited? How credible and persuasive will they be to readers? What other kinds of sources might work better?

- Are all quotations introduced with appropriate signal phrases (such as "As Tyson argues, . . .") and blended smoothly into the writer's sentences?

- Are all visual sources labeled, introduced, and commented upon?

Organization and Style

- How are the parts of the argument organized? Is this organization effective?

- Will readers understand the relationships among the claims, supporting reasons, warrants, and evidence? If not, how might those connections be clearer? Is the function of every visual clear? Are more transitions needed? Would headings or graphic devices help?

- Are the transitions or links from point to point, sentence to sentence, and paragraph to paragraph clear and effective? If not, how could they be improved?

- Are all visuals carefully integrated into the text? Is each visual introduced and commented on to point out its significance? Is each visual labeled as a figure or a table and given a caption as well as a citation?
- Is the style suited to the subject? Is it too formal, casual, or technical? Can it be improved?
- Which sentences seem effective? Which ones seem weaker, and how could they be improved? Should short sentences be combined, and any longer ones be broken up?
- How effective are the paragraphs? Too short or too long? How can they be improved?
- Which words or phrases seem effective? Do any seem vague or inappropriate for the audience or the writer's purpose? Are technical or unfamiliar terms defined?

Spelling, Punctuation, Mechanics, Documentation, and Format

- Are there any errors in spelling, punctuation, capitalization, and the like?
- Is the documentation appropriate and consistent? (See Chapter 22.)
- Does the paper or project follow an appropriate format? Is it appropriately designed and attractively presented?

PROJECTS •

1. What kinds of reviews or evaluations do you consult most often or read regularly—those of TV shows, sports teams, video games, fashions, fishing gear, political figures? Try composing an argument of evaluation in your favorite genre: make and defend a claim about the quality of some object, item, work, or person within your area of interest or special knowledge. Let the paper demonstrate an expertise you have gained by your reading. If it helps, model your evaluation upon the work of a reviewer or expert you particularly respect.

2. Prepare a project in which you challenge what you regard as a wrongheaded evaluation, providing sound reasons and solid evidence for challenging this existing and perhaps commonly held view. Maybe you believe that a classic novel you had to read in high school is overrated or that people who criticize video games really don't understand them. Explain why the topic of your evaluation needs to be reconsidered and provide reasons, evidence, and, if necessary, different criteria of evaluation for doing so. For an example of this type of evaluation, see Sean Kamperman's "The Wikipedia Game" on pp. 232–36.

3. Write an evaluation in which you compare or assess the contributions or achievements of two or three notable people working within the same field or occupation. They may be educators, entrepreneurs, artists, legislators, editorial cartoonists, fashion designers, programmers, athletes—you name it. While your first instinct might be to rank these individuals and pick a "winner," this evaluation will work just as well if you can help readers appreciate the different paths by which your subjects have achieved distinction.

4. Within this chapter, the authors claim that criteria of evaluation can change depending on times and circumstances: "In good times, people may demand homes with soaring entryways, lots of space, and premium appliances. In tougher times, they may care more about efficient use of space, quality insulation, and energy-efficient stoves and dishwashers." Working in a group, discuss several scenarios of change and then explore how those circumstances could alter the way we evaluate particular objects, activities, or productions. For example, what impact might global warming have upon the way we determine desirable places to live or vacation? How might a continued economic downturn change the criteria by which we judge successful careers or good educational paths for our children? If people across the globe continue to put on weight, how might standards of personal beauty or fashion alter? If government institutions continue to fall in public esteem, how might we modify our expectations for elected officials? Following the discussion, write a paper or prepare a project in which you explore how one scenario for change might revise customary values and standards of evaluation.

The Wikipedia Game: Boring, Pointless, or Neither?

SEAN KAMPERMAN

When most people think about Wikipedia—the self-styled "free, Web-based, collaborative, multilingual encyclopedia project"—they are likely reminded of the preliminary research they did for that term paper on post-structuralism, or of the idle minutes they may've spent exploring an interesting topic just for the heck of it—the neuroanatomy of purple-striped jellyfish, for example, or *Jersey Shore*. First and foremost a layman's tool, Wikipedia has struggled to find legitimacy alongside more reputable reference sources such as *Encyclopaedia Britannica*, even in spite of the outstanding quality of many of its entries. But fortunately for the makers of the Free Encyclopedia—and for the rest of us—Wikipedia's usefulness goes far beyond its intended "encyclopedic" purpose. Under the right circumstances, it can be as much a source of entertainment as one of knowledge and self-improvement.

A prime example of this fact is a phenomenon identified as the Wikipedia game—or, as it's now known to users of Apple and Android smart phones, "WikiHunt." WikiHunt is a simple game whose rules draw upon the unique architectural features of wikis, in that players

Opening paragraph provides a context and a subtle evaluative thesis: "Wikipedia's usefulness goes far beyond its intended 'encyclopedic' purpose."

WikiHunt is introduced as a cultural phenomenon.

Sean Kamperman wrote "The Wikipedia Game: Boring, Pointless, or Neither?" in spring 2010 for a lower-division course on rhetoric and media at the University of Texas at Austin. In his topic proposal he briefly described Wikipedia games familiar to many students and then indicated what he intended to explore: "A lot of scholars have been very critical of Wikipedia—some going so far as to discourage its use altogether, even for the purpose of gathering background info. Does the fact that games like these use Wikipedia detract from their educational value? Or do the games in some way rebut these criticisms, demonstrating that the practical uses of user-generated online encyclopedias go beyond traditional research and, by extension, considerations of factual correctness?" His paper is the answer to those questions.

perform "moves" by following the links that connect one Wikipedia entry to another. Driven by cultural conditions of dilettantism and the spurts of creativity that tend to come on in times of extreme boredom, dozens if not hundreds of Wikipedia users in high school computer labs, college dormitories, and professional workspaces around the globe have "discovered" the game on their own. Some have even gone so far as to claim sole proprietorship—as in the case of two of my friends, who swear they invented the game while sitting through a lecture on academic dishonesty. Questions of original authorship aside, the Wikipedia game would appear to be a bona fide grassroots phenomenon—and one well worth examining if we consider its possible implications for learning and education.

If you've never played the Wikipedia game, it's fun—educational—and, for the most part, free; indeed, all you'll need is one or more friends, two computers, and an Internet connection. To begin, navigate to the Wikipedia homepage and click the "Random article" link on the left-hand side of the screen. As advertised, this link will lead you and your friend to two randomly generated Wikipedia articles. The objective from here is to get from your article to your opponent's using nothing but links to other articles. These links, which appear within the text of the articles themselves, are bits of hypertext denoted in blue; click on any of them, and you'll be instantly transported to another article and another set of links. Depending on which version of the rules you're going by, either the player who finishes first or the one who gets to his or her opponent's page using the fewest number of links is the winner. Easy, right?

Not exactly. What makes the Wikipedia game hard—and coincidentally, what makes it so much fun—is the vastness of the Web site's encyclopedic content. Click the "Random article" button enough times, and you'll see a pattern emerge: the majority of articles that pop up are short ones covering extremely obscure topics, usually having to do with something related to European club soccer. Entries such as these, labeled "orphans" for their relative

Understanding that not every reader will know WikiHunt, Kamperman offers a detailed explanation.

The paper returns to its thesis when it notes how unexpectedly hard WikiHunt is.

paucity of length and links, in fact comprise the majority of Wikipedia articles. So the chances of you or your opponent hitting the randomly-generated-article jackpot and getting a "Jesus" or an "Adolf Hitler"—two pages with tons of links—are pretty slim. Rather, the task at hand usually requires that players navigate from orphan to orphan, as was the case in a game I played just last night with my friends David and Paige. They were unlucky enough to pull up an article on the summer village of Whispering Hills, Alberta, and I was no less unfortunate to get one on "blocking," an old 3D computer animation technique that makes characters and objects look like they're moving. Between these two pages, we were supplied with a total of nineteen links—they had nine doors to choose from, whereas I had ten. That's not a lot to work with. As you can probably surmise, games like this one take more than a few idle minutes—not to mention a heck of a lot of brainpower and spontaneous strategizing.

Kamperman uses his own experience to show precisely how WikiHunt tracks users' processes of thought and "knowledge sets."

Indeed, what makes the Wikipedia game interesting is that it welcomes comparison between the players' respective strategies and methods for getting from point A to point B, highlighting differences between their thought processes and respective knowledge sets. To elaborate using the aforementioned example, I initially knew nothing about either Whispering Hills, Alberta, or "Blocking (animation)." What I did know, however, was that in order to get to Canada, I'd have to go through the good old U.S. of A. So I clicked a link at the bottom of the page entitled "Categories: animation techniques," and from there looked for a well-known technique that I knew to be associated with an American software company. Selecting "Power-Point animation," I was led from there to the article on Microsoft—which, thanks to the company's late '90s monopolistic indiscretions, furnished me with a link to the U.S. Department of Justice. Five clicks later and I was in Alberta, looking for a passageway to Whispering Hills, one of the province's smallest, obscurest villages. I finally found it in a series of lists on communities in Alberta—but not before my opponents beat me to the punch and got to my page on "blocking" first. David, a computer science major, had taken a different approach to clinch the win; rather than drawing upon his knowledge of a macroscopic, big-picture subject like geography, he skipped from the article on Canada to a page entitled "Canadian industrial research and development organizations," from which he quickly bored through twelve articles on various topics in the computer sciences before falling on "Blocking (animation)." In his case, specialized knowledge was the key to winning.

But did David and Paige really win? Perhaps—but in the wide world of the Wikipedia game, there are few hard-and-fast rules to go by. Whereas my opponents got to their destination quicker than I, my carefully planned journey down the funnel from big ("United States") to small ("List of summer villages in Alberta") got me to Whispering Hills using two fewer links than they. So in this example, one sees not a clear-cut lesson on how to win the game, but rather a study in contrasting styles. A player can rely on specialized knowledge, linking quickly to familiar domains and narrowing the possibilities from there; or, she/he may choose to take a slower, more methodical approach, employing abstract, top-down reasoning skills to systematically sift through broader categories of information. Ultimately, victory is possible in either case.

Its more casual, entertaining uses aside, Wikipedia gets a bad rap, especially in the classroom. Too many college professors and high school English teachers have simply written it off, some even going so far as to expressly forbid their students from using it while at school. These stances and attitudes are understandable. Teaching students how to find good sources and properly credit them is hard enough without the competing influence of the Wikipedia community, whose definition of an acceptably accurate source seems to extend not only to professionally or academically vetted articles, but to blogs as well, some obviously plagiarized. But to deny Wikipedia a place in the classroom is to deny both students and teachers alike the valuable experience of playing a game that shows us not only what we know, but how we know—how our brains work when posed with the everyday challenge of having to connect ostensibly unrelated pieces of information, and furthermore, how they work differently in that respect.

Knowledge building is a connective or associative process, as the minds behind Wikipedia well know. A casual perusal of any Wikipedia article reveals reams and reams of blue hypertext—bits of text that, when set in isolation, roughly correspond to discrete categories of information about the world. In a sense, the visual rhetoric of Wikipedia invokes the verbal rhetoric of exploration, prompting intrepid Web-using truth seekers to go sailing through a bright blue sea of information that is exciting by virtue of its seeming limitlessness. It should comfort teachers to know that, in quickly navigating through linked knowledge categories to reach their respective destinations, Wikipedia gamers aren't relying too much on their understanding of the articles themselves; rather, what they're relying on is their ability to understand relationships.

The fact that so many people have independently found the fun at the heart of Wikipedia should be a heads-up. The Wikipedia game is a grassroots technological innovation that sheds new light on what it means to know—and, perhaps more importantly, one that reminds us that, yes, learning can be fun. It isn't too hard to imagine versions of the game that could be played by kids in school, and how teachers could then use the game to learn more about the stuff of their trade—namely, learning and how it works. So the next time you hear a friend, teacher, or coworker dismiss the Free Encyclopedia as "unreliable" or "unacademic," do knowledge a favor and challenge them to the following:

"Villa of Livia" to "List of Montreal Expos
    broadcasters" . . .

. . . no click-backs . . .

. . . twenty links or less.

Go.

My Awkward Week with Google Glass

HAYLEY TSUKAYAMA

The Washington
Post/Getty Images

April 29, 2014

It's a Wednesday night, and I'm turning heads on the sidewalk. People are slowing halfway down the block as I approach. They're whispering about me as I walk through the room. Strangers are watching me, sometimes even stopping me on the street.

Why? Because I'm wearing Google Glass. And I hate it.

I shouldn't feel this way. I like new technology—I've been a tech reporter at the *Washington Post* for more than three years. And I admire the vision of technology that Google promises Glass can offer: a device that lets you keep track of e-mails, texts and other messages in a seamless way—all through a screen that's perched just over your right eye.

Headed into a week with Glass, on loan from a co-worker, I was prepared to review a buggy product. Glass, after all, is still in testing, and has only been released to developers, media and just a handful of "normal" people who were willing to spend $1,500 on an untested product. I expected tension headaches from constantly trying to focus on a floating screen above my line of vision. (I got only one headache, for what it's worth.) I even prepared myself to be comfortable talking aloud to the product in public because you can control Glass through voice commands.

What I wasn't prepared for was the attention I got. Sporting Glass put me among only a handful of people in Washington, and that meant getting a lot of looks. Most of it was good attention from curious people, but it still made me miserable. For wallflowers like me, wearing something that draws constant attention is more or less my personal idea of hell.

I've heard just about every privacy concern raised about Glass, but, as the one wearing the device, I wasn't expecting that the privacy most

---

Hayley Tsukayama covers consumer technology for the *Washington Post*.

invaded would be my own. That type of anxiety should lessen over time, particularly as Google works with designer labels such as Luxottica's Oakley and Ray-Ban to make prettier models. But anyone who opts to buy Glass should be ready and willing to become a constant topic of conversation and to answer questions from strangers. Wearing Google Glass in public is like wearing a sandwich-board that says "Talk to me!" And, given the rare but highly publicized fights, robberies and other major incidents some Glass users have experienced, I was a little wary about wearing the device in public.

In the name of fairness, though, I did wear them—nearly everywhere: to work, to the grocery store, out with friends, even to choir rehearsal. Here's a sample of what I heard (or overheard) from friends and strangers in the week I spent with Glass:

"Is she wearing Google Glass?" "Is that what I think that is?" "Are you recording, like, right now?" "You look ridiculous."

Or, my personal favorite, delivered deadpan, from a friend: "Oh, *Hayley*."

But beyond the personal privacy issues, I found that Google Glass is an intriguing device that has a lot of flaws. After more than two years in development, the number of remaining technical bugs is surprising.

On the hardware side, the problems ranged from the device becoming too warm—sometimes after just 10 minutes of use—to needing to be charged multiple times a day. The sensors on the device were far from perfect, and there were many times when I had to re-tap, re-swipe or (and maybe this was the worst part) jerk my head up repeatedly to wake up the device when it went dormant. I probably reset the device at least half a dozen times in the course of normal use because it wouldn't respond to my frantic taps, or refused to connect to my smartphone even when there were no other network problems.

Glass works better with Google's Android phones (in my case, an HTC One M8 on loan from HTC) than with the iPhone, if only because the integration between the Google systems is much smoother. As for software, developers have been smart about designing Glass apps to minimize the amount of data bombarding users. Big names such as Facebook, Twitter and CNN provide a strong app core for Glass. The CNN app, for example, will let you see headlines for top stories, or by subject, and serves headlines, photos and short video.

There are other apps that would be nice to have, however, particularly more photo apps to take advantage of the point-of-view vantage you get with the device.

The iPhone experience with Glass is improving. In fact, Google added a feature allowing Glass users to see iPhone text notifications during the week I wore the device. And some functions of Glass, such as the ability to project what a Glass user sees to a paired phone, were fantastic and useful in ways I didn't anticipate.

But though I tried, very hard, to make Glass a part of my life, I simply didn't feel comfortable with the screen hovering just out of my line of sight. I didn't get any direct challenges about filming others without their permission—not that I ever did film people without permission—but nearly every person who questioned me about Glass asked if I was filming.

What struck me most, however, was what happened when I let others try on the device, giving me a glimpse of how I appeared when I was wearing Glass: a conversation partner who was like a dinner guest who keeps looking at the door, as if to check if there's another person in the room they'd rather be talking to. Think of every person wearing earbuds or a Bluetooth headset who has annoyed you for the same reason. Now multiply it by a factor of 10.

All of which goes against what Glass is supposedly all about: the idea that you can avoid those awkward moments when you try to sneak a peek at your smartphone, which is always much more obvious than you think.

After a few earnest days of trying to make the thing work, I stopped trying to force the issue and used it as I would in real life—in situations when I needed to watch something hands-free, or when I wasn't required to actively engage with other people. In those cases, Glass worked as promised. It delivered updates to keep me informed without overwhelming me and acted as a useful second screen to my smartphone.

But that also meant that, more often than not, Glass ended up perched on the top of my head—the way you wear your sunglasses indoors—or discreetly tucked into my bag, in order to keep it from being the only subject of conversation.

Would I buy Google Glass? Not now, especially with that $1,500 price tag. The device has a lot of evolving to do before it's ready for the world. The world has some evolving to do before it's ready for Glass, too.

11
Causal Arguments

Left to right: c. byatt-norman/Shutterstock; Robyn Beck/AFP/Getty Images; AP Photo/Jeff Roberson

In spite of the fact that they have thrived for over fifty million years, around nine years ago colonies of bees started dying . . . and dying. Are pesticides the cause? Or perhaps it's the move agriculture has made from planting cover crops like alfalfa and clover that create natural fertilizers to using synthetic fertilizers that cater to crop monocultures but leave no food support for bees? Scientists believe a combination of these factors account for the current loss of bees.

Small business owners and big companies alike still seem reluctant to hire new employees. Is it because of complex government regulations, continuing uncertainties about health care costs, worries about debt, improvements in productivity—or all of the above? People needing jobs want to know.

Most state governments use high taxes to discourage the use of tobacco products. But when anti-smoking campaigns and graphic warning labels convince people to quit smoking, tax revenues decline, reducing support for health and education programs. Will raising taxes even higher restore that lost revenue?

Understanding Causal Arguments

Americans seem to be getting fatter, so fat in fact that we hear often about the "obesity crisis" in the United States. But what is behind this rise in weight? Rachel Berl, writing for *U.S. News and World Report*, points to unhealthy foods and a sedentary lifestyle:

> "There is no single, simple answer to explain the obesity patterns" in America, says Walter Willett, who chairs the department of nutrition at the Harvard School of Public Health. "Part of this is due to lower incomes and education, which result in purchases of cheap foods that are high in refined starch and sugar. More deeply, this also reflects lower public investment in education, public transportation, and recreational facilities," he says. The bottom line: cheap, unhealthy foods mixed with a sedentary lifestyle have made obesity the new normal in America. And that makes it even harder to change, Willett says.
>
> —Rachel Pomerance Berl

Many others agree that as processed fast food and other things such as colas have gotten more and more affordable, consumption of them has gone up, along with weight. But others offer different theories for the rise in obesity.

Whatever the reasons for our increased weight, the consequences can be measured by everything from the width of airliner seats to the rise of diabetes in the general population. Many explanations are offered

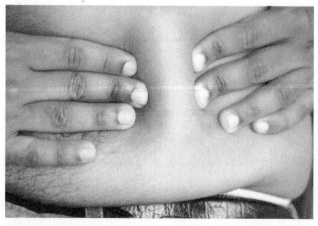

© Bartomeu Amengual/age fotostock

by scientists, social critics, and health gurus, and some are refuted. Figuring out what's going on is a national concern—and an important exercise in cause-and-effect argument.

Causal arguments—from the causes of poverty in rural communities to the consequences of ocean pollution around the globe—are at the heart of many major policy decisions, both national and international. But arguments about causes and effects also inform many choices that people make every day. Suppose that you need to petition for a grade change because you were unable to turn in a final project on time. You'd probably enumerate the reasons for your failure—the death of your cat, followed by an attack of the hives, followed by a crash of your computer—hoping that an associate dean reading the petition might see these explanations as tragic enough to change your grade. In identifying the causes of the situation, you're implicitly arguing that the effect (your failure to submit the project on time) should be considered in a new light. Unfortunately, the administrator might accuse you of faulty causality (see p. 80) and judge that failure to complete the project is due more to your procrastination than to the reasons you offer.

Causal arguments exist in many forms and frequently appear as part of other arguments (such as evaluations or proposals). It may help focus your work on causal arguments to separate them into three major categories:

Arguments that state a cause and then examine its effects

Arguments that state an effect and then trace the effect back to its causes

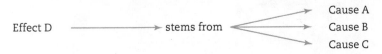

Arguments that move through a series of links: A causes B, which leads to C and perhaps to D

Cause A → leads to Cause B → leads to Cause C → leads to Effect D

Arguments That State a Cause and Then Examine Its Effects

What would happen if Congress suddenly came together and passed immigration reform that gave millions of people in the United States a legal pathway to citizenship? Before such legislation could be enacted, the possible effects of this "cause" would have to be examined in detail and argued intensely. Groups on various sides of this hot-button issue are actually doing so now, and the sides present very different scenarios. In this debate, you'd be successful if you could convincingly describe the consequences of such a change. Alternatively, you could challenge the causal explanations made by people you don't agree with. But speculation about causes and effects is always risky because life is complicated.

Consider the following passage from researcher Gail Tverberg's blog *Our Finite World*, from 2011, describing possible consequences of the commitment to increase the production of ethanol from corn:

> At the time the decision was made to expand corn ethanol production, we seemed to have an excess of arable land, and corn prices were low. Using some corn for ethanol looked like it would help farmers, and also help increase fuel for our vehicles. There was also a belief that cellulosic ethanol production might be right around the corner, and could substitute, so there would not be as much pressure on food supplies.
>
> Now the situation has changed. Food prices are much higher, and the number of people around the world with inadequate food supply

Paresh Nath, cartoonist for India's *National Herald*, personifies the causes for a world food crisis in this item from March 2011. © Paresh Nath, Cagle Cartoons, Inc.

is increasing. The ethanol we are using for our cars is much more in direct competition with the food people around the world are using, and the situation may very well get worse, if there are crop failures.

—Gail Tverberg, *Our Finite World*

Note that the researcher here begins by pointing out the cause-effect relationship that the government was hoping for and then points to the potential effects of that policy when circumstances change. As it turns out, using corn for fuel did have many unintended consequences, for example, inflating the price not only of corn but of wheat and soybeans as well, leading to food shortages and even food riots around the globe.

Arguments That State an Effect and Then Trace the Effect Back to Its Causes

This type of argument might begin with a specific effect (a catastrophic drop in sales of music CDs) and then trace it to its most likely causes (the introduction of MP3 technology, new modes of music distribution, a preference for single song purchases). Or you might examine the reasons that music executives offer for their industry's dip and decide whether their causal analyses pass muster.

Like other kinds of causal arguments, those tracing effects to a cause can have far-reaching significance. In 1962, for example, the scientist Rachel Carson seized the attention of millions with a famous causal argument about the effects that the overuse of chemical pesticides might have on the environment. Here's an excerpt from the beginning of her book-length study of this subject. Note how she begins with the effects before saying she'll go on to explore the causes:

[A] strange blight crept over the area and everything began to change. Some evil spell had settled on the community: mysterious maladies swept the flocks of chickens; the cattle and sheep sickened and died. Everywhere was a shadow of death. The farmers spoke of much illness among their families. . . . There had been several sudden and unexplained deaths, not only among adults but even among children, who would be stricken suddenly while at play and die within a few hours. The roadsides, once so attractive, were now lined with browned and withered vegetation as though swept by fire. These, too, were silent, deserted by all living things. Even the streams were now lifeless. Anglers no longer visited them, for all the fish had died.

In the gutters under the eaves and between the shingles of the roofs, a white granular powder still showed a few patches; some weeks before it had fallen like snow upon the roofs and lawns, the fields and streams. No witchcraft, no enemy action had silenced the rebirth of new life in this stricken world. The people had done it themselves. . . . What has silenced the voices of spring in countless towns in America? This book is an attempt to explain.

—Rachel Carson, *Silent Spring*

Today, one could easily write a causal argument of the first type about *Silent Spring* and the environmental movement that it spawned.

Arguments That Move through a Series of Links: A Causes B, Which Leads to C and Perhaps to D

In an environmental science class, for example, you might decide to argue that, despite reductions in acid rain, tightened national regulations regarding smokestack emissions from utility plants are still needed for the following reasons:

1. Emissions from utility plants in the Midwest still cause significant levels of acid rain in the eastern United States.
2. Acid rain threatens trees and other vegetation in eastern forests.
3. Powerful lobbyists have prevented midwestern states from passing strict laws to control emissions from these plants.
4. As a result, acid rain will destroy most eastern forests by 2030.

In this case, the first link is that emissions cause acid rain; the second, that acid rain causes destruction in eastern forests; and the third, that states have not acted to break the cause-and-effect relationship that is established by the first two points. These links set the scene for the fourth link, which ties the previous points together to argue from effect: unless X, then Y.

RESPOND •

The causes of some of the following events and phenomena are well known and frequently discussed. But do you understand these causes well enough to spell them out to someone else? Working in a group, see how well (and in how much detail) you can explain each of the following events or phenomena. Which explanations are relatively clear, and which seem more open to debate?

earthquakes/tsunamis

popularity of Lady Gaga or Taylor Swift or the band Wolf Alice

Cold War

Edward Snowden's leak of CIA documents

Ebola crisis in western Africa

popularity of the *Transformers* films

swelling caused by a bee sting

sharp rise in cases of autism or asthma

climate change

Characterizing Causal Arguments

Causal arguments tend to share several characteristics.

They Are Often Part of Other Arguments.

Many stand-alone causal arguments address questions that are fundamental to our well-being: *Why are juvenile asthma and diabetes increasing so dramatically in the United States? What are the causes of the rise in cases of malaria in Africa, and what can we do to counter this rise? What will happen to Europe if its birthrate continues to decline?*

But causal analyses often work to support other arguments — especially proposals. For example, a proposal to limit the time that children spend playing video games might first draw on a causal analysis to establish that playing video games can have bad results — such as violent behavior, short attention spans, and decreased social skills. The causal analysis provides a rationale that motivates the proposal. In this way, causal analyses can be useful in establishing good reasons for arguments in general.

They Are Almost Always Complex.

The complexity of most causal relationships makes it difficult to establish causes and effects. For example, in 2011 researchers at Northwestern University reported a startling correlation: youths who participated in church activities were far more likely to grow into obese adults than their counterparts who were not engaged in religious activities. How does one even begin to explain such a peculiar and unexpected finding? Too many church socials? Unhealthy food at potluck meals? More regular social engagement? Perhaps.

Or consider the complexity of analyzing the causes of food poisoning when they strike large populations: in 2008, investigators spent months trying to discover whether tomatoes, cilantro, or jalapeño peppers were the cause of a nationwide outbreak of salmonella. More than seventeen states were affected. But despite such challenges, whenever it is possible to demonstrate convincing causal connections between X and Y, we gain important knowledge and powerful arguments. That's why, for example, great effort went into establishing an indisputable link between smoking and lung cancer. Once proven, decisive legal action could finally be taken to warn smokers.

They Are Often Definition Based.

One reason that causal arguments are complex is that they often depend on careful definitions. Recent figures from the U.S. Department of Education, for example, show that the number of high school dropouts is rising and that this rise has caused an increase in youth unemployment. But exactly how does the study define *dropout*? A closer look may suggest that some students (perhaps a lot) who drop out later "drop back in" and complete high school or that some who drop out

"*The rise in unemployment, however, which was somewhat offset by an expanding job market, was countered by an upturn in part-time dropouts, which, in turn, was diminished by seasonal factors, the anticipated summer slump, and, over-all, a small but perceptible rise in actual employment.*"

Causal arguments can also be confusing. © Ed Arno/The New Yorker Collection/ The Cartoon Bank

become successful entrepreneurs or business owners. Further, how does the study define *employment*? Until you can provide definitions for all key terms in a causal claim, you should proceed cautiously with your argument.

They Usually Yield Probable Rather Than Absolute Conclusions.

Because causal relationships are almost always complex or subtle, they seldom can yield more than a high degree of probability. Consequently, they are almost always subject to criticism or open to charges of false causality. (We all know smokers who defy the odds to live long, cancer-free lives.) Scientists in particular are wary when making causal claims.

Even after an event, proving precisely what caused it can be hard. During the student riots of the late 1960s, for example, a commission was charged with determining the causes of riots on a particular campus. After two years of work and almost a thousand pages of evidence and reports, the commission was unable to pinpoint anything but a broad network of contributing causes and related conditions. And how many years is it likely to take to unravel all the factors responsible for the extended recession and economic decline in the United States that began in 2008? After all, serious scholars are still arguing about the forces responsible for the Great Depression of 1929.

To demonstrate that X caused Y, you must find the strongest possible evidence and subject it to the toughest scrutiny. But a causal argument doesn't fail just because you can't find a single compelling cause. In fact, causal arguments are often most effective when they help readers appreciate how tangled our lives and landscapes really are.

Developing Causal Arguments

Exploring Possible Claims

To begin creating a strong causal claim, try listing some of the effects—events or phenomena—that you'd like to know the causes of:

- Why do college tuition costs routinely outstrip the rate of inflation?
- What's really behind the slow pace of development of alternative energy sources?
- Why are almost all the mothers in animated movies either dead to begin with or quickly killed off?

- Why is same-sex marriage more acceptable to American society than it was a decade ago?
- Why do so few younger Americans vote, even in major elections?

Or try moving in the opposite direction, listing some phenomena or causes you're interested in and then hypothesizing what kinds of effects they may produce:

- How will the growing popularity of e-readers change our relationships to books?
- What will happen as the result of efforts to repeal the Affordable Health Care Act?
- What will be the consequences if more liberal (or conservative) judges are appointed to the U.S. Supreme Court?
- What will happen as China and India become dominant industrialized nations?

Read a little about the causal issues that interest you most, and then try them out on friends and colleagues. They might suggest ways to refocus or clarify what you want to do or offer leads to finding information about your subject. After some initial research, map out the causal relationship you want to explore in simple form:

X might cause (or might be caused by) Y for the following reasons:

1.

2.

3. (add more as needed)

Such a statement should be tentative because writing a causal argument should be an exercise in which you uncover facts, not assume them to be true. Often, your early assumptions (*Tuition was raised to renovate the stadium*) might be undermined by the facts you later discover (*Tuition doesn't fund the construction or maintenance of campus buildings*).

You might even decide to write a wildly exaggerated or parodic causal argument for humorous purposes. Humorist Dave Barry does this when he explains the causes of El Niño and other weather phenomena: "So we see that the true cause of bad weather, contrary to what they have been claiming all these years, is TV weather forecasters, who have also single-handedly destroyed the ozone layer via overuse of hair spray." Most of the causal reasoning you do, however, will take a serious approach to subjects that you, your family, and your friends care about.

RESPOND.

Working with a group, write a big *Why?* on a sheet of paper or computer screen, and then generate a list of *why* questions. Don't be too critical of the initial list:

Why

—*do people laugh?*

—*do swans mate for life?*

—*do college students binge drink?*

—*do teenagers drive fast?*

—*do babies cry?*

—*do politicians take risks on social media?*

Generate as lengthy a list as you can in fifteen minutes. Then decide which of the questions might make plausible starting points for intriguing causal arguments.

© Bill Coster/age fotostock

Defining the Causal Relationships

In developing a causal claim, you can examine the various types of causes and effects in play in a given argument and define their relationship. Begin by listing all the plausible causes or effects you need to consider. Then decide which are the most important for you to analyze or the easiest to defend or critique. The following chart on "Causes" may help you to appreciate some important terms and relationships.

Type of Causes	What It Is or Does	What It Looks Like
Sufficient cause	Enough for something to occur on its own	Lack of oxygen is sufficient to cause death Cheating on an exam is sufficient to fail a course
Necessary cause	Required for something to occur (but in combination with other factors)	Fuel is necessary for fire Capital is necessary for economic growth
Precipitating cause	Brings on a change	Protest march ignites a strike by workers Plane flies into strong thunderstorms
Proximate cause	Immediately present or visible cause of action	Strike causes company to declare bankruptcy Powerful wind shear causes plane to crash
Remote cause	Indirect or underlying explanation for action	Company was losing money on bad designs and inept manufacturing Wind shear warning failed to sound in cockpit
Reciprocal causes	One factor leads to a second, which reinforces the first, creating a cycle	Lack of good schools leads to poverty, which further weakens education, which leads to even fewer opportunities . . .

Even the most everyday causal analysis can draw on such distinctions among reasons and causes. What persuaded you, for instance, to choose the college you decided to attend? *Proximate* reasons might be the location of the school or the college's curriculum in your areas of interest. But what are the *necessary* reasons—the ones without which your choice of that college could not occur? Adequate financial support? Good test scores and academic record? The expectations of a parent?

Once you've identified a causal claim, you can draw out the reasons, warrants, and evidence that can support it most effectively:

Claim	Certain career patterns cause women to be paid less than men.
Reason	Women's career patterns differ from men's.
Warrant	Successful careers are made during the period between ages twenty-five and thirty-five.
Evidence	Women often drop out of or reduce work during the decade between ages twenty-five and thirty-five to raise families.

Claim	Lack of community and alumni support caused the football coach to lose his job.
Reason	Ticket sales and alumni support have declined for three seasons in a row despite a respectable team record.
Warrant	Winning over fans is as important as winning games for college coaches in smaller athletic programs.
Evidence	Over the last ten years, coaches at several programs have been sacked because of declining support and revenues.

RESPOND●

Here's a schematic causal analysis of one event, exploring the difference among precipitating, necessary, and sufficient causes. Critique and revise the analysis as you see fit. Then create another of your own, beginning with a different event, phenomenon, incident, fad, or effect.

Event: Traffic fatality at an intersection

Precipitating cause: A pickup truck that runs a red light, totals a Prius, and injures its driver

Necessary cause: Two drivers who are navigating Friday rush-hour traffic (if no driving, then no accident)

Sufficient cause: A truck driver who is distracted by a cell-phone conversation

Supporting Your Point

In drafting your causal argument, you'll want to do the following:

● Show that the causes and effects you've suggested are highly probable and backed by evidence, or show what's wrong with the faulty causal reasoning you may be critiquing.

● Assess any links between causal relationships (what leads to or follows from what).

● Show that your explanations of any causal chains are accurate, or identify where links in a causal chain break down.

● Show that plausible cause-and-effect explanations haven't been ignored or that the possibility of multiple causes or effects has been considered.

In other words, you will need to examine your subject carefully and find appropriate ways to support your claims. There are different ways to accomplish that goal.

For example, in studying effects that are physical (as they would be with diseases or climate conditions), you can offer and test *hypotheses*, or theories about possible causes. That means researching such topics thoroughly because you'll need to draw upon authorities and research articles for your explanations and evidence. (See Chapter 17, "Academic Arguments," and Chapter 18, "Finding Evidence.") Don't be surprised if you find yourself debating which among conflicting authorities make the most plausible causal or explanatory arguments. Your achievement as a writer may be simply that you present these differences in an essay, leaving it to readers to make judgments of their own—as John Tierney does in "Can a Playground Be Too Safe?" at the end of this chapter (see p. 268).

But not all the evidence in compelling causal arguments needs to be strictly scientific or scholarly. Many causal arguments rely on **ethnographic observations**—the systematic study of ordinary people in their daily routines. How would you explain, for example, why some people step aside when they encounter someone head-on and others do not? In an argument that attempts to account for such behavior, investigators Frank Willis, Joseph Gier, and David Smith observed "1,038 displacements involving 3,141 persons" at a Kansas City shopping mall. In results that surprised the investigators, "gallantry" seemed to play a significant role in causing people to step aside for one another—more so than other causes that the investigators had anticipated (such as deferring to someone who's physically stronger or higher in status). Doubtless you've read of other such studies, perhaps in psychology courses. You may even decide to do a little fieldwork on your own—which raises the possibility of using personal experiences in support of a causal argument.

Indeed, people's experiences generally lead them to draw causal conclusions about things they know well. Personal experience can also help build your credibility as a writer, gain the empathy of listeners, and thus support a causal claim. Although one person's experiences cannot ordinarily be universalized, they can still argue eloquently for causal relationships. Listen to Sara Barbour, a recent graduate of Columbia University, as she draws upon her own carefully described experiences to bemoan what may happen when e-readers finally displace printed books:

> In eliminating a book's physical existence, something crucial is lost forever. Trapped in a Kindle, the story remains but the book can no longer be scribbled in, hoarded, burned, given, or received. We may be

able to read it, but we can't share it with others in the same way, and its ability to connect us to people, places, and ideas is that much less powerful.

I know the Kindle will eventually carry the day—an electronic reader means no more embarrassing coffee stains, no more library holds and renewals, no more frantic flipping through pages for a lost quote, or going to three bookstores in one afternoon to track down an evasive title. Who am I to advocate the doom of millions of trees when the swipe of a finger can deliver all 838 pages of *Middlemarch* into my waiting hands?

But once we all power up our Kindles something will be gone, a kind of language. Books communicate with us as readers—but as important, we communicate with each other through books themselves. When that connection is lost, the experience of reading—and our lives—will be forever altered.

—Sara Barbour, "Kindle vs. Books: The Dead Trees Society,"
Los Angeles Times, June 17, 2011

All these strategies—testing hypotheses, presenting experimental evidence, and offering personal experience—can help you support a causal argument or undermine a causal claim you regard as faulty.

RESPOND ●

One of the fallacies of argument discussed in Chapter 5 is the *post hoc, ergo propter hoc* ("after this, therefore because of this") fallacy. Causal arguments are particularly prone to this kind of fallacious reasoning, in which a writer asserts a causal relationship between two entirely unconnected events. When Angelina Jolie gave birth to twins in 2008, for instance, the stock market rallied by nearly six hundred points, but it would be difficult to argue that either event is related to the other.

Because causal arguments can easily fall prey to this fallacy, you might find it instructive to create and defend an absurd connection of this kind. Begin by asserting a causal link between two events or phenomena that likely have no relationship: *The enormous popularity of* Doctor Who *is partially due to global warming.* Then spend a page or so spinning out an imaginative argument to defend the claim. It's OK to have fun with this exercise, but see how convincing you can be at generating plausibly implausible arguments.

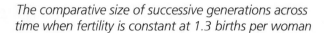

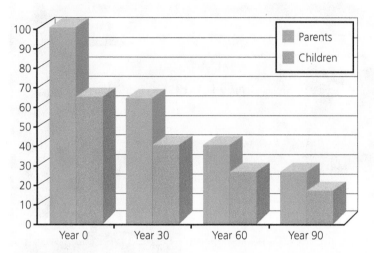

A simple graph can provide dramatic evidence for a causal claim—in this case, the effect of reduced fertility rates on a population. Data from Statistics Bureau, MIC; Ministry of Health, Labour and Welfare

Considering Design and Visuals

You may find that the best way to illustrate a causal relationship is to present it visually. Even a simple bar graph or chart can demonstrate a relationship between two variables that might be related to a specific cause, like the one above showing the dramatic effects of lowered birth-rates. The report that uses this figure explores the effects that such a change would have on the economies of the world.

Or you may decide that the most dramatic way to present important causal information about a single issue or problem is via an infographic, cartoon, or public service announcement. Our arresting example on the next page is part of a campaign by People for the Ethical Treatment of Animals (PETA). An organization that advocates for animal rights, PETA promotes campaigns that typically try to sway people to adopt vegetarian diets by depicting the practices of the agriculture industry as cruel.

PETA's ad campaign expands its focus to environmentalists by explaining through causal links why they should consider vegetarian diets. Courtesy of People for the Ethical Treatment of Animals; peta.org

(Many of us have also seen their celebrity anti-fur campaigns; see p. 100 for one example.) Their "Meat's Not Green!" campaign, however, attempts to reach an audience that might not buy into the animal rights argument. Instead, it appeals to people who have environmentalist beliefs by presenting data that claims a causal link between animal farming and environmental destruction. How much of this data surprises you?

GUIDE to writing a causal argument

● Finding a Topic

You're entering a causal argument when you:

- state a cause and then examine its effects: *The ongoing economic downturn has led more people to return to college to enhance their job market credentials.*

- describe an effect and trace it back to its causes: *There has been a recent surge in the hiring of part-time contract workers, likely due to the reluctance of businesses to hire permanent employees who would be subject to new health care regulations.*

- trace a string of causes to figure out why something happened: *The housing and financial markets collapsed in 2008 after government mandates to encourage homeownership led banks to invent questionable financial schemes in order to offer subprime mortgages to borrowers who bought homes they could not afford with loans they could not pay back.*

- explore plausible consequences (intended or not) of a particular action, policy, or change: *The ban on incandescent lightbulbs may draw more attention to climate change than any previous government action.*

Spend time brainstorming possibilities for causal arguments. Many public issues lend themselves to causal analysis and argument: browse the homepage of a newspaper or news source on any given day to discover plausible topics. Consider topics that grow from your own experiences.

It's fair game, too, to question the accuracy or adequacy of existing arguments about causality. You can write a strong paper by raising doubts about the facts or assumptions that others have made and perhaps offering a better causal explanation on your own.

● Researching Your Topic

Causal arguments will lead you to many different resources:

- current news media—especially magazines and newspapers (online or in print)

- online databases

- scholarly journals

- books written on your subject (here you can do a keyword search, either in your library or online)
- blogs, Web sites, or social networking sites

In addition, why not carry out some field research? Conduct interviews with appropriate authorities on your subject, create a questionnaire aimed at establishing a range of opinions on your subject, or arrange a discussion forum among people with a stake in the issue. The information you get from interviews, questionnaires, or open-ended dialogue might provide ideas to enrich your argument or evidence to back up your claims.

● Formulating a Claim

For a conventional causal analysis, try to formulate a claim that lets readers know where you stand on some issue involving causes and effects. First, identify the kind of causal argument that you expect to make (see pp. 241–45 for a review of these kinds of arguments) or decide whether you intend, instead, to debunk an existing cause-and-effect claim. Then explore your relationship to the claim. What do you know about the subject and its causes and effects? Why do you favor (or disagree with) the claim? What significant reasons can you offer in support of your position?

End this process by formulating a thesis—a complete sentence that says, in effect, *A causes (or does not cause or is caused by) B*, followed by a summary of the reasons supporting this causal relationship. Make your thesis as specific as possible and be sure that it's sufficiently controversial or intriguing to hold a reader's interest. Of course, feel free to revise any such claim as you learn more about a subject.

For causal topics that are more open-ended and exploratory, you may not want to take a strong position, particularly at the outset. Instead, your argument might simply present a variety of reasonable (and possibly competing) explanations and scenarios.

● Examples of Causal Claims

- Right-to-carry gun laws have led to increased rates of crime in states that have approved such legislation.
- Sophisticated use of social media is now a must for any political candidate who hopes to win.
- Grade inflation is lowering the value of a college education.

- The proliferation of images in film, television, and computer-generated texts is changing the way we read and use information.

- Experts don't yet agree on the long-term impact that sophisticated use of social media will have on American political campaigns, though some effects are already evident.

● Preparing a Proposal

If your instructor asks you to prepare a proposal for your project, here's a format that may help:

State your thesis completely. If you're having trouble doing so, try outlining it in Toulmin terms:

    Claim:

    Reason(s):

    Warrant(s):

Alternatively, you might indicate an intention to explore a particular causal question in your project, with the thesis perhaps coming later.

- Explain why this issue deserves attention. What's at stake?

- Identify whom you hope to reach through your argument and why this group of readers would be interested in it.

- Briefly discuss the key challenges you anticipate in preparing your argument.

- Determine what research strategies you'll use. What sources do you expect to consult?

- Briefly identify and explore the major stakeholders in your argument and what alternative perspectives you may need to consider as you formulate your argument.

● Considering Format and Media

Your instructor may specify that you use a particular format and/or medium. If not, ask yourself these questions to help you make a good choice:

- What format is most appropriate for your causal argument? Does it call for an academic essay, a report, an infographic, a brochure, or something else?

- What medium is most appropriate for your argument? Would it be best delivered orally to a live audience? Presented as an audio essay or podcast? Presented in print only or in print with illustrations?
- Will you need visuals, such as moving or still images, maps, graphs, charts—and what function will they play in your argument? Make sure they are not just "added on" but are necessary components of the argument.

● Thinking about Organization

Your causal argument will likely include elements such as the following:

- a specific causal claim somewhere in the paper—or the identification of a significant causal issue
- an explanation of the claim's significance or importance
- evidence sufficient to support each cause or effect—or, in an argument based on a series of causal links, evidence to support the relationships among the links
- a consideration of other plausible causes and effects, and evidence that you have thought carefully about these alternatives before offering your own ideas

● Getting and Giving Response: Questions for Peer Response

Your instructor may assign you to a group for the purpose of reading and responding to each other's drafts. If not, ask for responses from serious readers or consultants at a writing center. Use the following questions to evaluate a colleague's draft. Be sure to illustrate your comments with examples; specific comments help more than general observations.

The Claim

- Does the claim state a causal argument?
- Does the claim identify clearly what causes and effects are being examined?
- What about the claim will make it appeal to readers?
- Is the claim too sweeping? Does it need to be qualified? How might it be narrowed and focused?
- How strong is the relationship between the claim and the reasons given to support it? How could that relationship be made more explicit?

Evidence for the Claim

- What's the strongest evidence offered for the claim? What, if any, evidence needs to be strengthened?

- Is enough evidence offered to show that these causes are responsible for the identified effect, that these effects result from the identified cause, or that a series of causes and effects are linked? If not, what additional evidence is needed? What kinds of sources might provide this evidence?

- How credible will the sources be to potential readers? What other sources might be more persuasive?

- Is evidence in support of the claim analyzed logically? Is more discussion needed?

- Have alternative causes and effects been considered? Have objections to the claim been carefully considered and presented fairly? Have these objections been discussed?

Organization and Style

- How are the parts of the argument organized? Is this organization effective?

- Will readers understand the relationships among the claims, supporting reasons, warrants, and evidence? If not, how might those connections be clearer? Is the function of every visual clear? Are more transitions needed? Would headings or graphic devices help?

- Are the transitions or links from point to point, sentence to sentence, and paragraph to paragraph clear and effective? If not, how could they be improved?

- Are all visuals (or other elements such as audio or video clips) carefully integrated into the text? Is each visual introduced and commented on to point out its significance? Is each visual labeled as a figure or a table and given a caption as well as a citation?

- Is the style suited to the subject? Is it too formal, casual, or technical? Can it be improved?

- Which sentences seem effective? Which ones seem weaker, and how could they be improved? Should short sentences be combined, and any longer ones be broken up?

- How effective are the paragraphs? Too short or too long? How can they be improved?

- Which words or phrases seem effective? Do any seem vague or inappropriate for the audience or the writer's purpose? Are technical or unfamiliar terms defined?

Spelling, Punctuation, Mechanics, Documentation, and Format

- Are there any errors in spelling, punctuation, capitalization, and the like?
- Is the documentation appropriate and consistent? (See Chapter 22.)
- Does the paper or project follow an appropriate format? Is it appropriately designed and attractively presented?

PROJECTS •

1. Develop an argument exploring one of the cause-and-effect topics mentioned in this chapter. Just a few of those topics are listed below:

   Disappearance of honeybees in the United States

   Causes of long-term unemployment or declining job markets

   Using the tax code to discourage/encourage specific behaviors (i.e., smoking, eating unhealthy foods, hiring more workers)

   Increasing numbers of obese children and/or adults

   Ramifications of increasing amounts of time spent on social media sites

   Results of failing to pass immigration reform legislation

   Repercussions of U.S. ethanol policy

   What is lost/gained as paper books disappear

2. Write a causal argument about a subject you know well, even if the topic does not strike you as particularly "academic": *What accounts for the popularity of* The Hunger Games *trilogy? What are the likely consequences of students living more of their lives via social media? How are video games changing the way students you know learn? Why do women love shoes?* In this argument, be sure to separate precipitating or proximate causes from sufficient or necessary ones. In other words, do a deep and revealing causal analysis about your subject, giving readers new insights.

3. John Tierney's essay "Can a Playground Be Too Safe?" (see p. 268) explores some unintended consequences of noble-minded efforts in recent decades to make children's playgrounds safer. After reading the Tierney piece, list any comparable situations you know of where unintended consequences may have undermined the good (or maybe even bad?) intentions of those who took action or implemented some change. Choose the most intriguing situation, do the necessary research, and write a causal argument about it.

4. Raven Jiang's "Dota 2: The Face of Professional Gaming" (see p. 264) argues that crowdfunding and netstreaming are two major causes in the rise of big-money professional gaming, which he sees as a phenomenon that is here to stay ("Watch out NFL, America's sport is about to change"). In a project of your own, describe the causes that have led to a particular effect on your campus or in your community or place of work. You may point out, as Jiang does, both advantages and disadvantages of the change brought about by the causes you analyze.

Dota 2: The Face of Professional Gaming

RAVEN JIANG

August 5, 2014

The introductory paragraph presents the "effect": a huge rise in professional online gaming.

Just over a week ago, history was made when a team of five young Chinese men left Seattle with $5 million in winnings. The game they were playing was not poker but "Dota 2," a multiplayer online game made by the Bellevue-based gaming company Valve. This year's annual "Dota 2" Internationals tournament, the fourth one since its creation, presented the largest prize pool ever seen in professional gaming—a total of $10.9 million. ESPN covered the matches and it seemed like every media outlet was trying to get in on the story, if only as a human interest piece. There is a sense that we are entering new uncharted territories.

A causal claim is stated.

Since the early 2000s, much has been written and said about the slow but steady rise of professional video gaming. What happened this month at Seattle is a coming-of-age story that we are all familiar with, but it is also so much more. A confluence of factors had brought the 2014 "Dota 2" Internationals into the mainstream consciousness and they represent an interesting microcosm of the technological forces that are shaping our future, gaming and otherwise.

The first cause is introduced: crowdfunding.

Kickstarter brought the idea of crowdfunding into our daily lives, but Valve made it addictive with "Dota 2." Unlike past video gaming tournaments that relied solely on sponsorships for prize money, which were often the first thing on the chopping boards when it came to corporate budget cuts, the Internationals were almost

---

Raven Jiang is an undergraduate at Stanford University, studying computer science. His piece was first published in the *Stanford Daily*, a student-produced newspaper founded in 1892.

entirely crowdfunded via in-game item purchases by online players. In the weeks leading up to the event, fans could purchase tournament-related in-game items to contribute to the prize pool and to eventually earn vanity visual effects that they could show off in-game on their characters. And just like a Kickstarter campaign, there was a counter tracking the amount raised, with final rewards that fans earn determined by the final total—think Kickstarter fundraising goals. For example, the reward for hitting $3.5 million this time was access to special chat emoticons. In this way, much like purchasing swag at an indie concert, fans not only contribute to the prize pool but feel like they get something back in return.

The benefits of crowdfunding are stated.

So, fans pay both to support the goal of having a more exciting tournament with bigger stakes and to gain personal items; Valve takes a cut as profits and professional Dota players get to make a career out of their passion. As Michael Scott once said, this is a win-win-win outcome. The final prize pool of $10.9 million was more than three times that of last year. To put that into perspective, the second placing team this year won more money than last year's winning team. That's a growth rate that would make Bernie Madoff jealous.

The author points out benefits to the winners as well as the viewers.

The successful use of crowdfunding by Valve is a great example of the value of crowdfunding as a whole. The reason why corporate sponsorships have historically been unreliable is because they are a poor indirect proxy for consumer demand. Much like the homemade gadgets that find their audience on Kickstarter, Valve is tapping into an underserved demand by getting the consumers to directly pay for the cost of production.

The other major force behind the modern "Dota 2" juggernaut is live game streaming. YouTube brought us video sharing and Netflix brought us the Internet's take on cable TV, but online gaming is helping to turn a very different form of visual entertainment into its own industry. Just like the Super Bowl, we now have the huge

The second major cause is presented to support the claim.

events that draw millions of viewers in the likes of the Internationals. But beyond that familiar format, there is also a burgeoning cottage industry of individual gamers who stream their gaming sessions live online and make money off of advertising and product placements. A popular full-time game streamer can take home a six-digit income doing what his parents say will never amount to much, probably right in their basement.

The prevalence of game streaming has created the interesting situation in which many fans of popular online games seldom ever actually feel the need to play them, because watching is so much less stressful, less time-consuming, and more readily accessible. In some sense, "Dota 2," a game notorious for its complex game mechanics, can probably thank the rise of stream watching for the success of its annual championship events, because let's face it: If every sports fan had to be able to play the game in order to understand and enjoy watching it, then college football would be bankrupt. With the professionalization of online gaming that parallels the paths taken by its traditional counterparts, it is no wonder Google recently decided to fork out a cool billion dollars to acquire the major game streaming site Twitch.tv.

The point is that online gaming is going to be a big deal. And it is a big deal not just because video gaming is becoming big money, but because its rise is symbolic of the same technological shifts that are changing all other aspects of our lives.

The author gives proof that online video gaming is already big time in South Korea and the United States.

The future is already here in South Korea, where professional "Starcraft" gamers are literally national celebrities. Significant milestones like the recent "Dota 2" Internationals suggest that the U.S. is on its way there. Watching the live stream of the Internationals with its extremely professional production value, the seasoned commentators throwing team and player stats at each other and the incredible amount of skill and concentration exhibited by the competitors, an alien visitor from Alpha Centauri would be hard-pressed to say what exactly differentiates "Dota 2" from sports. (I suppose there has not been any accusation of steroid abuse. Yet.)

That said, it is not all rainbows and unicorns. There is a general feeling that this year's matches at the Internationals have not been as exciting and eventful as last year's. Perhaps the unprecedented prize pool this year was causing players to be more risk-averse, leading to fewer clutch plays and comebacks from behind. Both of the teams in the final were also Chinese, who are known for being more methodological both in play style and training processes. The old fan favorite Na'Vi, the Eastern European past championship winners known for their dramatic comebacks and eccentric play styles, did not manage to get into the final four this year. Still, even if "Dota 2" does falter, it has already pushed the boundaries for professional gaming and paved the way for the future.

Watch out NFL, America's sport is about to change.

The downsides of the dramatic rise in online gaming are presented.

The concluding sentence assures readers that even if Dota 2 itself fails, what it represents has already had a major impact on the future of gaming.

Can a Playground Be Too Safe?

JOHN TIERNEY

A childhood relic: jungle gyms, like this one in Riverside Park in Manhattan, have disappeared from most American playgrounds in recent decades. © Dith Pran/The New York Times/Redux

When seesaws and tall slides and other perils were disappearing from New York's playgrounds, Henry Stern drew a line in the sandbox. As the city's parks commissioner in the 1990s, he issued an edict concerning the ten-foot-high jungle gym near his childhood home in northern Manhattan.

"I grew up on the monkey bars in Fort Tryon Park, and I never forgot how good it felt to get to the top of them," Mr. Stern said. "I didn't want to see that playground bowdlerized. I said that as long as I was parks commissioner, those monkey bars were going to stay."

John Tierney is a journalist and coauthor of the book *Willpower: Rediscovering the Greatest Human Strength* (2011). He writes the science column "Findings" for the *New York Times*, where this piece was originally published on July 18, 2011. You will note that, as a journalist, Tierney cites sources without documenting them formally. An academic version of this argument might offer both in-text citations and a list of sources at the end.

His philosophy seemed reactionary at the time, but today it's shared by some researchers who question the value of safety-first playgrounds. Even if children do suffer fewer physical injuries—and the evidence for that is debatable—the critics say that these playgrounds may stunt emotional development, leaving children with anxieties and fears that are ultimately worse than a broken bone.

"Children need to encounter risks and overcome fears on the playground," said Ellen Sandseter, a professor of psychology at Queen Maud University in Norway. "I think monkey bars and tall slides are great. As playgrounds become more and more boring, these are some of the few features that still can give children thrilling experiences with heights and high speed."

After observing children on playgrounds in Norway, England, and Australia, Dr. Sandseter identified six categories of risky play: exploring heights, experiencing high speed, handling dangerous tools, being near dangerous elements (like water or fire), rough-and-tumble play (like wrestling), and wandering alone away from adult supervision. The most common is climbing heights.

"Climbing equipment needs to be high enough, or else it will be too boring in the long run," Dr. Sandseter said. "Children approach thrills and risks in a progressive manner, and very few children would try to climb to the highest point for the first time they climb. The best thing is to let children encounter these challenges from an early age, and they will then progressively learn to master them through their play over the years."

Sometimes, of course, their mastery fails, and falls are the common form of playground injury. But these rarely cause permanent damage, either physically or emotionally. While some psychologists—and many parents—have worried that a child who suffered a bad fall would develop a fear of heights, studies have shown the opposite pattern: A child who's hurt in a fall before the age of nine is less likely as a teenager to have a fear of heights.

By gradually exposing themselves to more and more dangers on the playground, children are using the same habituation techniques developed by therapists to help adults conquer phobias, according to Dr. Sandseter and a fellow psychologist, Leif Kennair, of the Norwegian University for Science and Technology.

"Risky play mirrors effective cognitive behavioral therapy of anxiety," they write in the journal *Evolutionary Psychology*, concluding that this "anti-phobic effect" helps explain the evolution of children's fondness for thrill-seeking. While a youthful zest for exploring heights might not seem adaptive—why would natural selection favor children who risk death before they have a chance to reproduce?—the dangers seemed to be outweighed by the benefits of conquering fear and developing a sense of mastery.

"Paradoxically," the psychologists write, "we posit that our fear of children being harmed by mostly harmless injuries may result in more fearful children and increased levels of psychopathology."

The old tall jungle gyms and slides disappeared from most American playgrounds across the country in recent decades because of parental concerns, federal guidelines, new safety standards set by manufacturers and—the most frequently cited factor—fear of lawsuits.

Shorter equipment with enclosed platforms was introduced, and the old pavement was replaced with rubber, wood chips, or other materials designed for softer landings. These innovations undoubtedly prevented some injuries, but some experts question their overall value.

"There is no clear evidence that playground safety measures have lowered the average risk on playgrounds," said David Ball, a professor of risk management at Middlesex University in London. He noted that the risk of some injuries, like long fractures of the arm, actually increased after the introduction of softer surfaces on playgrounds in Britain and Australia.

"This sounds counterintuitive, but it shouldn't, because it is a common phenomenon," Dr. Ball said. "If children and parents believe they are in an environment which is safer than it actually is, they will take more risks. An argument against softer surfacing is that children think it is safe, but because they don't understand its properties, they overrate its performance."

Reducing the height of playground equipment may help toddlers, but it can produce unintended consequences among bigger children. "Older children are discouraged from taking healthy exercise on playgrounds because they have been designed with the safety of the very young in mind," Dr. Ball said. "Therefore, they may play in more dangerous places, or not at all."

Fear of litigation led New York City officials to remove seesaws, merry-go-rounds, and the ropes that young Tarzans used to swing from one platform to another. Letting children swing on tires became taboo because of fears that the heavy swings could bang into a child.

"What happens in America is defined by tort lawyers, and unfortunately that limits some of the adventure playgrounds," said Adrian Benepe, the current parks commissioner. But while he misses the Tarzan ropes, he's glad that the litigation rate has declined, and he's not nostalgic for asphalt pavement.

"I think safety surfaces are a godsend," he said. "I suspect that parents who have to deal with concussions and broken arms wouldn't agree that playgrounds have become too safe." The ultra-safe enclosed platforms of the 1980s and 1990s may have been an overreaction, Mr. Benepe said, but lately there have been more creative alternatives.

"The good news is that manufacturers have brought out new versions of the old toys," he said. "Because of height limitations, no one's building the old monkey bars anymore, but kids can go up smaller climbing walls and rope nets and artificial rocks."

Still, sometimes there's nothing quite like being ten feet off the ground, as a new generation was discovering the other afternoon at Fort Tryon Park. A soft rubber surface carpeted the pavement, but the jungle gym of Mr. Stern's youth was still there. It was the prime destination for many children, including those who'd never seen one before, like Nayelis Serrano, a ten-year-old from the South Bronx who was visiting her cousin.

When she got halfway up, at the third level of bars, she paused, as if that was high enough. Then, after a consultation with her mother, she continued to the top, the fifth level, and descended to recount her triumph.

"I was scared at first," she explained. "But my mother said if you don't try, you'll never know if you could do it. So I took a chance and kept going. At the top I felt very proud." As she headed back for another climb, her mother, Orkidia Rojas, looked on from a bench and considered the pros and cons of this unfamiliar equipment.

"It's fun," she said. "I'd like to see it in our playground. Why not? It's kind of dangerous, I know, but if you just think about danger you're never going to get ahead in life."

12
Proposals

Left to right: © Florian Kopp/agefotostock.com; spaxiax/Shutterstock; AP Photo/Eric Gay

A student looking forward to spring break proposes to two friends that they join a group that will spend the vacation helping to build a school in a Haitian village.

The members of a club for undergrad business majors talk about their common need to create informative, appealing, interactive résumés. After much talk, three members suggest that the club develop a résumé app especially for business majors looking for a first job.

A project team at a large architectural firm works for three months developing a response to an RFP (request for proposal) to convert a university library into a digital learning center.

Understanding and Categorizing Proposals

We live in an era of big proposals—complex programs for health care reform, bold dreams to privatize space exploration, multibillion-dollar designs for high-speed rail systems, ceaseless calls to improve education, and so many other such ideas brought down to earth by sobering proposals for budget reform and deficit reduction. As a result, there's often more talk than action because persuading people (or legislatures) to do something—or *anything!*—is always hard. But that's what *proposal arguments* do: they provide thoughtful reasons for supporting or sometimes resisting change.

Such arguments, whether national or local, formal or casual, are important not only on the national scene but also in all of our lives. How many proposals do you make or respond to in one day? A neighbor might suggest that you volunteer to help clean up an urban creek bed; a campus group might demand that students get better seats at football games; a supervisor might ask for ideas to improve customer satisfaction at a restaurant; you might offer an ad agency reasons to hire you as a summer intern—or propose to a friend that you take in the latest zombie film. In each case, the proposal implies that some action should take place and suggests that there are sound reasons why it should.

This cartoon, by Steve Breen, suggests that high-speed rail proposals are going to run into a major obstacle in California. By permission of Steve Breen and Creators Syndicate, Inc.

In their simplest form, proposal arguments look something like this:

A should do B because of C.

```
┌──────── A ────────┐┌──────────── B ────────────┐
```
Our student government should endorse the Academic Bill of Rights
```
┌────────────────────── C ──────────────────────┐
```
because students should not be punished in their courses for their personal political views.

Proposals come at us so routinely that it's not surprising that they cover a dizzyingly wide range of possibilities. So it may help to think of proposal arguments as divided roughly into two kinds—those that focus on specific practices and those that focus on broad matters of policy. Here are several examples of each kind:

Proposals about Practices

- The college should allow students to pay tuition on a month-by-month basis.
- Commercial hotels should stop opposing competitors like Airbnb.
- College athletes should be paid for the services they provide.

Proposals about Policies

- The college should adopt a policy guaranteeing that students in all majors can graduate in four years.
- The United Nations should make saving the oceans from pollution a global priority.
- Major Silicon Valley firms should routinely reveal the demographic makeup of their workforces.

RESPOND •

People write proposal arguments to solve problems and to change the way things are. But problems aren't always obvious: what troubles some people might be no big deal to others. To get an idea of the range of problems people face on your campus (some of which you may not even have thought of as problems), divide into groups, and brainstorm about things that annoy you on and around campus, including wastefulness in the cafeterias, 8:00 a.m. classes, and long lines for football or concert tickets. Ask each group to aim for at least a dozen gripes. Then choose three problems, and as a group, discuss how you'd prepare a proposal to deal with them.

Characterizing Proposals

Proposals have three main characteristics:

1. They call for change, often in response to a problem.
2. They focus on the future.
3. They center on the audience.

Proposals always call for some kind of action. They aim at getting something done—or sometimes at *preventing* something from being done. Proposals marshal evidence and arguments to persuade people to choose a course of action: *Let's build a completely green house. Let's oppose the latest Supreme Court ruling on Internet privacy. Let's create a campus organization for first-generation college students. Let's ban drones from campus airspace, especially at sporting events.* But you know the old saying, "You can lead a horse to water, but you can't make it drink." It's usually easier to *convince* audiences what a good course of action is than to *persuade* them to take it (or pay for it). Even if you present a cogent proposal, you may still have work to do.

Proposal arguments must appeal to more than good sense. Ethos matters, too. It helps if a writer suggesting a change carries a certain gravitas earned by experience or supported by knowledge and research. If your word and credentials carry weight, then an audience is more likely to listen to your proposal. So when the commanders of three *Apollo* moon missions, Neil Armstrong, James Lovell, and Eugene Cernan, wrote an open letter to President Obama expressing their dismay at his administration's decision to cancel NASA's plans for advanced spacecraft and new lunar missions, they won a wide audience:

> For The United States, the leading space faring nation for nearly half a century, to be without carriage to low Earth orbit and with no human exploration capability to go beyond Earth orbit for an indeterminate time into the future, destines our nation to become one of second or even third rate stature. While the President's plan envisages humans traveling away from Earth and perhaps toward Mars at some time in the future, the lack of developed rockets and spacecraft will assure that ability will not be available for many years.
>
> Without the skill and experience that actual spacecraft operation provides, the USA is far too likely to be on a long downhill slide to mediocrity. America must decide if it wishes to remain a leader in space. If it does, we should institute a program which will give us the very best chance of achieving that goal.

But even their considerable ethos was not enough to carry the day with the space agency and the man who made the decision.

All that remains of the American space program?
Michael Williamson/The Washington Post/Getty Images

Yet, as the space program example obviously demonstrates, proposal arguments focus on the future—what people, institutions, or governments should do over the upcoming weeks, months, or, in the NASA moon-mission example, decades. This orientation toward the future presents special challenges, since few of us have crystal balls. Proposal arguments must therefore offer the best evidence available to suggest that actions we recommend will achieve what they promise.

In May 2014, Senator Elizabeth Warren introduced legislation aimed at reducing student loan debt, in part by allowing for refinancing. In an interview in *Rolling Stone*, Senator Warren explained:

> Homeowners refinance their loans when interest rates go down. Businesses refinance their loans. But right now, there's no way for students to be able to do that. I've proposed that we reduce the interest rate on the outstanding loan debt to the same rate Republicans and Democrats came together last year to set on new loans [3.86 percent]. For millions of borrowers, that would cut interest rates in half or more.

Yet Warren's proposal soon came under fire, particularly from senators who argued that the proposed bill did little to reduce borrowing or lower

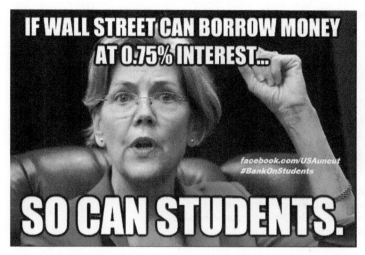

http://www.ClassWarfareExists.com

the cost of higher education. So despite the concerns of bankers and economists that the $1.1 trillion student loan debt is dampening the national economy, the bill was turned aside on June 11, 2014.

Which raises the matter of audiences, and we are left asking whether Senator Warren's bill spoke equally well to students, parents, bankers, and members of Congress. Some of those audiences failed to be convinced.

Some proposals are tailored to general audiences; consequently, they avoid technical language, make straightforward and relatively simple points, and sometimes use charts, graphs, and tables to make data comprehensible. You can find such arguments, for example, in newspaper editorials, letters to the editor, and political documents like Senator Warren's proposed legislation. And such appeals to a broad group make sense when a proposal—say, to finance new toll roads or build an art museum—must surf on waves of community support and financing.

But often proposals need to win the approval of specific groups or individuals (such as financiers, developers, public officials, and legislators) who have the power to make change actually happen. Such arguments will usually be more technical, detailed, and comprehensive than those aimed at the general public because people directly involved with an issue have a stake in it. They may be affected by it themselves and thus have in-depth knowledge of the subject. Or they may be responsible for implementing the proposal. You can expect them to have specific

Proposals have to take audience values into account. Shooting deer, even when they're munching on garden flowers, is unacceptable to most suburbanites. Ron Sanford/Science Source®/ Photo Researchers

questions about it and, possibly, formidable objections. So identifying your potential audiences is critical to the success of any proposal. On your own campus, for example, a plan to alter admissions policies might be directed both to students in general and (perhaps in a different form) to the university president, members of the faculty council, and admissions officers.

An effective proposal also has to be compatible with the values of the audience. Some ideas may make good sense but cannot be enacted. For example, many American towns and cities have a problem with expanding deer populations. Without natural predators, the deer are moving closer to homes, dining on gardens and shrubbery, and endangering traffic. Yet one obvious and feasible solution—culling the herds through hunting—is usually not saleable to communities (perhaps too many people remember *Bambi*).

RESPOND ●

Work in a group to identify about half a dozen problems on your campus or in the local community, looking for a wide range of issues. (Don't focus on problems in individual classes.) Once you have settled on these issues, then use various resources—the Web, the phone book (if you can find one), a campus directory—to locate specific people, groups, or offices whom you might address or influence to deal with the issues you have identified.

Developing Proposals

In developing a proposal, you will have to do some or all of the following:

- Define a problem that needs a solution or describe a need that is not currently addressed.
- Make a strong claim that addresses the problem or need. Your solution should be an action directed at the future.
- Show why your proposal will fix the problem or address the need.
- Demonstrate that your proposal is feasible.

This might sound easy, but writing a proposal argument can be a process of discovery. At the outset, you think you know exactly what ought to be done, but by the end, you may see (and even recommend) other options.

Defining a Need or Problem

To make a proposal, first establish that a need or problem exists. You'll typically dramatize the problem that you intend to fix at the beginning of your project and then lead up to a specific claim. But in some cases, you could put the need or problem right after your claim as the major reason for adopting the proposal:

> Let's ban cell phones on campus now. Why? Because we've become a school of walking zombies. No one speaks to or even acknowledges the people they meet or pass on campus. Half of our students are so busy chattering to people that they don't participate in the community around them.

How can you make readers care about the problem you hope to address? Following are some strategies:

- Paint a vivid picture of the need or problem.
- Show how the need or problem affects people, both those in the immediate audience and the general public as well.
- Underscore why the need or problem is significant and pressing.
- Explain why previous attempts to address the issue may have failed.

For example, in proposing that the military draft be restored in the United States or that all young men and women give two years to national service (a tough sell!), you might begin by drawing a picture of a younger generation that is self-absorbed, demands instant gratification, and doesn't understand what it means to participate as a full member of society. Or you might note how many young people today fail to develop the life skills they need to strike out on their own. Or like congressional representative Charles Rangel (D-New York), who regularly proposes a Universal National Service Act, you could define the issue as a matter of fairness, arguing that the current all-volunteer army shifts the burden of national service to a small and unrepresentative sample of the American population. Speaking on CNN on January 26, 2013, Rangel said:

> Since we replaced the compulsory military draft with an all-volunteer force in 1973, our nation has been making decisions about wars without worry over who fights them. I sincerely believe that reinstating the draft would compel the American public to have a stake in the wars we fight as a nation. That is why I wrote the Universal National Service Act, known as the "draft" bill, which requires all men and women between ages 18 and 25 to give two years of service in any capacity that promotes our national defense.

Of course, you would want to cite authorities and statistics to prove that any problem you're diagnosing is real and that it touches your likely audience. Then readers *may* be ready to hear your proposal.

File this cartoon under "anticipate objections to your proposal." © Mike Keefe/Cagle Cartoons, Inc.

In describing a problem that your proposal argument intends to solve, be sure to review earlier attempts to fix it. Many issues have a long history that you can't afford to ignore (or be ignorant of). Understand too that some problems seem to grow worse every time someone tinkers with them. You might pause before proposing any new attempt to reform the current system of financing federal election campaigns when you discover that previous reforms have resulted in more bureaucracy, more restrictions on political expression, and more unregulated money flowing into the system. *"Enough is enough"* can be a potent argument when faced with such a mess.

RESPOND●

If you review "Let's Charge Politicians for Wasting Our Time" at the end of this chapter, a brief proposal by political and culture writer/blogger Virginia Postrel, you'll see that she spends quite a bit of time pointing out the irritation caused by unwanted political robocalls to her landline, even though she recognizes that such calls are illegal on cell phones. Does this focus on the landline take away from her proposal that the politicians should have to pay a fee for such calls as well as for unsolicited email messages they send, a proposal also put forward by technology guru Esther Dyson? Would you advise her to revise her argument—and if so, how?

Making a Strong and Clear Claim

After you've described and analyzed a problem, you're prepared to offer a fix. Begin with your claim (a proposal of what X or Y should do), followed by the reason(s) that X or Y should act and the effects of adopting the proposal:

Claim	Communities should encourage the development of charter schools.
Reason	Charter schools are not burdened by the bureaucracy that is associated with most public schooling.
Effects	Instituting such schools will bring more effective education to communities and offer an incentive to the public schools to improve their programs.

Having established a claim, you can explore its implications by drawing out the reasons, warrants, and evidence that can support it most effectively:

Claim   In light of a recent U.S. Supreme Court decision that ruled that federal drug laws cannot be used to prosecute doctors who prescribe drugs for use in suicide, our state should immediately pass a bill legalizing physician-assisted suicide for patients who are terminally ill.

Reason   Physician-assisted suicide can relieve the suffering of those who are terminally ill and will die soon.

Warrant   The relief of suffering is desirable.

Evidence   Oregon voters have twice approved the state's Death with Dignity Act, which has been in effect since 1997, and to date the suicide rate has not risen sharply, nor have doctors given out a large number of prescriptions for death-inducing drugs. Several other states are considering ballot initiatives in favor of doctor-assisted suicide.

The *reason* sets up the need for the proposal, whereas the *warrant* and *evidence* demonstrate that the proposal is just and could meet its objective. Your actual argument would develop each point in detail.

RESPOND●

For each problem and solution below, make a list of readers' likely objections to the solution offered. Then propose a solution of your own, and explain why you think it's more workable than the original.

Problem   Future deficits in the Social Security system
Solution   Raise the age of retirement to seventy-two.

Problem   Severe grade inflation in college courses
Solution   Require a prescribed distribution of grades in every class: 10% A; 20% B; 40% C; 20% D; 10% F.

Problem   Increasing rates of obesity in the general population
Solution   Ban the sale of high-fat sandwiches and entrees in fast-food restaurants.

Problem   Inattentive driving because drivers are texting
Solution   Institute a one-year mandatory prison sentence for the first offense.

Problem   Increase in sexual assaults on and around campus
Solution   Establish a 10:00 p.m. curfew on weekends.

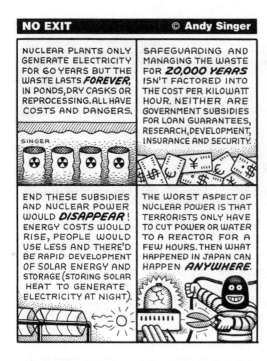

A proposal argument in four panels. You might compare this argument with Taylor Pearson's "Why You Should Fear Your Toaster More Than Nuclear Power" in Chapter 8. © Andy Singer/ Cagle Cartoons, Inc.

Showing That the Proposal Addresses the Need or Problem

An important but tricky part of making a successful proposal lies in relating the claim to the need or problem that it addresses. Facts and probability are your best allies. Take the time to show precisely how your solution will fix a problem or at least improve upon the current situation. Sometimes an emotional appeal is fair play, too. Here's former NBA player John Amaechi using that approach when he asks superstar Kobe Bryant of the L.A. Lakers not to appeal a $100,000 penalty he received for hurling an antigay slur at a referee:

> Kobe, stop fighting the fine. You spoke ill-advised words that shot out like bullets, and if the emails I received from straight and gay young people and sports fans in Los Angeles alone are anything to go by, you did serious damage with your outburst.
>
> A young man from a Los Angeles public school emailed me. You are his idol. He is playing up, on the varsity team, he has your posters all over his room, and he hopes one day to play in college and then in the NBA with you. He used to fall asleep with images of passing

Left: John Amaechi; right: Kobe Bryant. Left: Chris Goodney/Bloomberg News/Getty Images; right: © Lucy Nicholson/Reuters/LANDOV

you the ball to sink a game-winning shot. He watched every game you played this season on television, but this week he feels less safe and less positive about himself because he stared adoringly into your face as you said the word that haunts him in school every single day.

Kobe, stop fighting the fine. Use that money and your influence to set a new tone that tells sports fans, boys, men, and the society that looks up to you that the word you said in anger is not OK, not ever. Too many athletes take the trappings of their hard-earned success and leave no tangible legacy apart from "that shot" or "that special game."

—John Amaechi, "A Gay Former NBA Player
Responds to Kobe Bryant"

The paragraph describing the reaction of the schoolboy provides just the tie that Amaechi needs between his proposal and the problem it would address. The story also gives his argument more power.

Alternatively, if you oppose an idea, these strategies work just as well in reverse: if a proposal doesn't fix a problem, you have to show exactly why. Here are a few paragraphs from an editorial posting by Doug Bandow for *Forbes* in which he refutes a proposal for reinstating military conscription:

All told, shifting to conscription would significantly weaken the military. New "accessions," as the military calls them, would be less bright, less well educated, and less positively motivated. They would be less likely to stay in uniform, resulting in a less experienced force. The armed forces would be less effective in combat, thereby costing America more lives while achieving fewer foreign policy objectives.

Why take such a step?

One argument, most recently articulated by Thomas Ricks of the Center for a New American Security, is that a draft would save "the government money." That's a poor reason to impress people into service.

First, conscription doesn't save much cash. It costs money to manage and enforce a draft—history demonstrates that not every inductee would go quietly. Conscripts serve shorter terms and reenlist less frequently, increasing turnover, which is expensive. And unless the government instituted a Czarist lifetime draft, everyone beyond the first ranks would continue to expect to be paid.

Second, conscription shifts rather than reduces costs. Ricks suggested that draftees should "perform tasks currently outsourced at great cost to the Pentagon: paperwork, painting barracks, mowing lawns, driving generals around." Better to make people do grunt work than to pay them to do it? Force poorer young people into uniform in order to save richer old people tax dollars. Ricks believes that is a good reason to jail people for refusing to do as the government demands?

The government could save money in the same way by drafting FBI agents, postal workers, Medicare doctors, and congressmen. Nothing warrants letting old politicians force young adults to pay for Washington's profligacy. Moreover, by keeping some people who want to serve out while forcing others who don't want to serve in—creating a veritable evasion industry along the way—conscription would raise total social costs. It would be a bad bargain by any measure.

—Doug Bandow, "A New Military Draft Would Revive
a Very Bad Old Idea"

Finally, if your own experience backs up your claim or demonstrates the need or problem that your proposal aims to address, then consider using it to develop your proposal (as John Amaechi does in addressing his proposal to Kobe Bryant). Consider the following questions in deciding when to include your own experiences in showing that a proposal is needed or will in fact do what it claims:

- Is your experience directly related to the need or problem that you seek to address or to your proposal about it?

- Will your experience be appropriate and speak convincingly to the audience? Will the audience immediately understand its significance, or will it require explanation?

- Does your personal experience fit logically with the other reasons that you're using to support your claim?

Be careful. If a proposal seems crafted to serve mainly your own interests, you won't get far.

Showing That the Proposal Is Feasible

To be effective, proposals must be *feasible*—that is, the action proposed can be carried out in a reasonable way. Demonstrating feasibility calls on you to present evidence—from similar cases, from personal experience, from observational data, from interview or survey data, from Internet research, or from any other sources—showing that what you propose can indeed be done with the resources available. "Resources available" is key: if the proposal calls for funds, personnel, or skills beyond reach or reason, your audience is unlikely to accept it. When that's the case, it's time to reassess your proposal, modify it, and test any new ideas against these revised criteria. This is also when you can reconsider proposals that others might suggest are better, more effective, or more workable than yours. There's no shame in admitting that you may have been wrong. When drafting a proposal, ask friends to think of counterproposals. If your own proposal can stand up to such challenges, it's likely a strong one.

Considering Design and Visuals

Because proposals often address specific audiences, they can take a number of forms—a letter, a memo, a Web page, a feasibility report, an infographic, a brochure, a prospectus, or even an editorial cartoon (see Andy Singer's "No Exit" item on p. 283). Each form has different design requirements. Indeed, the design may add powerfully to—or detract significantly from—the effectiveness of the proposal. Typically, though, proposals are heavy in photographs, tables, graphs, comparison charts, and maps, all designed to help readers understand the nature of a problem and how to solve it. Needless to say, any visual items should be handsomely presented: they contribute to your ethos.

Lengthy reports also usually need headings—or, in an oral report, slides—that clearly identify the various stages of the presentation. Those headings, which will vary, would include items such as Introduction, Nature of the Problem, Current Approaches or Previous Solutions,

Proposal/Recommendations, Advantages, Counterarguments, Feasibility, Implementation, and so on. So before you produce a final copy of any proposal, be sure its design enhances its persuasiveness.

A related issue to consider is whether a graphic image might help readers understand key elements of the proposal—what the challenge is, why it demands action, and what exactly you're suggesting—and help make the idea more attractive. That strategy is routinely used in professional proposals by architects, engineers, and government agencies.

For example, the artist rendering below shows the Bionic Arch, a proposed skyscraper in Taiwan designed by architect Vincent Callebaut. As a proposal, this one stands out because it not only suggests an addition to the city skyline, but it also offers architectural innovations to make the structure more environmentally friendly. If you look closely, you'll notice that each floor of the building includes suspended "sky gardens" that, according to the proposal, will help solve the problem of city smog by siphoning away toxic fumes. According to Callebaut, "The skyscraper reduces our ecological footprint in the urban area. It respects the environment and gives a new symbiotic ecosystem for the biodiversity of Taiwan. The Bionic Arch is the new icon of sustainable development." Who wouldn't support a building that looked great *and* helped clean the air?

The Bionic Arch proposes to do more than add retail and office space. AP/Wide World Photos

GUIDE to writing a proposal

● **Finding a Topic or Identifying a Problem**

You're entering a proposal argument when you:

- make a claim that supports a change in practice: *Bottled water should carry a warning label describing the environmental impact of plastic.*

- make a claim that supports a change in policy: *Government workers, especially legislators and administrative officials, should never be exempt from laws or programs imposed on other citizens.*

- make a claim that resists suggested changes in practice or policy: *The surest way to guarantee that HOV lanes on freeways improve traffic flow is not to build any.*

- explore options for addressing existing issues or investigate opportunities for change: *Urban planners need to examine the long-term impact digital technologies may have on transportation, work habits, housing patterns, power usage, and entertainment opportunities in cities of the future.*

Since your everyday experience often calls on you to consider problems and to make proposals, begin your brainstorming for topics with practical topics related to your life, education, major, or job. Or make an informal list of proposals that you would like to explore in broader academic or cultural areas—problems you see in your field or in the society around you. Or do some freewriting on a subject of political concern, and see if it leads to a call for action.

● **Researching Your Topic**

For many proposals, you can begin your research by consulting the following types of sources:

- newspapers, magazines, reviews, and journals (online and print)
- television or radio news reports
- online databases
- government documents and reports
- Web sites, blogs, social networking sites, listservs, or newsgroups
- books
- experts in the field, some of whom might be right on your campus

Consider doing some field research, if appropriate—a survey of student opinions on Internet accessibility, for example, or interviews with people who have experienced the problem you are trying to fix.

Finally, remember that your proposal's success can depend on the credibility of the sources you use to support it, so evaluate each source carefully (see Chapter 19).

● Formulating a Claim

As you think about and explore your topic, begin formulating a claim about it. To do so, come up with a clear thesis that makes a proposal and states the reasons that this proposal should be adopted. To start formulating a claim, explore and respond to the following questions:

- What do I know about the proposal that I'm making?
- What reasons can I offer to support my proposal?
- What evidence do I have that implementing my proposal will lead to the results I want?

Rather than make a specific proposal, you may sometimes want to explore the range of possibilities for addressing a particular situation or circumstance. In that case, a set of open-ended questions might be a more productive starting point than a focused thesis, suggesting, for instance, what goals any plausible proposal might have to meet.

● Examples of Proposal Claims

- Because lowering the amount of fuel required to be blended with ethanol would lower greenhouse gas emissions by millions of tons and decrease land use that is releasing unhealthy amounts of carbon into the atmosphere, the EPA proposal to reduce ethanol produced from corn should be adopted.
- Every home should be equipped with a well-stocked emergency kit that can sustain inhabitants for at least three days in a natural disaster.
- Congress should repeal the Copyright Extension Act, since it disrupts the balance between incentives for creators and the right of the public to information as set forth in the U.S. Constitution.
- To simplify the lives of consumers and eliminate redundant products, industries that manufacture rechargeable batteries should agree on a design for a universal power adapter.

- People from different economic classes, age groups, political philosophies, and power groups (government, Main Street, Wall Street) all have a stake in reforming current budget and tax policies. But how do we get them to speak and to listen to each other? That is the challenge we face if we hope to solve our national economic problems.

Preparing a Proposal

If your instructor asks you to prepare a proposal for your project, here's a format that may help:

State the thesis of your proposal completely. If you're having trouble doing so, try outlining it in Toulmin terms:

Claim:

Reason(s):

Warrant(s):

Alternatively, you might describe your intention to explore a particular problem in your project, with the actual proposal (and thesis) coming later.

- Explain why this issue deserves attention. What's at stake?
- Identify and describe those readers whom you hope to reach with your proposal. Why is this group of readers appropriate? Can you identify individuals who can actually fix a problem?
- Briefly discuss the major difficulties that you foresee for your proposal. How will you demonstrate that the action you propose is necessary and workable? Persuade the audience to act? Pay for the proposal?
- Determine what research strategies you'll use. What sources do you expect to consult?

Considering Format and Media

Your instructor may specify that you use a particular format and/or medium. If not, ask yourself these questions to help you make a good choice:

- What format is most appropriate for your proposal? Does it call for an academic essay, a report, an infographic, a brochure, or something else?
- What medium is most appropriate for your argument? Would it be best delivered orally to a live audience? Presented as an audio essay or podcast? Presented in print only or in print with illustrations?

- Will you need visuals, such as moving or still images, maps, graphs, charts—and what function will they play in your argument? Make sure they are not just "added on" but are necessary components of the argument.

● Thinking about Organization

Proposals can take many different forms but generally include the following elements:

- a description of the problem you intend to address or the state of affairs that leads you to propose the action
- a strong and specific proposal, identifying the key reasons for taking the proposed action and the effects that taking this action will have
- a clear connection between the proposal and a significant need or problem
- a demonstration of ways in which the proposal addresses the need
- evidence that the proposal will achieve the desired outcome
- a consideration of alternative ways to achieve the desired outcome and a discussion of why these may not be feasible
- a demonstration that the proposal is feasible and an explanation of how it may be implemented

● Getting and Giving Response: Questions for Peer Response

Your instructor may assign you to a group for the purpose of reading and responding to each other's drafts. If not, ask for responses from serious readers or consultants at a writing center. Use the following questions to evaluate a colleague's draft. Since specific comments help more than general observations, be sure to illustrate your comments with examples. Some of the questions below assume a conventional, thesis-driven project, but more exploratory, open-ended proposal arguments also need to be clearly phrased, organized, and supported with evidence.

The Claim

- Does the claim clearly call for action? Is the proposal as clear and specific as possible? Is it realistic or possible to accomplish?
- Is the proposal too sweeping? Does it need to be qualified? If so, how?

- Does the proposal clearly address the problem that it intends to solve? If not, how could the connection be strengthened?
- Is the claim likely to get the audience to act rather than just to agree? If not, how could it be revised to do so?

Evidence for the Claim

- Is enough evidence furnished to get the audience to support the proposal? If not, what kind of additional evidence is needed? Does any of the evidence provided seem inappropriate or otherwise ineffective? Why?
- Is the evidence in support of the claim simply announced, or are its significance and appropriateness analyzed? Is a more detailed discussion needed?
- Are objections that readers might have to the claim or evidence adequately and fairly addressed?
- What kinds of sources are cited? How credible and persuasive will they be to readers? What other kinds of sources might work better?
- Are all quotations introduced with appropriate signal phrases (such as "As Tyson argues, . . .") and blended smoothly into the writer's sentences?
- Are all visual sources labeled, introduced, and commented upon?

Organization and Style

- How are the parts of the argument organized? Is this organization effective?
- Will readers understand the relationships among the claims, supporting reasons, warrants, and evidence? If not, how might those connections be clearer? Is the function of every visual clear? Are more transitions needed? Would headings or graphic devices help?
- Are the transitions or links from point to point, sentence to sentence, and paragraph to paragraph clear and effective? If not, how could they be improved?
- Are all visuals carefully integrated into the text? Is each visual introduced and commented on to point out its significance? Is each visual labeled as a figure or a table and given a caption as well as a citation?
- Is the style suited to the subject? Is it too formal, casual, or technical? Can it be improved?

- Which sentences seem effective? Which ones seem weaker, and how could they be improved? Should short sentences be combined, and any longer ones be broken up?

- How effective are the paragraphs? Too short or too long? How can they be improved?

- Which words or phrases seem effective? Do any seem vague or inappropriate for the audience or the writer's purpose? Are technical or unfamiliar terms defined?

Spelling, Punctuation, Mechanics, Documentation, and Format

- Are there any errors in spelling, punctuation, capitalization, and the like?

- Is the documentation appropriate and consistent? (See Chapter 22.)

- Does the paper or project follow an appropriate format? Is it appropriately designed and attractively presented?

PROJECTS •

1. Identify a proposal currently in the news or one advocated unrelentingly by the media that you *really* don't like. It may be a political initiative, a cultural innovation, a transportation alternative, or a lifestyle change. Spend time studying the idea more carefully than you have before. And then compose a proposal argument based on your deeper understanding of the proposal. You may still explain why you think it's a bad idea. Or you may endorse it, using your new information and your interesting perspective as a former dissenter.

2. The uses and abuses of technology and media—from smartphones and smartwatches to social networks—seem to be on everyone's mind. Write a proposal argument about some pressing dilemma caused by the digital screens that are changing (ruining?) our lives. You might want to explain how to bring traditional instructors into the digital age or establish etiquette for people who walk in traffic using handheld electronic devices. Or maybe you want to keep parents off of social networks. Or maybe you have a great idea for separating professional and private lives online. Make your proposal in some pertinent medium: print op-ed, cartoon, photo essay, infographic, set of PowerPoint or Prezi slides, podcast.

3. Write a proposal to yourself diagnosing some minor issue you would like to address, odd behavior you'd like to change, or obsession you'd like to curb. Explore the reasons behind your mania and the problems it causes you and others. Then come up with a plausible proposal to resolve the issue and prove that you can do it. Make the paper hilarious.

4. Working in a group initially, come up with a list of problems—local, national, or international—that seem just about insoluble, from persuading nations to cut down on their CO_2 emissions to figuring out how to keep tuition costs in check. After some discussion, focus on just one or two of these matters and then discuss not the issues themselves but the general reasons that the problems have proven intractable. What exactly keeps people from agreeing on solutions? Are some people content with the status quo? Do some groups profit from the current arrangements? Are alternatives to the status quo just too costly or not feasible for other reasons? Do people find change uncomfortable? Following the discussion, work alone or collaboratively on an argument that examines the general issue of *change*: What makes it possible in any given case? What makes it difficult? Use the problems you have discussed as examples to illustrate your argument. Your challenge as a writer may be to make such an open-ended discussion interesting to general readers.

A Call to Improve Campus Accessibility

MANASI DESHPANDE

Courtesy of
Manasi Deshpande

INTRODUCTION

Wes Holloway, a sophomore at the University of Texas at Austin (UT), never considered the issue of campus accessibility during his first year on campus. But when an injury his freshman year left him wheelchair-bound, he was astonished to realize that he faced an unexpected challenge: maneuvering around the UT campus. Hills that he had effortlessly traversed became mountains; doors that he had easily opened became anvils; and streets that he had mindlessly crossed became treacherous terrain. Says Wes: "I didn't think about accessibility until I had to deal with it, and I think most people are the same way."

The paper opens with a personal example and dramatizes the issue of campus accessibility.

For the ambulatory individual, access for the mobility impaired on the UT campus is easy to overlook. Automatic door entrances and bathrooms with the universal handicapped symbol make the campus seem sufficiently accessible. But for many students and faculty at UT, including me, maneuvering the UT campus in a wheelchair is a daily experience of stress and frustration. Although the University has made a concerted and continuing effort to improve access, students and faculty with physical disabilities still suffer from discriminatory hardship, unequal opportunity to succeed, and lack of independence.

Both problem and solution are previewed here, with more details provided in subsequent sections of the paper.

Manasi Deshpande wrote a longer version of this essay for a course preparing her to work as a consultant in the writing center at the University of Texas at Austin. We have edited it to emphasize the structure of her complex proposal. Note, too, how she reaches out to a general audience to make an argument that might seem to have a narrow constituency. This essay is documented using MLA style.

The introduc-
tion's final
paragraph
summarizes the
argument.

The University must make campus accessibility a higher priority and take more seriously the hardship that the campus at present imposes on people with mobility impairments. Better accessibility would also benefit the numerous students and faculty with temporary disabilities and help the University recruit a more diverse body of students and faculty.

ASSESSMENT OF CURRENT EFFORTS

The author's
fieldwork
(mainly inter-
views) enhances
her authority
and credibility.

The current state of campus accessibility leaves substantial room for improvement. There are approximately 150 academic and administrative buildings on campus (Grant). Eduardo Gardea, intern architect at the Physical Plant, estimates that only about nineteen buildings comply fully with the Americans with Disabilities Act (ADA). According to Penny Seay, PhD, director of the Center for Disability Studies at UT Austin, the ADA in theory "requires every building on campus to be accessible." However, as Bill Throop, associate director of the Physical Plant, explains, there is "no legal deadline to make the entire campus accessible"; neither the ADA nor any other law mandates that certain buildings be made compliant by a certain time. Though not bound by specific legal obligation, the University should strive to fulfill the spirit of the law and recognize campus accessibility as a pressing moral obligation.

The paper uses
several layers
of headings
to organize
its diverse
materials.

THE BENEFITS OF CHANGE

Benefits for People with Permanent Mobility Impairments

Improving campus accessibility would significantly enhance the quality of life of students and faculty with mobility impairments. The campus at present poses discriminatory hardship on these individuals by making daily activities such as getting to class and using the bathroom unreasonably difficult. Before Wes Holloway leaves home, he must plan his route carefully to avoid hills, use ramps that are easy to maneuver, and enter the side of the building with the accessible entrance. As he goes to class, Wes must go out of his way to avoid poorly paved sidewalks and roads. Sometimes he cannot avoid them and must take an uncomfortable and bumpy ride across potholes and uneven pavement. If his destination does not have an automatic door, he must wait for someone to open the door for him because it is too heavy for him to open himself. To get into Burdine Hall, he has to ask a stranger to push him through the heavy narrow doors because his fingers would get crushed if he pushed himself. Once in the classroom, Wes must find a suitable place to sit, often far away from his classmates because stairs block him from the center of the room.

The author outlines the challenges faced by a student with mobility impairment.

Other members of the UT community with mobility impairments suffer the same daily hardships as Wes. According to Mike Gerhardt, student affairs administrator of Services for Students with Disabilities (SSD), approximately eighty students with physical disabilities, including twenty to twenty-five students using wheelchairs, are registered with SSD. However, the actual number of students with mobility impairments is probably higher because some students choose not to seek services from SSD. The current state of campus accessibility discriminates against all individuals with physical disabilities in the unnecessary hardship it imposes and in the ways it denies them independence.

Accessibility issues are given a human face with examples of the problems that mobility-impaired people face on campus.

Benefits for People with Temporary Mobility Impairments

In addition to helping the few members of the UT campus with permanent mobility impairments, a faster rate of accessibility improvement would also benefit the much larger population of people with temporary physical disabilities. Many students and faculty will become temporarily disabled from injury at some point during their time at the University. They will encounter difficulties similar to those facing people with permanent disabilities, including finding accessible entrances, opening doors without

The author broadens the appeal of her proposal by showing how improved accessibility will benefit everyone on campus.

automatic entrances, and finding convenient classroom seating. And, according to Dr. Jennifer Maedgen, assistant dean of students and director of SSD, about 5 to 10 percent of the approximately one thousand students registered with SSD at any given time have temporary disabilities. By improving campus accessibility, the University would in fact reach out to all of its members, even those who have never considered the possibility of mobility impairment or the state of campus accessibility.

Numbers provide hard evidence for an important claim.

Benefits for the University

The author offers a new but related argument: enhanced accessibility could bolster recruitment efforts.

Better accessibility would also benefit the University as a whole by increasing recruitment of handicapped individuals and thus promoting a more diverse campus. When prospective students and faculty with disabilities visit the University, they might decide not to join the UT community because of poor access. On average, about one thousand students, or 2 percent of the student population, are registered with SSD. Mike Gerhardt reports that SSD would have about 1,500 to 3,000 registered students if the University reflected the community at large with respect to disability. These numbers suggest that the University can recruit more students with disabilities by taking steps to ensure that they have an equal opportunity to succeed.

COUNTERARGUMENTS

The paper briefly notes possible objections to the proposal.

Arguments against devoting more effort and resources to campus accessibility have some validity but ultimately prove inadequate. Some argue that accelerating the rate of accessibility improvements and creating more efficient services require too much spending on too few people. However, this spending actually enhances the expected quality of life of all UT community members rather than just the few with permanent physical disabilities. Unforeseen injury can leave anyone with a permanent or temporary disability at any time. In making decisions about campus accessibility, administrators must realize that having a disability is not a choice and that bad luck does not discriminate. They should consider how their decisions would affect their campus experience if they became disabled. Despite the additional cost, the University should make accessibility a priority and accommodate more accessibility projects in its budget.

RECOMMENDATIONS

Foster Empathy and Understanding for Long-Term Planning

The University should make campus accessibility a higher priority and work toward a campus that not only fulfills legal requirements but also provides a user-friendly environment for the mobility impaired. It is difficult for the ambulatory person to empathize with the difficulties faced by these individuals. Recognizing this problem, the University should require the administrators who allocate money to ADA projects to use wheelchairs around the campus once a year. Administrators must realize that people with physical disabilities are not a small, distant, irrelevant group; anyone can join their ranks at any time. Administrators should ask themselves if they would find the current state of campus accessibility acceptable if an injury forced them to use a wheelchair on a permanent basis.

In addition, the University should actively seek student input for long-term improvements to accessibility. The University is in the process of creating the ADA Accessibility Committee, which, according to the office of the Dean of Students' Web site, will "address institutionwide, systemic issues that fall under the scope of the Americans with Disabilities Act." Students should play a prominent and powerful role in this new ADA Accessibility Committee. The Committee should select its student representatives carefully to make sure that they are driven individuals committed to working for progress and representing the interests of students with disabilities. The University should consider making Committee

After establishing a case for enhanced campus accessibility, the author offers specific suggestions for action.

positions paid so that student representatives can devote sufficient time to their responsibilities.

Improve Services for the Mobility Impaired

The University should also work toward creating more useful, transparent, and approachable services for its members with physical disabilities by making better use of online technology and helping students take control of their own experiences.

First, SSD can make its Web site more useful by updating it frequently with detailed information on construction sites that will affect accessible routes. The site should delineate alternative accessible routes and approximate the extra time required to use the detour. This information would help people with mobility impairments to plan ahead and avoid delays, mitigating the stress of maneuvering around construction sites.

The University should also develop software for an interactive campus map. The software would work like MapQuest or Google Maps but would provide detailed descriptions of accessible routes on campus from one building to another. It would be updated frequently with new ADA improvements and information on construction sites that impede accessible routes.

Since usefulness of services is most important for students during their first encounters with the campus, SSD should hold one-on-one orientations for new students with mobility impairments. SSD should inform students in both oral and written format of their rights and responsibilities and make them aware of problems that they will encounter on the campus. Beyond making services more useful, these orientations would give students the impression of University services as open and responsive, encouraging students to report problems that they encounter and assume the responsibility of self-advocacy.

As a continuing resource for people with physical disabilities, the SSD Web site should include an anonymous

forum for both general questions and specific complaints and needs. Many times, students notice problems
but do not report them because they find visiting or calling SSD time-consuming or because they do not wish to
be a burden. The anonymity and immediate feedback
provided by the forum would allow for more freedom of
expression and provide students an easier way to solve
the problems they face.

Services for the mobility impaired should also
increase their transparency by advertising current accessibility projects on their Web sites. The University should
give its members with mobility impairments a clearer
idea of its efforts to improve campus accessibility.
Detailed online descriptions of ADA projects, including
the cost of each project, would affirm its resolve to create
a better environment for its members with physical
disabilities.

Conclusion

Although the University has made progress in accessibility improvements on an old campus, it must take bolder
steps to improve the experience of its members with
mobility impairments. At present, people with permanent mobility impairments face unreasonable hardship,
unequal opportunity to succeed, and lack of independence. To enhance the quality of life of all of its members
and increase recruitment of disabled individuals, the
University should focus its resources on increasing
the rate of accessibility improvements and improving
the quality of its services for the mobility impaired.

The writer reiterates her full proposal.

As a public institution, the University has an obligation to make the campus more inclusive and serve as an
example for disability rights. With careful planning and a
genuine desire to respond to special needs, practical and
cost-effective changes to the University campus can significantly improve the quality of life of many of its members and prove beneficial to the future of the University
as a whole.

WORKS CITED

Gardea, Eduardo. Personal interview, 24 Mar. 2005.

Gerhardt, Michael. Personal interview, 8 Apr. 2005.

Grant, Angela. "Making Campus More Accessible." *Daily Texan Online,* 14 Oct. 2003, www.dailytexanonline.com/2003/11/14/making-campus-more-accessible.

Holloway, Wesley Reed. Personal interview, 5 Mar. 2005.

Maedgen, Jennifer. Personal interview, 25 Mar. 2005.

Office of the Dean of Students. ADA Student Forum. *University of Texas at Austin,* 6 Apr. 2005, ddce.utexas.edu/disability/2005/04/april-6th-ada-student-forums/.

Seay, Penny. Personal interview, 11 Mar. 2005.

Throop, William. Personal interview, 6 Apr. 2005.

Let's Charge Politicians for Wasting Our Time

VIRGINIA POSTREL

There's an election today here in California, and that means my landline at home is ringing constantly with robocalls from assorted public figures whose recorded voices urge me to get out and vote for their favorite candidates. One called the other day while I was conducting an interview on the mobile phone I use for most purposes. I didn't answer, but it interrupted the flow of the conversation. Yesterday I picked up the receiver to find five voice mails, all from recorded political voices (including two identical messages from the same sheriff candidate).

Our phone number is on the National Do Not Call Registry, but those rules for telemarketers don't apply to political campaigns. The folks who make the laws aren't about to do away with a technique that works.

Political robocalls are illegal to mobile phones but OK to most landlines, as long as they meet disclosure requirements. Everyone I know hates such calls, and even political consultants know they're a problem. "Some voters get turned off by too many robocalls," cautions a political-strategy website. The cumulative annoyance, it warns, means that voters may resent yours even if they're rare. Yep.

Recorded, automatically dialed messages arguably constitute a legitimate and potentially important form of political speech. If I weren't so annoyed, I might actually like to know who's endorsing whom for sheriff. But it's ridiculous that the only way to limit the onslaught is to pay someone $24.99 to tell organizations, who may or may not listen, that I don't want them bothering me.

Here's a better idea: You should be able to set a charge for calling you. Every number that isn't on your "free" list would automatically be assessed a fee. The phone company would get a percentage of the revenue, and you'd be able to adjust the fee to different levels at different times of the day or for different seasons. (The nearer the election, the higher I'd make my charge.) If candidates really think it's valuable to call me, they should

Virginia Postrel posted this column on the Bloomberg View on June 3, 2014. She has also written for *Forbes*, the *Wall Street Journal*, the *New York Times*, and the *Atlantic*.

be willing to pay. Otherwise, they're just forcing me to subsidize their political efforts with my time and attention.

Technology investor Esther Dyson has for years been pushing a similar idea for e-mail. Unsolicited phone calls are much more annoying, and the technological challenges of "reversing the charges" should be much easier. Although you can't track down the true scamsters who break the do-not-call law and peddle fraudulent schemes from phony numbers, the politicians and charities that pester us for support aren't trying to hide. They're just trying to get something scarce and precious—our time and attention—for free.

GLOSSARY

academic argument writing that is addressed to an audience well informed about the topic, that aims to convey a clear and compelling point in a somewhat formal style, and that follows agreed-upon conventions of usage, punctuation, and formats.

accidental condition in a definition, an element that helps to explain what's being defined but isn't essential to it. An accidental condition in defining a bird might be "ability to fly" because most, but not all, birds can fly. (See also *essential condition* and *sufficient condition*.)

ad hominem **argument** a fallacy of argument in which a writer's claim is answered by irrelevant attacks on his/her character.

allusion an indirect reference. Saying "watch out or you'll create the next Edsel" contains an allusion to the Ford Edsel, a disastrously unpopular and unsuccessful product of the late 1950s.

analogy an extended comparison between something unfamiliar and something more familiar for the purpose of illuminating or dramatizing the unfamiliar. An analogy might, say, compare nuclear fission (less familiar) to a pool player's opening break (more familiar).

anaphora a figure of speech involving repetition, particularly of the same word at the beginning of several clauses.

antithesis the use of parallel structures to call attention to contrasts or opposites, as in *Some like it hot; some like it cold.*

antonomasia use of a title, epithet, or description in place of a name, as in *Your Honor* for *Judge.*

argument (1) a spoken, written, or visual text that expresses a point of view; (2) the use of evidence and reason to discover some version of the truth, as distinct from *persuasion*, the attempt to change someone else's point of view.

artistic appeal support for an argument that a writer creates based on principles of reason and shared knowledge rather than on facts and evidence. (See also *inartistic appeal*.)

assumption a belief regarded as true, upon which other claims are based.

assumption, cultural a belief regarded as true or commonsensical within a particular culture, such as the belief in individual freedom in American culture.

audience the person or persons to whom an argument is directed.

authority the quality conveyed by a writer who is knowledgeable about his/her subject and confident in that knowledge.

background the information a writer provides to create the context for an argument.

backing in Toulmin argument, the evidence provided to support a warrant.

bandwagon appeal a fallacy of argument in which a course of action is recommended on the grounds that everyone else is following it.

begging the question a fallacy of argument in which a claim is based on the very grounds that are in doubt or dispute: *Rita can't be the bicycle thief; she's never stolen anything.*

causal argument an argument that seeks to explain the effect(s) of a cause, the cause(s) of an effect, or a causal chain in which A causes B, B causes C, C causes D, and so on.

ceremonial argument an argument that deals with current values and addresses questions of praise and blame. Also called *epideictic*, ceremonial arguments include eulogies and graduation speeches.

character, appeal based on a strategy in which a writer presents an authoritative, credible self-image in order to gain the trust of an audience.

circumstantial evidence in legal cases, evidence from which conclusions cannot be drawn directly but have to be inferred.

claim a statement that asserts a belief or truth. In arguments, most claims require supporting evidence. The claim is a key component in Toulmin argument.

classical oration a highly structured form of an argument developed in ancient Greece and Rome to defend or refute a thesis. The oration evolved to include six parts—*exordium, narratio, partitio, confirmatio, refutatio,* and *peroratio.*

confirmatio the fourth part of a classical oration, in which a speaker or writer offers evidence for the claim.

connotation the suggestions or associations that surround most words and extend beyond their literal meaning, creating associational effects. *Slender* and *skinny* have similar meanings, for example, but carry different connotations, the former more positive than the latter.

context the entire situation in which a piece of writing takes place, including the writer's purpose(s) for writing; the intended audience; the time and place of writing; the institutional, social, personal, and other influences on the piece of writing; the material conditions of writing (whether it's, for instance, online or on paper, in handwriting or in print); and the writer's attitude toward the subject and the audience.

conviction the belief that a claim or course of action is true or reasonable. In a proposal argument, a writer must move an audience beyond conviction to action.

credibility an impression of integrity, honesty, and trustworthiness conveyed by a writer in an argument.

criterion (*plural* criteria) in evaluative arguments, a standard by which something is measured to determine its quality or value.

deductive reasoning a process of thought in which general principles are applied to particular cases.

definition, argument of an argument in which the claim specifies that something does or doesn't meet the conditions or features set forth in a definition: *Pluto is not a major planet.*

deliberative argument an argument that deals with action to be taken in the future, focusing on matters of policy. Deliberative arguments include parliamentary debates and campaign platforms.

delivery the presentation of an argument.

dogmatism a fallacy of argument in which a claim is supported on the grounds that it's the only conclusion acceptable within a given community.

either/or choice a fallacy of argument in which a complicated issue is misrepresented as offering only two possible alternatives, one of which is often made to seem vastly preferable to the other.

emotional appeal a strategy in which a writer tries to generate specific emotions (such as fear, envy, anger, or pity) in an audience to dispose it to accept a claim.

enthymeme in Toulmin argument, a statement that links a claim to a supporting reason: *The bank will fail* (claim) *because it has lost the support of its largest investors* (reason). In classical rhetoric, an enthymeme is a syllogism with one term understood but not stated: *Socrates is mortal because he is a human being.* (The understood term is *All human beings are mortal.*) (See also *syllogism.*)

epideictic argument See *ceremonial argument.*

equivocation a fallacy of argument in which a lie is given the appearance of truth, or in which the truth is misrepresented in deceptive language.

essential condition in a definition, an element that must be part of the definition but, by itself, isn't enough to define the term. An essential condition in defining a bird might be "winged": all birds have wings, yet wings alone don't define a bird since some insects and mammals also have wings. (See also *accidental condition* and *sufficient condition.*)

ethical appeal See *character, appeal based on,* and *ethos.*

ethnographic observation a form of field research involving close and extended observation of a group, event, or phenomenon; careful and detailed note-taking during the observation; analysis of the notes; and interpretation of that analysis.

ethos the self-image a writer creates to define a relationship with readers. In arguments, most writers try to establish an ethos that suggests authority, fairness, and credibility.

evaluation, argument of an argument in which the claim specifies that something does or doesn't meet established criteria: *The Nikon D4s is the most sophisticated digital SLR camera currently available.*

evidence material offered to support an argument. (See *artistic appeal* and *inartistic appeal.*)

example, definition by a definition that operates by identifying individual examples of what's being defined: *sports car—Corvette, Viper, Miata, Cayman.*

exordium the first part of a classical oration, in which a speaker or writer tries to win the attention and goodwill of an audience while introducing a subject.

experimental evidence evidence gathered through experimentation; often evidence that can be quantified (for example, a survey of students before and after an election might yield statistical evidence about changes in their attitudes toward the candidates). Experimental evidence is frequently crucial to scientific arguments.

fact, argument of an argument in which the claim can be proved or disproved with specific evidence or testimony: *The winter of 2012 was the warmest on record for the United States.*

fallacy of argument a flaw in the structure of an argument that renders its conclusion invalid or suspect. (See ad hominem *argument, bandwagon appeal, begging the question, dogmatism, either/or choice, equivocation, false authority, faulty analogy, faulty causality, hasty generalization, non sequitur, scare tactic, sentimental appeal, slippery slope,* and *straw man.*)

false authority a fallacy of argument in which a claim is based on the expertise of someone who lacks appropriate credentials.

faulty analogy a fallacy of argument in which a comparison between two objects or concepts is inaccurate or inconsequential.

faulty causality a fallacy of argument making the unwarranted assumption that because one event follows another, the first event causes the second. Also called *post hoc, ergo propter hoc,* faulty causality forms the basis of many superstitions.

firsthand evidence data—including surveys, observations, personal interviews, etc.—collected and personally examined by the writer. (See also *secondhand evidence.*)

forensic argument an argument that deals with actions that have occurred in the past. Sometimes called *judicial arguments,* forensic arguments include legal cases involving judgments of guilt or innocence.

formal definition a definition that identifies something first by the general class to which it belongs (see *genus*) and then by the characteristics that distinguish it from other members of that class (see *species*): *Baseball is a game* (genus) *played on a diamond by opposing teams of nine players who score runs by circling bases after striking a ball with a bat* (species).

genus in a definition, the general class to which an object or a concept belongs: *baseball is a sport; green is a color.*

grounds in Toulmin argument, the evidence provided to support a claim and reason—that is, an *enthymeme.*

hard evidence support for an argument using facts, statistics, testimony, or other evidence the writer finds.

hasty generalization a fallacy of argument in which an inference is drawn from insufficient data.

hyperbole use of overstatement for special effect.

hypothesis a well-informed guess at what the conclusion of one's research will reveal. Hypotheses must be tested against evidence, opposing arguments, and so on.

immediate reason the cause that leads directly to an effect, such as an automobile accident that results in an injury to the driver. (See also *necessary reason* and *sufficient reason*.)

inartistic appeal support for an argument using facts, statistics, eyewitness testimony, or other evidence the writer finds rather than creates. (See also *artistic appeal*.)

inductive reasoning a process of thought in which particular cases lead to general principles.

infotention a term coined by Howard Rheingold to describe the digital literacy skills of managing the technology we use and synthesizing the information we find online.

intended readers the actual, real-life people whom a writer consciously wants to address in a piece of writing.

invention the process of finding and creating arguments to support a claim.

inverted word order moving grammatical elements of a sentence out of their usual order (subject-verb-object/complement) for special effect, as in *Tired I was; sleepy I was not.*

invitational argument a term used by Sonja Foss and Cindy Griffin to describe arguments that are aimed not at vanquishing an opponent but at inviting others to collaborate in exploring mutually satisfying ways to solve problems.

invoked readers the readers implied in a text, which may include some whom the writer didn't consciously intend to reach. An argument that refers to *those who have experienced a major trauma*, for example, invokes all readers who have undergone this experience.

irony use of language that suggests a meaning in contrast to the literal meaning of the words.

kairos the opportune moment; in arguments, the timeliness of an argument and the most opportune ways to make it.

line of argument a strategy or an approach used in an argument. Argumentative strategies include appeals to the heart (emotional appeals), to character (ethical appeals), and to facts and reason (logical appeals).

logical appeal a strategy in which a writer uses facts, evidence, and reason to convince audience members to accept a claim.

logos See *logical appeal.*

metaphor a figure of speech that makes a comparison, as in *The ship was a beacon of hope.*

metonymy a rhetorical trope in which a writer uses a particular object to stand for a general concept, as in referring to businesspeople as "suits" or to the English monarchy as "the crown."

narratio the second part of a classical oration, in which a speaker or writer presents the facts of a case.

necessary reason a cause that must be present for an effect to occur; for example, infection with a particular virus is a necessary reason for the development of mumps. (See also *immediate reason* and *sufficient reason.*)

non sequitur a fallacy of argument in which claims, reasons, or warrants fail to connect logically; one point doesn't follow from another: *If you're really my friend, you'll lend me five hundred dollars.*

operational definition a definition that identifies an object by what it does or by the conditions that create it: *A line is the shortest distance between two points.*

oxymoron a rhetorical trope that states a paradox or contradiction, as in "jumbo shrimp."

parallelism use of similar grammatical structures or forms for clarity, emphasis, and/or artfulness: *in the classroom, on the playground, and at the mall.*

paraphrase a restatement of the meaning of a piece of writing using different words from the original.

partitio the third part of a classical oration, in which a speaker or writer divides up the subject and explains what the claim will be.

patchwriting a misuse of sources in which a writer's phrase, clause, or sentence stays too close to the original language or syntax of the source.

pathos, appeal to See *emotional appeal.*

peroratio the sixth and final part of a classical oration, in which a speaker or writer summarizes the case and moves the audience to action.

persuasion the act of seeking to change someone else's point of view.

plagiarism the act of using the words, phrases, and expressions of others without proper citation or acknowledgment.

precedents actions or judgments in the past that have established a pattern or model for subsequent decisions. Precedents are particularly important in legal cases.

premise a statement or position regarded as true and upon which other claims are based.

propaganda an argument advancing a point of view without regard to reason, fairness, or truth.

proposal argument an argument in which a claim is made in favor of or opposing a specific course of action: *Sport-utility vehicles should have to meet the same fuel economy standards as passenger cars.*

purpose the goal of an argument. Purposes include entertaining, informing, convincing, exploring, and deciding, among others.

qualifiers words or phrases that limit the scope of a claim: *usually; in a few cases; under these circumstances.*

qualitative argument an argument of evaluation that relies on non-numerical criteria supported by reason, tradition, precedent, or logic.

quantitative argument an argument of evaluation that relies on criteria that can be measured, counted, or demonstrated objectively.

quantitative data the sort of data that can be observed and counted.

reason in writing, a statement that expands a claim by offering evidence to support it. The reason may be a statement of fact or another claim. In Toulmin argument, a reason is attached to a claim by a warrant, a statement that establishes the logical connection between claim and supporting reason. (See also *Toulmin argument.*)

rebuttal an answer that challenges or refutes a specific claim or charge. Rebuttals may also be offered by writers who anticipate objections to the claims or evidence they offer.

rebuttal, conditions of in Toulmin argument, potential objections to an argument. Writers need to anticipate such conditions in shaping their arguments.

red herring a fallacy of argument in which a writer abruptly changes the topic in order to distract readers from potentially objectionable claims.

refutatio the fifth part of a classical oration, in which a speaker or writer acknowledges and refutes opposing claims or evidence.

reversed structures a figure of speech that involves the inversion of clauses: *What is good in your writing is not original; what is original is not good.*

rhetoric the art of persuasion. Western rhetoric originated in ancient Greece as a discipline to prepare citizens for arguing cases in court.

rhetorical analysis an examination of how well the components of an argument work together to persuade or move an audience.

rhetorical questions questions posed to raise an issue or create an effect rather than to get a response: *You may well wonder, "What's in a name?"*

rhetorical situation the relationship between topic, author, audience, and other contexts (social, cultural, political) that determine or evoke an appropriate spoken or written response.

Rogerian argument an approach to argumentation based on the principle, articulated by psychotherapist Carl Rogers, that audiences respond best when they don't feel threatened. Rogerian argument stresses trust and urges those who disagree to find common ground.

scare tactic a fallacy of argument presenting an issue in terms of exaggerated threats or dangers.

scheme a figure of speech that involves a special arrangement of words, such as inversion.

secondhand evidence any information taken from outside sources, including library research and online sources. (See also *firsthand evidence*.)

sentimental appeal a fallacy of argument in which an appeal is based on excessive emotion.

signifying a distinctive trope found extensively in African American English in which a speaker or writer cleverly and often humorously needles another person.

simile a comparison that uses *like* or *as*: *My love is like a red, red rose* or *I wandered lonely as a cloud.*

slippery slope a fallacy of argument exaggerating the possibility that a relatively inconsequential action or choice today will have serious adverse consequences in the future.

species in a definition, the particular features that distinguish one member of a genus from another: *Baseball is a sport* (genus) *played on a diamond by teams of nine players* (species).

stacking the deck a fallacy of argument in which the writer shows only one side of an argument.

stance the writer's attitude toward the topic and the audience.

stasis theory in classical rhetoric, a method for coming up with appropriate arguments by determining the nature of a given situation: a question of fact; of definition; of quality; or of policy.

straw man a fallacy of argument in which an opponent's position is misrepresented as being more extreme than it actually is, so that it's easier to refute.

sufficient condition in a definition, an element or set of elements adequate to define a term. A sufficient condition in defining God, for example, might be "supreme being" or "first cause." No other conditions are necessary, though many might be made. (See also *accidental condition* and *essential condition*.)

sufficient reason a cause that alone is enough to produce a particular effect; for example, a particular level of smoke in the air will set off a smoke alarm. (See also *immediate reason* and *necessary reason*.)

summary a presentation of the substance and main points of a piece of writing in very condensed form.

syllogism in formal logic, a structure of deductive logic in which correctly formed major and minor premises lead to a necessary conclusion:

Major premise	All human beings are mortal.
Minor premise	Socrates is a human being.
Conclusion	Socrates is mortal.

testimony a personal experience or observation used to support an argument.

thesis a sentence that succinctly states a writer's main point.

Toulmin argument a method of informal logic first described by Stephen Toulmin in *The Uses of Argument* (1958). Toulmin argument describes the key components of an argument as the claim, reason, warrant, backing, and grounds.

trope a figure of speech that involves a change in the usual meaning or signification of words, such as *metaphor*, *simile*, and *analogy*.

understatement a figure of speech that makes a weaker statement than a situation seems to call for. It can lead to powerful or to humorous effects.

values, appeal to a strategy in which a writer invokes shared principles and traditions of a society as a reason for accepting a claim.

warrant in Toulmin argument, the statement (expressed or implied) that establishes the logical connection between a claim and its supporting reason.

Claim	Don't eat that mushroom.
Reason	It's poisonous.
Warrant	What is poisonous should not be eaten.

ACKNOWLEDGMENTS

Doug Bandow. "A New Military Draft Would Revive a Very Bad Old Idea" from *Forbes*, July 16, 2012, copyright © 2012 by Forbes LLC. All rights reserved. Used by permission and protected by the Copyright Laws of the United States. The printing, copying, redistribution, or retransmission of this Content without express written permission is prohibited.

Sara Barbour. From "Kindle vs. Books: The Dead Trees Society," first published in the *Los Angeles Times*, June 17, 2011. Reprinted by permission of the author.

David Brooks. "It's Not about You" from the *New York Times*, May 31, 2011. Copyright © 2011 by The New York Times. All rights reserved. Used by permission and protected by the Copyright Laws of the United States. The printing, copying, redistribution, or retransmission of this Content without express written permission is prohibited.

Edye Deloch-Hughes. From "So God Made a Black Farmer Too," reprinted by permission of the author. http://eldhughes.com/2013/02/05/so-god-made-a-farmer-dodge-ram/

Jon Dolan. "Drake, 'Draft Day'" by Jon Dolan, from *Rolling Stone*, Issue 1207, April 24, 2014. Copyright © 2014 by Rolling Stone, LLC. All rights reserved. Used by permission.

Roger Ebert. From a review of *Toy Story* (1995). Used by permission of Ebert Digital, LLC.

Neil Irwin. "What the Numbers Show about N.F.L. Player Arrests" from the *New York Times*, September 13, 2014. Copyright © 2014 by The New York Times. All rights reserved. Used by permission and protected by the Copyright Laws of the United States. The printing, copying, redistribution, or retransmission of this Content without express written permission is prohibited.

Raven Jiang. "Dota 2: The Face of Professional Gaming" from the *Stanford Daily*, August 5, 2014, is reprinted by permission of the *Stanford Daily* and Raven Jiang.

Joyce Xinran Liu. "Friending: The Changing Definition of Friendship in the Social Media Era" by Joyce Xinran Liu, from *Vitamin IMC*, March 6, 2014. Reprinted by permission of the author.

Walter Russell Mead. From "It All Begins with Football," first published in the *American Interest*, December 4, 2011. Reprinted by permission of the author.

Virginia Postrel. "Let's Charge Politicians for Wasting Our Time" from *Bloomberg View*, June 3, 2014. Reprinted by permission of Bloomberg L.P. Copyright © 2014. All rights reserved.

Deborah Tannen. "Why Is 'Compromise' Now a Dirty Word?," first published in *Politico*, June 15, 2011. Copyright © Deborah Tannen. Used by permission of the author.

John Tierney. "Can a Playground Be Too Safe?" by John Tierney from the *New York Times*, July 18, 2011. Copyright © 2011 by The New York Times. All rights reserved. Used by permission and protected by the Copyright Laws of the United States. The printing, copying, redistribution, or retransmission of this Content without express written permission is prohibited.

Hayley Tsukayama. "My Awkward Week with Google Glass" from the *Washington Post*, April 29, 2014. Copyright © 2014 by The Washington Post Company. All rights reserved. Used by permission and protected by the Copyright Laws of the United States. The printing, copying, redistribution, or retransmission of this Content without express written permission is prohibited.

INDEX

academic arguments, 379–411
  data collection for, 420–26
  developing, 385–95
  samples of, 396–405
  understanding, 380–84
academic integrity, 455–64
accuracy, of print sources, 431
ad hominem arguments, 78–79
advertisement, citing, in MLA style, 484
afterword, citing, in MLA style, 474
Alexie, Sherman, 103–4, 311
Alleman, Heather Tew, 79
allusion, 318
Amaechi, John, 283–84
American Psychological Association (APA). *See* APA style
analogies, 319–20
  faulty, 84–85
  as logical structure for argument, 68
anaphora, 326–27
Anderson, Wes, 424
anecdotes, in Toulmin argument, 132
Angelou, Maya, 316
annotated bibliography, 454
anthologies, in MLA style, 469
antithesis, 327
antonomasia, 320
anxiety, public speaking and, 357–58
APA style
  content notes in, 490
  example of, 500–502
  first text page in, 500
  in-text citations in, 487–90
  online sources in, 489–90, 494–98, 499
  other sources in, 498–99
  quotations in, 445
  References list in, 490–99, 502
  signal verbs in, 447
  title page in, 500
  for visuals, 341
appeals, 21–26
  emotional, 23
  ethical, 23–24
  logical, 24–26
arguments, 11. *See also specific types and topics*
  academic, 379–411
  arrangement and media of, 101–2
  causal, 240–71
  classifying, 52
  to convince, 7
  cultural contexts for, 66–67
  definitional, 18, 185–209
  emotion-based, 9, 34–36, 38–39
  evaluations and, 19, 210–39
  to explore, 11
  factual, 17–18, 51–70, 152–84
  fallacies of, 71–86
  about future, 14
  to inform, 7
  kinds of, 17–21
  logical appeals as, 24, 33, 51–70
  to make decisions, 10
  makers of, 91–92
  media uses in, 101

multimedia, 361–75
occasions for, 12–17
to persuade, 8–9
about present, 14–16
presentation methods, 344–60
proposal, 20
reasons for, 6–12
rhetoric and, 11
sentence structure and, 312–13
structuring, 101–2, 121–50
style in, 102–4, 307–29
Toulmin, 65–66, 130–44
for understanding, 11
understanding purpose of, 90–91
visual, 104, 330–43
Aristotle
on classifying arguments, 52
enthymeme and, 65–66
on ethos, 42
on forensic arguments, 13
on rhetoric, 12
Armstrong, Neil, 275
Arnold, Eve, 335
articles, citing
in APA style, 492, 495
in MLA style, 469, 475, 476
Web journals, in MLA style, 478
artistic proofs, 52–53
artwork, citing, in MLA style, 483
attention, managing, 437
audience. *See also* readers
for academic argument, 387
appeals to, 21–26
assessing, 347
connecting with, 43–45
identifying and appealing to,
92–95
for multimedia arguments, 369
for new media, 365–67
for proposals, 278
for sources, 431
authorities, in Toulmin argument,
132

authority
claims of, 45–47
establishing, 46
images for, 335–37
authors
in APA style, 487–89, 490
in MLA style, 467–68, 472–75
reliability of, 420–21
of sources, 430

Bandow, Doug, 284–85
bandwagon appeals fallacy, 75–76
Barbour, Sara, 253–54
bar charts, 391
Barry, Dave, 249
Bechdel, Alison, 222, 223
begging the question fallacies, 81
beliefs, core principles and, 44
Bennett, Lerone, Jr., 327
Berl, Rachel Pomerance, 241
Bernstein, Richard, 46
bias
in questionnaires, 422
in sources, 428–29
Biba, Erin, 323
bibliographic notes, in MLA style,
471–72
Bibliography, in APA style, 490
blogs, 373–74
reliability of, 429
books, citing
in MLA style, 472–74
online in MLA style, 478
in series, in MLA style, 475
"both/and" solutions, 11
Boxer, Sarah, 394
boxes, 340
Boyle, Jamie, 384
brackets, for quotations, 445
Breen, Mike, 273
Brooks, David, 44
"It's Not about You," 105, 106–8

Brown, Emma, 19
Brown, Tiffany Lee, 325
Bryant, Kobe, 283
Bush, George W., 38

Calegari, Nínive, 68
Callebaut, Vincent, 287
"Call to Improve Campus
    Accessibility, A" (Deshpande),
    295–302
"Can a Playground Be Too Safe?"
    (Tierney), 268–71
captions, in MLA style, 469–70
Carlisle, Julia, 102
Carr, Nicholas, 173
Carretta, Vincent, 161
Carroll, James, 41
Carson, Rachel, 244–45
cartoon, citing, in MLA style, 484
Castro, Jason, 393
causal arguments, 240–71
    categorizing, 246–48
    conclusions in, 248
    defining relationships in, 250–52
    design and visuals in, 254–55,
        256
    developing, 248–56
    moving through series of links,
        245–46
    organizing, 260, 261
    as parts of other arguments, 242
    reviewing, 260–62
    samples of, 264–67, 268–71
    stating cause and examining
        effects, 243–44
    stating effect and tracing to
        causes, 244–46
    style for, 261–62
    supporting point in, 252–54
    Toulmin terms for, 259
    types of, 243–46
    writing guidelines for, 257–62

cause and effect. *See* causal
    arguments
ceremonial arguments, 14–15
ceremonial rhetoric, 211
Cernan, Eugene, 275
character arguments. *See* ethical
    appeals (ethos)
charts. *See also* graphs
    bar, 391
    citing in MLA style, 471, 484
    pie charts, 340
Chidiac, George, 344, 348–50
"China: The Prizes and Pitfalls of
    Progress" (Xue), 406–9
Chisholm, Latisha, 15
Chokshi, Niraj, 58–59
Chou, Hui-Tzu Grace, 56–57
Chung, Jack, 384
circumstantial evidence, 437–38
citations. *See also* documentation
    in academic argument, 392
    documentation principles and,
        458–59
    for paraphrases, 440
cited passage, MLA style for, 461
claims
    for academic argument, 386
    for causal arguments, 248–50,
        258–59
    for definitional arguments, 194,
        196–97, 200
    developing or supporting, 450
    in evaluations, 219–21, 226, 227,
        229
    examples of, 137
    for factual arguments, 168
    in proposals, 281–83, 289, 291–92
    refining, 160–61
    in rhetorical analysis, 98–99, 101,
        112–13, 115–16
    tentative, 193–94
    in Toulmin argument, 130–31,
        139, 149

clarification, sources for, 447–51
class discussions, 345–46
classical oration, 122–25
    parts of, 122, 123
climactic order, in presentation,
    354–55
Cloud, John, 21
collaborations
    acknowledging, 462–63
    in MLA style, 474
colloquial words and phrases, 310
colons, 315
color, emotional responses to, 334
common sense, in straight talk, 94
composition, of rhetorical analysis,
    89–90
compromise, Tannen on, 144,
    145–48
computer software, citing
    in APA style, 496
    in MLA style, 481
concepts, defining, 449
conclusions, in presentations,
    351–52
conditions of rebuttal, 141–42
conference proceedings, citing, in
    MLA style, 475
confirmatio, 122
connecting with audience,
    trustworthiness and
    credibility for, 43–45
connotation, 311
content, of presentation, 347
content notes, in APA style, 490
context, in rhetorical analysis, 88, 115
copyrighted material, 456, 459
    checking for, 343
    fair use of, 460
    notice or symbol for, 459
    permission for Internet sources,
    459–60
core principles, beliefs and, 44
Costas, Bob, 37, 222

counterarguments, highlighting,
    450–51
"crap detection," 153, 432–34
Creative Commons license, 459
credentials, of authors, publishers,
    or sponsors, 430
credibility
    building with audiences, 92–93
    images for, 335–37
    style and, 102
    tone and, 45
    trustworthiness and, 43–45
credit(s)
    for collaborative work, 463
    for copyrighted material, 460
crediting sources, 458–59
Crews, Harry, 393
critical reading, for pathos, 29–31
critical thinking
    about character-based
        arguments, 42–43
    about hard evidence, 52–55
    about own arguments, 33–34
cross-cultural communications, 126
Cruz, Ted, 4
Crystal, David, 441, 443
cultural contexts
    ethos and, 49
    logos and, 66–67
    "normal" thinking and, 27
    organization of argument and, 150
    of rhetorical situation, 415
    speaking up in class and, 346
    style issues and, 329
cultural Web sites, 364
currency, of print sources, 431

dashes, 216
data
    collecting, 420–26
    quantitative, 413
    from research sources, 415–19

databases, 416–17
  articles in MLA style, 480
  articles in APA style, 495–96
  searching, 419
decision-making, arguments for, 10
Declaration of Independence,
    classical oration structure of,
    124–25
deductive reasoning, 121
  syllogism as, 63–64, 65
definitional arguments, 18, 185–209
  claims for, 194, 196–97
  design and visuals in, 197–98
  developing, 193–98
  kinds of definition and, 189–93
  matching claims to, 196–97
  organization in, 204
  samples of, 207, 208–9
  style in, 204
  Toulmin argument and, 195
definitional claims, 200, 201
definitions
  in causal arguments, 247–48
  of concepts, 449
  crafting of, 195–96
  by example, 192–93
  formal, 189–90
  operational, 190–92
degree, as logical structure for
    argument, 67
deliberative arguments, 14
delivery, of presentation, 357–59
Deloch-Hughes, Edye, 88–89
Derse, Elizabeth, 393
Deshpande, Manasi, 450
  "Call to Improve Campus
    Accessibility, A," 295–302
design
  in causal arguments, 254–55
  in definitional arguments,
    197–98
  ethos reflected in, 337–38
  in evaluations, 223, 224

of factual argument, 164–66
information conveyed by, 340
of multimedia arguments,
    369–70
for pathos, 332–33
in proposals, 286–87
details, for presentation, 350–51
diagrams, 341. See also graphics
Dickens, Charles, 163–64, 328
diction, in presentation, 352–53
digital documents, 390. See also Web
    sites
digital sources. See also online
    sources
  analyzing, 100
  in MLA style, 476
DiIulio, John J., Jr., 55–56
discussions, class and public,
    345–46
dissertations, citing
  in APA style, 498
  in MLA style, 481
documentation, 465–503. See also
    APA style; MLA style
  for academic argument, 388–89
  principles of, 458–59
  in rhetorical analysis, 117
  systems of, 388–89
documented sources, 100
Dodick, David W., 382
dogmatism fallacies, 77–78
Dohn, Jeremiah, 373
Dolan, Jon, 310
domain names, assessing, 433
"Dota 2: The Face of Professional
    Gaming" (Jiang), 264–67
Douglass, Frederick, 127–28
drafts
  of questionnaires, 424
  reflecting on, 391–92
drawings, 341
Dubner, Stephen J., 155
DVD, citing, in APA style, 498

Eastwood, Clint, 314
Ebert, Roger, 216–17, 218
Edge, Nicholas, 56–57
editing, 392
editions, citing
 in APA style, 492
 in MLA style, 474
editor, citing
 in APA style, 492
 in MLA style, 473
editorials, citing, in MLA style, 476
Edwards, Russell, 438
Eggers, Dave, 68
either/or choices, 72–73
electronic sources. *See* online
 sources
ellipsis marks, 314, 316
 for quotations, 445
email, citing
 in APA style, 489–91, 498
 in MLA style, 480
emotional appeals (pathos), 9, 23,
 28–39, 139
 arguments based on, 38–39
 arguments sustained with, 34–36
 fallacies of, 72–76
 humor in, 36–38
 images and visual design for,
 332–33
 logical claims and, 33–34
 rhetorical analysis of, 95–97
 using, 31–34
Englehart, Bob, 7, 8
enthymeme, 65–66, 139
entire works, in MLA style, 469
epideictic arguments, 14–15, 16, 211
Epstein, Eve, 325–26
Equiano, Olaudah, 161
equivocations, as fallacies, 82
ethical appeals (ethos), 23–24
 authority through, 45–47, 49
 character-based arguments and,
 40–50

critical thinking about, 42–43
cultural context for argument
 and, 49
fallacies of, 76–79
honesty about motives and,
 47–48
in own writing, 48
personal image and, 336
rhetorical analysis of, 97–98
trustworthiness, credibility, and,
 43–45
visuals for, 335
ethnographic observations, in
 causal arguments, 253
ethos. *See* ethical appeals (ethos)
evaluations, 19, 210–39
 characterizing, 214–17
 claims in, 219–21, 226, 227, 229
 criteria of, 212–14, 218–19
 design and visuals for, 223, 224
 developing, 217–24
 evidence in, 221–22, 223, 229
 format and media for, 228
 organization of, 228, 229–30
 of print sources, 430–32
 qualitative and quantitative,
 214–17
 reviewing, 228–30
 samples of, 232–36, 237–39
 of sources, 427–35
 style in, 229–30
 Toulmin structure for, 227
 writing guidelines for, 225
evidence, 412–26
 for academic arguments,
 387–88
 analyzing, 101
 backing, 138–39
 choosing, 161–63
 circumstantial, 437–38
 critical thinking about, 52–55
 for definitional argument claims,
 203

evidence *(continued)*
    in evaluations, 221–22, 223, 229
    for factual arguments, 171
    hard, 214
    presenting, 163–64, 221–22, 223
    from research sources, 415–19
    for rhetorical analysis, 115, 116,
        413–15
    in Toulmin argument, 131–33,
        139
evocative language, in emotional
    appeals, 96–97
examples, definitions by, 192–93
exclamation point, 314
exordium, 122
experiments, data collection
    through, 420
explanatory notes, in MLA style,
    471–72
exploratory arguments, 11

Facebook, friending on, 208–9, 323
facts. *See also* data
    as evidence, 55–57
    in Toulmin argument, 132
factual arguments, 17–18, 51–70,
    152–84
    characterizing, 154–55
    design and visuals and, 164–66
    developing, 155–66
    graphics for, 54
    hypotheses in, 154–55, 159
    issues for, 157–58
    reason and common sense in,
        63–67
    rhetorical analysis of, 98–100
    samples of, 174–79, 180–84
    samples of claims for, 168
    statistics for, 57–60
    surveys and polls for, 60–62
    testimonies and narratives for,
        62–63

    in Toulmin terms, 169
    writing guides for, 167–72
"fair use," 460
Fallaci, Oriana, 414
fallacies, 71–86
    defined, 71–72
    of emotional argument,
        72–76
    of ethical argument, 76–79
    of logical argument, 79–86
Fallon, Claire, 309
false authority appeals, 76–77
Fantz, Ashley, 59
faulty analogy fallacies, 84–85
faulty causality fallacies, 80–81
field research, assessing, 434–35
figurative language, 317–28
film, citing
    in APA style, 498
    in MLA style, 482–83
fonts, 198, 337–38
forensic arguments, 13
foreword, citing, in MLA style, 474
formal definitions, 189–90
formality, 329
formal style, 309
format
    for causal arguments, 259–60
    for definitional argument, 202
    for evaluations, 228
    for factual argument, 169–70
    for proposals, 290–91
    for rhetorical analysis, 114, 117
Fortgang, Tal, 47–48
Foss, Sonja, 12, 126
Fournier, Ron, 46
Fox, Susannah, 380
Freakonomics (Dubner and Levitt),
    155
"Friending: The Changing Definition
    of Friendship in the Social
    Media Era" (Liu), 208–9
future, arguments about, 14

Gargus, J. Jay, 382
Geaghan-Breiner, Charlotte, 386
  "Where the Wild Things
    Should Be: Healing Nature
    Deficit Disorder through the
    Schoolyard," 396–405
Gearhart, Sally Miller, 127
genus, of terms, 189
Gerson, Michael, 64–65, 317
Gier, Joseph, 253
Goadsby, Peter J., 381
Google, 418
government document, citing
  in APA style, 493, 496
  in MLA style, 475
graphic narrative, citing
  in APA style, 493
  in MLA style, 474
graphics. See also design; visuals
  for definitional argument, 197,
    198
  for factual arguments, 54, 163,
    165
graphs, 341, 342. See also charts
  in causal arguments, 255
Greene, Brian, 325
Gregoire, Carolyn, 94–95
Griffin, Cindy, 12, 126
Gutting, Gary, 11

Hamilton, Tracy Brown, 78
hard evidence, 214
  critical thinking about, 52–55
Hard Times (Dickens), 163–64
Hari, Johann, 394
Harrop, Froma, 62–63
hasty generalization fallacies, 80
headings, 101, 340, 355, 389
Hemingway, Ernest, 432, 443
Himes, Chester, 324
Howard, Jennifer, 161
Howard, Rebecca Moore, 451–53

"How It Feels to Be Colored Me"
  (Hurston), 12
humor
  credibility through, 44
  in emotional appeals, 36–38
  ridicule as, 38
Hurston, Zora Neale, "How It Feels
  to Be Colored Me," 12
hyperbole, 320
hypotheses
  for factual arguments, 154–55, 168
  researching, 159

icon, as visual argument, 135
illustrations. See visuals
images. See visuals
IMRAD (Introduction, Methods,
  Research, and Discussion),
  170
inartistic proofs, 52–53
indents, for quotations, 445
indirect sources, in MLA style, 469
inductive reasoning, 121
infographics, 163, 165, 341, 342, 382
informal logic, Toulmin argument
  as, 65–66
information
  quality of, 100
  synthesizing, 438–53
  visual organization of, 339–40
informing, arguments for, 7
infotention, 436–37, 438
intellectual property, 455–56, 457
intended readers, 21–22
Interesting Narrative, The (Equiano),
  161
Internet. See also online entries;
  Web sites
  "crap detection" for information
    from, 153, 432–34
  permission for copyrighted
    sources, 459–60

Internet (*continued*)
    search options on, 418–19
    sites finding and posting errors
        about, 155–56
    sources on, 416–19
    value of, 380
interviews
    in APA style, 493
    data collection through, 421
    in MLA style, 482
in-text citations
    in APA style, 487–90
    in MLA style, 467–71
introductions
    to borrowed words and ideas,
        445–47
    citing in MLA style, 474
    in presentations, 351–52
    to terms, 449
inverted word order, 327
invitational arguments, 11, 126–29
invoked readers, 22
irony, 321
Irwin, Neil, "What the Numbers
    Show about N.F.L. Player
    Arrests," 180–84
"It's Not about You" (Brooks), 106–8

jargon, 311
Jiang, Raven, 263
    "Dota 2: The Face of Professional
        Gaming," 264–67
Jobs, Steve, 32
Johnson, Samuel, 187–88, 327
journal articles, citing, in APA style,
    493
journals, 417

kairos, 24–26
Kamperman, Sean, "Wikipedia
    Game, The: Boring, Pointless,
    or Neither?," 232–36

Kelly, Kevin, 331
keywords, for Internet searches, 418
King, Martin Luther, Jr., 354–55, 433
Kleege, Georgina, 32–33
Knight, Lindsey, 59
Kolb, Rachel, "Understanding
    Brooks's Binaries," 105, 109–11
Krugman, Paul, 85, 316

language, evocative, 96–97
Lanham, Richard, 437
Layton, Lyndsey, 19
lecture, citing, in MLA style, 484
LePatner, Barry, 23–24
Lessig, Lawrence, 344
Lessing, Doris, 327
"Let's Charge Politicians for Wasting
    Our Time" (Postrel), 303–4
letters, citing
    in APA style, 489
    in MLA style, 482
letter to the editor, citing
    in APA style, 493
    in MLA style, 476
Levitt, Steven, 155
Library of Congress Subject
    Headings (LCSH), 417
library resources, 416
listening, rhetorical, 126
literary works, citing, in MLA style,
    469
literature, reviewing, 448–59
Liu, Joyce Xinran, "Friending:
    The Changing Definition
    of Friendship in the Social
    Media Era," 208–9
logic
    reasoning as, 63
    Toulmin argument as, 65–66, 130
logical appeals (logos), 24, 33, 51–70,
    337
    cultural contexts for, 66–67
    fallacies of, 79–86

rhetorical analysis of, 98–100
  on Twitter, 367
  as visual images, 336
  visual images supporting, 339–43
logical structures
  analogies as, 68
  degree as, 67
  precedent as, 69–70
logos. *See* logical appeals (logos)
Lovell, James, 275

Madrigal, Alexis C., 308
magazine articles, citing, in MLA
  style, 476
Makau, Josina, 12
maps, 341
  citing in MLA style, 484
Marcus, Ruth, 321
market research, evaluation criteria
  and, 214
mashups, 459
Mayer, Jane, 314
McCorkle, Ben, 352–53
McLuhan, Marshall, 332
McWhorter, John, 99
Mead, Walter Russell, 34–35
mechanics, 45. *See also specific types
  of argument*
media. *See also* multimedia
  arguments
  for causal arguments, 259–60
  choice of, 336–37
  choosing, 355–57
  for definitional argument, 202
  for evaluations, 228
  for factual argument, 169–70
  old transformed by new, 362–64
  for presentation subject, 355–57
  for proposals, 290–91
  for rhetorical analysis, 114
  uses in arguments, 101
metaphor, 321
metonymy, 322–23

microform articles, citing, in MLA
  style, 481
MLA Handbook, 467. *See also* MLA
  style
MLA style
  for cited passage, 461
  on collaborative work, 463
  example of, 485–86
  explanatory and bibliographic
    notes in, 471–72
  guidelines for visuals in, 341
  in-text citations in, 467–71
  online sources in, 477–81
  other sources in, 481–83
  quotations in, 445
  for visuals in text, 461
  Works Cited list in, 472–84
Modern Language Association
  (MLA). *See* MLA style
motives, honesty about, 47–48
multimedia, new audiences for,
  365–67
multimedia arguments, 102, 332,
  361–75
  analyzing, 368–70
  new content in, 364–65
  Web sites and, 371–72
multiple authors, citing, in MLA
  style, 476
multivolume works, citing
  in APA style, 492
  in MLA style, 469, 474
"My Awkward Week with Google
  Glass" (Tsukayama), 237–39

narratio, 122
narratives, for factual arguments,
  62–63
Nath, Paresh, 243
newsgroups, 142
  citing, in APA style, 497
newspaper articles, citing, in APA
  style, 493

nonprint sources, 416
  in MLA style, 469–70
non sequitur arguments, 82–83
Noonan, Peggy, 316
"normal" thinking, 27
notes, in-text, 461
Novella, Steven, 83–84

Obama, Barack, 52
Obama, Michelle
  on Boko Haram kidnapping, 3, 4
  invitational argument used by,
    128–29
objections, conditions of rebuttal
    and, 141, 149
observations, data collection
    through, 420–21
O'Connor, Anahad, 7
online sources, 416–19
  in APA style, 489–90, 494–98,
    499
  assessing, 432–34
  in MLA style, 469, 478–81
  searching, 419
online video clip, citing, in MLA
    style, 483
operational definitions, 190–92
oration, classical, 122–25
organization of argument
  academic argument, 389–90
  causal argument, 260
  cultural context and, 150
  definitional argument, 202, 204
  evaluations, 228, 229
  factual arguments, 170, 171–72
  proposals, 291, 292–93
  rhetorical analysis, 114–15,
    116–17
  visual, of information, 339–40
Oster, Emily, 61
outlines, of Toulmin argument,
    143
oxymoron, 323

Paglia, Camille, 5, 8–9
pamphlet, citing, in MLA style, 475
papers, citing, in APA style, 498
parallelism, 327–28
  in presentation, 354–55
paraphrasing
  crediting, 459
  example of, 441–42
  guidelines for, 440–42
  as plagiarism, 462
  of sources, 438–39, 439–42
Parker, James, 424
Parker-Pope, Tara, 158
partitio, 122
patchwriting, 451–53
pathos. *See* emotional appeals
    (pathos)
Pearson, Taylor, 283, 447, 454
  "Why You Should Fear Your
    Toaster More Than Nuclear
    Power," 174–79
peer review. *See* reviewing
    arguments
Pena, Laura, 449, 450–51
performance, citing, in MLA style,
    484
periodicals, citing
  in APA style, 493
  in MLA style, 475–76
permission
  for copyrighted Internet sources,
    459–60
  request for, 460
peroratio, 122
personal experience
  authority through, 49
  data collection through, 424–25
  for factual claims, 62–63
  in Toulmin argument, 132
personal pronouns, 310
persuasion, arguments for, 8–9
Pew Research Center, 164, 380,
    381
Phillip, Abby, 69

photographs, 166
. citing in MLA style, 483–84
communicating through, 338
creating, 333
plagiarism, 452
academic integrity and, 455–64
paraphrase as, 462
Platt, Russell, 461
political Web sites, 364
Pollan, Michael, 33–34
polls, for factual arguments, 60–62
poster sessions, citing, in APA style, 498
post hoc, ergo propter hoc fallacies, 80–81
Postrel, Virginia, "Let's Charge Politicians for Wasting Our Time," 303–4
precedence, weight given to, 413
precedent, as logical structure for argument, 69–70
preface, citing, in MLA style, 474
Prensky, Marc, 14
present, arguments about, 14
presentation methods, 344–60
delivery and, 357–59
multimedia, 102, 332, 361–75
oral version with illustration, 353–54
preparation of, 346–60
print version of, 352–53
script for, 351–55
software for, 357
Web-based, 359, 371–72
primary research, 159
print documents, 390
print sources, 416
assessing, 430–32
professional style, 309
pronouns, personal, 310
proofreading, 392

proposals, 20, 272–304
categorizing, 273–74
for causal arguments, 259
characterizing, 275–78
claims in, 281–83, 289–90, 292
defining need or problem in, 279–81
for definitional argument, 201–2
demonstrating feasibility of, 286
design in, 286–87
developing, 279–93
for evaluations, 227
for factual arguments, 169
format and media for, 290–91
meeting need or problem in, 283–86
organization of, 291, 292–93
preparing, 290
reviewing, 291–93
for rhetorical analysis, 113–14
samples of, 295–302, 303–4
style of, 292–93
topic for, 288
Toulmin terms for, 290
visuals in, 286–87
Psaki, Jen, 4
Publication Manual of the American Psychological Association, guidelines for visuals in, 341. *See also* APA style
public discussions, 345–46
public domain, 343
publishers, reliability of, 420–21
punctuation
argument and, 314–17
in rhetorical analysis, 117
purpose
of arguments, 90–91
of assignment, 347

qualifiers, 140–41
to make reasonable claims, 161
qualitative evaluations, 215–17

quantitative data, 413
quantitative evaluations, 214–15
questionnaires, for surveys, 422–24
quotation marks, 441, 444
quotations, 340, 441, 443–45
    in APA style, 445
    guidelines for, 443–45
    in-text references for, 459
    in MLA style, 445

radio program, citing, in MLA style, 483
Rainie, Lee, 380
Rangel, Charles, 280
Ratcliffe, Krista, 126
readers
    intended, 21–22
    invoked, 22
reading, for pathos, 29–31
reasoning. *See also* factual arguments
    deductive, 63–64, 65, 121
    inductive, 121
reasons
    examples of, 137
    in Toulmin argument, 131–33, 149
rebuttals, conditions of, 141
red herring fallacies, 84
Reed, Rex, 320
References list, in APA style, 490–99, 502
reference works, citing
    in APA style, 492, 496
    in MLA style, 475, 479
refutatio, 122
relevance, of sources, 430
reliability, of sources, 428–29
repetition, in presentation, 354–55
republication, citing
    in APA style, 492
    in MLA style, 475

research
    for causal argument topic, 257–58
    data and evidence from, 415–19
    for definitional arguments, 199–200
    for evaluation topic, 225–26
    for factual argument hypothesis, 159
    field, 434–35
    for proposal topic, 288–89
    for rhetorical analysis topic, 112
resources. *See also* sources
    library, 416
    online, 417–19
reviewing arguments
    causal argument, 260–62
    definitional arguments, 203–4
    evaluations, 228–29
    factual arguments, 170–72
    for proposals, 291–93
    for rhetorical analysis, 115–17
reviews, citing
    in APA style, 494
    in MLA style, 476
Rheingold, Howard, 153, 432–33, 437
rhetoric, 12
    ceremonial or epideictic, 211
    kairos and, 24–26
    visual, 330
rhetorical analysis, 87–118
    as argument, 94–95
    of argument structure, 101
    of character, 97–98
    claims for, 112–13
    composing, 89–90
    of emotional arguments, 95–97
    examination of, 105–11
    facts and reason for, 98–100
    of maker of argument, 91–92
    proposal for, 113–14
    of purpose of argument, 90–91
    of style, 102–5
    writing guide to, 112–18

rhetorical listening, 126
rhetorical question, 323
rhetorical situation
    assessing for presentation, 347
    cultural context for, 415
    evidence for, 413–15
ridicule, as humor, 38
Robinson, Eugene, 316
Rodriguez, Natasha, 205
    "Who Are You Calling
        Underprivileged?," 206–7
Rogerian argument, 11, 12, 126
Rogers, Carl, 11, 126
Rose, Charlie, 73
Rosen, Christine, 5
Rosenbaum, Ron, 36–37, 96
Ross, Lauren, 162
Rowling, J. K., 43
Rubio, Marco, 29–30
running heads, 340. *See also*
    headings

sacred text, citing, in MLA style, 470
Sáenz, Benjamin, 321–22
San Luis, Natalie, 449–50
sans serif fonts, 338
scare tactics, 72
schemes, 318, 326–28
scholarly databases, 416
script, for presentation, 351–55
semicolon, 314–15
sentence fragments, 313
sentence structure, argument and,
    312–14
sentimental appeals fallacy, 74–75
serif fonts, 337–38
Shaw, Jeff, 459
signal words
    in APA style, 447
    to introduce borrowed words
        and ideas, 445–47
signifying, 323–24

signposts, in presentation, 352
simile, 325
Simmons, Ruth J., 15, 44
Singer, Andy, 283, 286
slang, 310
slippery slope fallacy, 74
Smith, David, 253
social media, 374
    in APA style, 497
    in MLA style, 480
    Twitter as, 3–5
    Web sites and, 364
software
    in APA style, 496
    in MLA style, 481
    presentation, 357
Solomon, Jack, 94
Sotomayor, Sonia, 308
sound recording, citing
    in APA style, 498
    in MLA style, 483
sources. *See also* research
    in academic argument, 392
    acknowledging, 461–62
    analyzing quality of, 100
    bias in, 428–29
    to clarify and support
        arguments, 447–51
    credibility of, 418
    crediting, 458–59
    evaluating, 159, 427–35
    number for academic argument,
        417
    online, 418, 432–34
    paraphrasing, 439–42
    permission for copyrighted
        Internet material, 459–60
    signal phrases for, 445–47
    synthesizing information and,
        438–53
    using, 159, 436–54
Sousanis, Nick, 384
speaking, for presentations, 357–59

specialization, of sources, 431
species, of terms, 189
speech
    citing in MLA style, 484
    logical appeals in, 52
spelling, in rhetorical analysis, 117
sponsors, reliability of, 420–21
square brackets, for quotations, 445
stacking the deck fallacies, 79
stasis theory, 17–21
statistics, for factual arguments,
    57–60
Stein, Nathaniel, 102–3, 314
Stiehm, Jamie, 78
straight talk, 94
straw man fallacies, 83–84
structure
    of argument, 67–70, 101–2,
        121–50
    of presentation, 347–50, 352
studies. *See* surveys
style, 307–29
    in academic arguments, 390
    in causal arguments, 261–62
    credibility and, 102
    cultural contexts and, 329
    in definitional arguments, 204
    in evaluations, 229–30
    in factual arguments, 171–72
    figurative language and, 317–28
    formality and, 329
    of presentation, 347–50
    of proposals, 292–93
    of rhetorical analysis, 102–5,
        116–17
    word choice and, 309–11
style of arguments, 102–5
subheadings, 101, 340, 355, 389
subject, of factual argument, 159
subject directory, online, 418
subscription service article, in MLA
    style, 480
Sullivan, Andrew, 322

summarizing
    guidelines for, 442–43
    of sources, 438–39
superscript, in APA text notes, 490
support, sources for, 447–51
surveys
    for factual arguments, 60–62
    questionnaires for, 422–24
syllogism, 63–65
synopsis, of rhetorical analysis,
    115
syntax, in presentation, 352–53
synthesis, of information, 438–53

Talbot, Margaret, 62
Tankersley, Reagan, 220
Tannen, Deborah
    Toulmin argument and, 144
    "Why Is 'Compromise' Now a
        Dirty Word?," 145–48
technical material, presenting,
    449–50
television program, citing
    in APA style, 498
    in MLA style, 483
tentative claim, 193–94
terms, introducing, 449
testimonies, for factual arguments,
    62–63
thesis, rhetorical analysis of, 99, 102
Thurman, Judith, 393
Tierney, John, 253, 263
    "Can a Playground Be Too Safe?,"
        268–71
timelines, 341
title page, in APA style, 500
titles, 340
title within title, citing, in MLA
    style, 475
Tommasini, Anthony, 196–97
tone, of academic argument, 390
Toor, Rachel, 319

topics
  for academic argument, 385
  for causal argument, 257
  for definitional argument, 199
  for evaluation, 225–26
  for factual argument, 167
  for proposal, 288
  for rhetorical analysis, 112
  rhetorical stance on, 386–87
Toulmin argument, 65–66, 130–44
  backing in, 138–39
  begging the question and, 81
  claims in, 130–31, 149
  conditions of rebuttal in, 141–42
  definition argument and, 195
  evidence and reasons in, 131–33,
    149
  outline of, 143
  qualifiers in, 140–41
  Tannen, Deborah, and, 144,
    145–48
  warrants in, 133–38
trademark, as visual image, 336
transitions, 101
translations, citing
  in APA style, 492
  in MLA style, 474
tropes, 318–26
Trudeau, Garry, 457
trustworthiness, credibility and,
  43–45
Tsukayama, Hayley, "My Awkward
  Week with Google Glass,"
  237–39
Turner, Fred, 383
Tverberg, Gail, 243–44
Twain, Mark, 84
tweet
  in APA style, 497
  in MLA style, 480
Twitter, 3–5, 365, 366–67
  Obama, Michelle, appeal on, 3
typefaces, 198, 337–38

understanding, arguments for, 11
"Understanding Brooks's Binaries"
  (Kolb), 109–11
understatement, 325–26
Uses of Argument, The (Toulmin), 130

values
  appeals to, 139
  arguments based on, 68
video, 372, 373
  citing in APA style, 498
  creating, 333
video game, citing, in MLA style,
  481
visual(s), 164–66
  in academic arguments, 390–91
  analysis of, 101
  APA style for, 341
  APA style for presentation
    guidelines, 341
  in causal arguments, 254–55, 256
  charts and graphs as, 340–41
  color in, 334
  communicating through, 338
  copyrights of, 343
  for credibility and authority,
    335–37
  data conveyed through, 340–41
  in definitional arguments, 197
  for ethos, 335
  in evaluations, 223, 224
  for factual argument, 164–66
  feelings conveyed through,
    333–34
  MLA style for, 461, 469–70
  for pathos, 332–33
  for presentations, 355–57
  professional guidelines for, 341,
    342
  in proposals, 286–87
  to support logos, 339–43
  using, 332–43

visual arguments, 104, 330–43
  icon as, 135
  power of, 331–32
visual signals, 340

Wales, Jimmy, 417
Wang, Kevin, 59
warrants, 53
  backing of, 138–39
  claims as, 53
  examples of, 137
  in Toulmin argument, 133–38
Warren, Elizabeth, 276–77
Weathers, Diane, 93
Webcasts, of live presentations, 359
Web site documents, citing
  in APA style, 496
  in MLA style, 476
Web sites
  in APA style, 495
  checking authors from, 448
  in MLA style, 476–77
  multimedia arguments and,
    371–72
  social, political, and cultural, 364
"What the Numbers Show about
  N.F.L. Player Arrests" (Irwin),
  180–84
"Where the Wild Things Should
  Be: Healing Nature Deficit
  Disorder through the
  Schoolyard" (Geaghan-
  Breiner), 396–405

"Who Are You Calling
  Underprivileged?"
  (Rodriguez), 206–7
"Why Is 'Compromise' Now
  a Dirty Word?" (Tannen),
  145–48
"Why You Should Fear Your Toaster
  More Than Nuclear Power"
  (Pearson), 174–79
wiki, 372–73
  in APA style, 497
  in MLA style, 479
Wikipedia, 369, 417–18
"Wikipedia Game, The: Boring,
  Pointless, or Neither?"
  (Kamperman), 232–36
Wilcox, Susan, 448–49
Williams, Terry Tempest, 46
Willis, Frank, 253
Wilsey, Sean, 222
"win/win" solutions, 11
Withers, Hannah, 162
Wolkowitz, Michael, 74
Womack, Philip, 315, 316
word choice, style and, 309–11
word order, inverted, 327
Works Cited list
  entries, 462
  in MLA style, 472–84, 486

Xue, Lan, "China: The Prizes
  and Pitfalls of Progress,"
  406–9